Understanding the Hebrew Bible:
A Reader's Guide

D1599283

Understanding the Hebrew Bible:
A Reader's Guide

BY

Elliott Rabin

KTAV Publishing House , Inc.
Jersey City, N.J.

Library of Congress Cataloging-in-Publication Data

Rabin, Elliott.
    Understanding the Hebrew Bible: a reader's guide / by Elliott Rabin.
        p. cm.
    Includes bibliographical reference and index.
        ISBN 0-88125-856-3 (hardcover) – ISBN 0-88125-871-7 (pbk.)   1.
Bible. O.T. – Criticism, interpretation, etc.   1. Title.
    BS117.3.R334 2005
    221.6–dc22

Published by
KTAV Publishing House, Inc.
930 Newark Avenue
Jersey City, NJ 07306
bernie@ktav.com
www.ktav.com
Tel. (201) 963-9524
Fax. (201) 963-0102

Typeset by Jerusalem Typesetting, www.jerusalemtype.com
Cover Design by S. Kim Glassman

To Adele, "my sister, my bride" (Song of Songs 4:12), and
Batia, our "delight every day" (Proverbs 8:30)

Acknowledgements

I owe an enormous debt to my friend Chanan Kessler for making judicious editorial comments and wise suggestions throughout. Without his help, this book would be in far worse condition than it is. Gratitude is also due to Professor Gary Rendsburg for his encouragement before the project ever got started and for his notes on the beginning chapters. My colleague Meryl Wheeler gladly volunteered to serve as a "target audience" – her careful observations on the introduction were invaluable. The cadre of biblical scholars at Indiana University taught me to appreciate the Bible as a sophisticated literary work. Over the years, professors such as James Ackerman and Luke Johnson have created an Eden of learning in a collegial atmosphere. I want especially to thank Bernie Levinson, who drummed into me everything I know about biblical Hebrew; Meir Sternberg, an intimidating first-semester presence who showed us how to discuss the Bible using the analytic tools of literary criticism; and most of all, my mentor and friend, Herb Marks. My fellow graduate student Jean-Pierre Sonnet continues to inspire me through his writing, his friendship, and his generous spirit. Thanks also go to my publisher, Bernie Scharfstein, for putting his faith in me to write this book. The crack editor Ilene McGrath did a wonderful job of whipping my prose into shape. I am deeply appereciative. At work, my charming associates at the Makor/Steinhardt Center of the 92nd Street Y have contributed through their humor and good wishes. Finally, my wife, Adele, was my toughest and most faithful reader. Without her love and support, this book would not exist.

Of course, all errors in fact or judgment, of omission or commission, are the fault of no one but myself.

Table of Contents

Preface

If you think about it, the Bible ought to be a simple book. Its dominant message – that there exists only one God who created and rules the world – presents a vastly simplified vision of the universe, compared with the accounts of divinity found in mythological stories. And yet the Bible is considerably longer and more complicated than most polytheistic epics. Why? The answer provides the first key for understanding the Bible: the Bible is not a book of doctrine. Statements of dogma are few and far between. It is a book that imparts its religious vision mostly through literary art, through stories and poems. The stories that the Bible tells, spanning enormous differences of time and circumstances, describe human responses to God's presence. God in the Bible does not merely exist and demand sacrifices. God speaks to people, challenging them generation after generation to live a life in God's image. The Bible might best be read as a chronicle of how people, from Adam and Eve down to Ezra and Esther, answered, or failed to answer, God's challenge.

Because the Bible is so long and complex, a guide can come in handy for the reader who wants to navigate its passages. This book charts the major currents of the Bible, enabling the reader to gain a sure sense of orientation no matter where he or she may land. *Understanding the Hebrew Bible* takes the large mass of writing compiled in this tome and organizes it according to different kinds of writing, called genres. The Bible contains six major genres – storytelling, law, history, prophecy, wisdom, and poetry – each one characterized by its own style and perspective reflecting different groups within ancient Israel. Understanding the Bible requires grasping what makes each of these genres "tick." This guide will enable the reader to open the Bible to any book and not feel lost. The reader will recognize the basic qualities of the writing and the assumptions for that genre; will know to what body of writings the book belongs; and will have a good sense of when the book was written. Other introductions to the Bible bog the reader down in a book-by-book analysis, or a focus on one genre – usually history – at the expense of the rest. The approach in this book offers the best method not only to understand the Bible, but also to read it with pleasure.

Above all, this book aims to impart the excitement of reading the Bible, to share some of the delights and surprises in store for the reader. Discover the Bible's astonishing scope – the unique diversity of material it contains, of interest to people who love history and literature, to those seeking psychological insight or the meaning of life and an encounter with God. Experience the awesome power of biblical writing: stories, speeches, and poems so immediate and direct that they can pierce the human heart millennia after they were written. Explore the drama of the history of the Jews and of their book – their national triumphs and catastrophes, the rapid alternation of sovereignty, conquest, and exile that produced a new conception of God and of the sacredness of writing. And enter into the fascinating world of biblical scholarship, which over the past two hundred years has continually changed our understanding of who wrote these texts, and for what purposes.

Many people turn to the Bible for answers; this guide aims to demonstrate that the Bible is primarily a book of questions, that for every idea it puts forth, it provokes the reader to interrogate and ponder further. Studying the Bible requires adjusting to its framework for asking what it believes to be the important questions. The Bible lays out some basic premises about the organization of the universe and the role of mankind, but it recognizes that principles never play out with mathematical clarity in the course of human affairs. Biblical stories purposefully entangle the reader in a web of dilemmas with no one simple moral. This book tries to answer some of the easy questions about the Bible and assist the reader in finding his or her path of exploring the more difficult and significant quandaries.

Understanding the Hebrew Bible is written for the general reader, in a clear and accessible style. It assumes no prior knowledge of the Bible and takes no particular position about the Bible's religious significance. Peoples of all faiths and creeds can read this book to learn about this remarkable collection of writings. It attempts neither to convert people to become religious nor to convince the religious to lose their faith; it seeks only to garner appreciation for the most influential book ever written. This guide offers insight to readers at all levels of acquaintance with the Bible. Beginners, we hope, will find the presentation an inviting start to their own discovery of the Bible. People with more knowledge of the Bible, whether from exposure in religious contexts or through personal study, can acquire a substantial and up-to-date grasp of the different parts of the Bible and the ways they fit into a larger whole. Even people highly familiar with the Bible are likely to find something here that will stimulate them to go back and reread their favorite biblical passages with new eyes.

This book originated as a class taught in a center for adult education. Although the chapters cover far more information than can be presented in a classroom, the book retains the format of class lessons, with suggested readings serving as a kind of syllabus for most of the material discussed in the chapters. Readers would do well to keep a copy of the Bible available for reference while reading this book. Even though all biblical citations are either quoted or paraphrased, the reader's enjoyment will be greater the more this book serves as a guide, rather than a substitute, for reading the Bible.

Some notes on the language used in this book. The word "Bible" refers to the Hebrew Bible or Jewish Bible. "Hebrew Bible" is now a standard term for the Jewish scriptures; its use here does not imply any knowledge of the Hebrew language. It would be too cumbersome to say "Hebrew Bible" every time the word Bible appears in the book, and besides, Hebrew Bible and Jewish Bible are not entirely accurate descriptions: some of the Bible is written in Aramaic – a related but different language than Hebrew – and the books discussed here carry religious significance for Christians as well as Jews. Christians know these books as the Old Testament, a term avoided here for its negative valuation of Judaism and the imposition of a perspective foreign to the writings under discussion (the writers of Leviticus did not consider its laws "old"). As is explained in the Introduction, the difference between the Hebrew Bible and the Old Testament lies more in the order of the books and the understanding of their significance than in the content within the books themselves. That content is nearly identical.

The Hebrew Bible as we know it is generally copied from the Leningrad Codex, the oldest complete version, dating from 1008 c.e. Most scholars today study the Hebrew in an edition called the Biblia Hebraica Stuttgartensia, which reproduces the Leningrad Codex and compares differences from other ancient versions of the Bible, such as the Septuagint, the Vulgate, and the Samaritan Pentateuch. Unlike the versions we read in translation, the Hebrew text contained no punctuation, no commas, quotation marks, upper or lower case, no division between sentences, not even vowels. The vowels, along with the current system of markings in the Hebrew text (called trope), which simultaneously indicate punctuation and serve as notes for chanting the Torah, came into circulation only by the ninth century. They were based upon received traditions, but we cannot know how precisely they reproduce the intent of the original. Chapter and verse divisions were not marked until the Middle Ages, by Christian scholar Stephen Langton, and were later adopted with slight changes by Jewish editors at the introduction of the printing press. Thus the standard Hebrew text of the Bible is similar but not exactly identical to the writings as they existed at the time of composition.

One final, thorny issue concerns the pronoun used for God. In the Bible, that pronoun is always masculine. When metaphorical language is applied to God, that language too is nearly always masculine: God is a "man of war," a "king," a "father." Biblical scholars debate to what degree people at the time of the Bible conceived of God as male. Later Jewish tradition interpreted this language not to refer to an actual gender, because God is not physical or "sexed." Rather, the pronoun and imagery project a sense of personal closeness with God, a conception of relationship which a gender-neutral term like "It" does not provide. (Bear in mind as well that Hebrew does not possess the neuter "it"; all objects are either masculine or feminine.) A translation that switches between He and She, while satisfying our contemporary desire to portray God in gender-neutral terms, can present confusion to the reader and does not reproduce the language of the Bible itself. Therefore, in order faithfully to reflect the original, this book retains the masculine pronoun but attempts to limit its use to occasions when repeating "God" or "Lord" would be awkward.

CHAPTER I

Introduction: There's More than One Way to Read the Bible

"Sweet sunny Holy Land! How pleasantly one reposes beneath thy tents."
– Heinrich Heine, upon reading the Bible

"A classic is a book that has never finished saying what it has to say."
– Italo Calvino

Objections to the Bible

"What does such an old book have to tell me?"

"I had enough of the Bible when it was shoved down my throat in Sunday school."

"I'm not interested in organized religion."

"The language is antiquated – full of words like 'thou' and 'shalt.'"

"I already know what's in it."

"It's too big – printed in two columns in small print. I don't have time to read it."

"God in the Bible is cruel – I can't relate to that."

"The Bible oppresses women and supports slavery."

Perhaps you've heard people give voice to complaints like these, or maybe you have expressed similar thoughts yourself. Such sentiments are perfectly understandable. Since the Bible is perhaps the greatest foundation of our society, it is bound to be taught, quoted, and interpreted in ways that support an enormous range of beliefs and positions. A saying from the rabbinic anthology *Ethics of the Fathers* teaches, "Don't make the Torah a crown for self-glorification, or a spade with which to dig," but few speakers and politicians over the centuries have been able to resist the temptation to shovel biblical quotations onto their arguments of whatever dubious merit. For many, a quotation from the Bible lends instant authority and the ring of truth to whatever point they are trying to make. The Bible has indeed been abused to justify the oppression of women ("Eve's sin") and slavery ("the curse of Ham"). But it has also provided a platform for the emancipation of the poor (Latin American Liberation Theology), and a quotation from the Bible still proclaims "liberty throughout the land and to all the inhabitants thereof" on the Liberty Bell. Feminists and antifeminists, pacifists and war hawks, conservative evangelicals and religious liberals, environmental advocates and even vegetarians – all are adept at pulling a line out of the Bible to support their positions.

The Bible's antiquity can make it seem, well, old. What relevance does a book written some 2,200 to 3,000 years ago have for the world today? How can we find meaning in laws about oxen and sacrifices? There are two good responses to this challenge. First, the Bible is not a book that has stood still. People have been reading it, and struggling to make sense of it, for thousands of years. Each generation has come up against the issue of the Bible's antiquity, its strangeness, from the perspective of that time and has found ways to interpret the Bible to give it new meaning. Interpretation has been the force breathing new life into the Bible throughout the ages. If you approach the Bible only as a monument to the past, it may appear insufferable. However, if you read it as an opportunity to insert your own creative insights, you can taste some of the excitement that animates these ancient letters.

Second, encountering the antiquity of the Bible – its "otherness" – removes us from the world in which we live, giving us a new perspective on our surroundings. It reminds us that the world did not always have cars and cell phones, or, for that matter, representative democracy. Reading the Bible can help us appreciate what is valuable in our society while no longer tolerating those things we would like to change. Just as we enter the world of the Bible when we read it, the Bible comes into our universe as well. It continues to surprise, astonish, delight, frustrate, and provoke the reader toward new insights and revelations of all kinds. For readers throughout the centuries, the world was created anew each time they opened the Good Book.

Why Bother to Read the Bible?

For millions of people, the Bible is primarily a spiritual guide. Biblical stories are not only about events that took place in the distant past; for believers, those events speak to us directly about our lives today and indicate the future direction of ourselves as well as our communities, our nation, even the fate of the world. There is no gap between the present and the world of the Bible; as it says in the Haggadah, the book read at the Passover seder, "In every generation a person is obligated to regard himself as if he personally had gone forth from Egypt." Beliefs and practices described in the Bible impart central lessons for us today, and the very act of reading the Book constitutes an important religious activity. In a passage from the Talmud recited every morning in Jewish ritual, the study of the Torah is declared the equivalent of a host of other good acts, including honoring one's parents and visiting the sick. Examples from the Christian tradition are similarly not hard to find: Saint Augustine, in his *Confessions*, mentions how a verse from Scripture selected at random inspired him to lead a life of religious faith. The whole idea of religion being centered upon a book originated with the Bible and is a crucial element of the religious history chronicled within its pages.

Many others have great respect for the Bible but are less certain of its absolute value and are reluctant to grant it full authority over their lives. For these readers, the Bible may serve not as an inerrant map, but rather as a tour book to life suggesting routes filled with potential comfort, meaning, and vision. For these people, even if the Bible is not approached as the source of literal Truth, it can offer ways of approaching the deepest questions of human life: the purpose of existence, the nature of reality and our relationship with nature, our role in the universe, the basis of morality, and the origins of evil. Whether or not we accept the Bible's answers, we may recognize that the Bible provides powerful, imaginative models for understanding the human condition.

Besides serving as a spiritual resource, the Bible makes several strong claims upon the attention of all literate people. It is the cornerstone upon which Judaism, Christianity, and to a certain extent, Islam – the major monotheistic religions – and their civilizations were built. None of these monuments of human culture can be understood without a solid grounding in the Bible. The very idea of monotheism is inconceivable without its biblical origin and unfolding. Beyond its religious influence, the Bible has also exerted a profound influence on a variety of secular institutions and associations, including legal codes, nationalist movements, and political advocacies from socialist to archconservative.

The Bible is unusual among the world's chief religious texts in being *a great read.* One does not need to be a religious adherent of the Bible to enjoy much of the writing within it, something that cannot be said of many other religious documents. In many households over the past several centuries, the Bible was the only book people owned, and there was so much good reading material in it that they did not want for other books. The variety of writing and the breathtaking literary power found in so many of its books render the Bible the source not only of literate religion, religion derived from it and based upon constant study of it, but also of a kind of *literary* religion, a religion for which the power of language to move the soul is inseparable from the creative power of the divine word. Think of the pathos of Job, Isaiah's hypnotic preaching, the depths and heights of prayer in the Psalms, the bitter cry of loss in Lamentations, Joseph and his brothers' long route to reconciliation, David's epic rise and slow decline, the subtle erotic playfulness of the Song of Songs. These and other sections of the Bible, each with vastly different messages and concerns, still burn with the passion, intensity, and clarity with which they were written. The overpowering rhetoric and imagery in many biblical books might be thought of as "poetry" because we're used to thinking of poetry as a form of language that is more compressed, rhythmic, and filled with more powerful imagery than other kinds of language. But biblical writing often exceeds poetry in the urgency and vehemence of its message. If "leisure" is considered an important aspect of poetry, then most biblical writing must be reckoned in another category altogether. It would be a shame to write off such towering works because one did not consider oneself "religious." Just as we can read Homer today with great pleasure without believing in the divinity of Athena and Zeus, so, too, is it possible to shudder at the awesome eloquence of the biblical writers while bracketing the question of one's faith in or relationship to the Bible's God.

For Jews, the Bible recounts the beginnings of the Jewish people and sets the framework – historical, intellectual, religious, cultural – for subsequent Jewish history and spiritual development. It has served as an inexhaustible quarry that Jews have mined for thousands of years. Poets, philosophers, rulers, judges, saints, sages, and scoundrels alike have turned to the Bible for inspiration. Prayers from the Bible contain the bedrock of the synagogue's three daily services. Weekly, the Shabbat morning service reaches its climax in the cantillation of the Torah portion, chanted to tunes passed down over the centuries with loving exactitude. Annually, nearly all the holidays throughout the year find their origins in biblically prescribed rituals. Throughout history, individual Jews have interwoven the fabric of their own lives with the skein of stories and sayings they've memorized from their earliest years. Tevye the dairyman, the unforgettable protagonist of *Fiddler on the Roof*, which is based on the classic stories by the Yiddish writer Sholem Aleichem, demonstrates in a highly humorous way how traditional Jews, whether lowly beggars or prominent rabbis, found expressions from the Bible teeming in their heads at every turn of their lives.

Why Bother to Read *This* Book?

Martin Luther, one of the most influential interpreters of the Bible, established as his chief interpretive principle the claim of *Sola Scriptura* – that the Bible can and should be explained by itself alone. According to him, no guides or commentaries are needed; all the means required for understanding the Bible are given within the book itself. In other words: just read it. Luther was arguing against the prevailing doctrines within the Catholic Church, which held that Church tradition was the sole legitimate guide for interpreting the Bible and that loyal churchgoers ought to let the priests tell them what to read and how to read it. In the Middle Ages, most people were illiterate and had neither the time nor tools to challenge the Church hierarchy. The Protestant revolution, along with the rise of the printing press, put a Bible in each household and required people to read it and understand it in their own way, as the spirit moved them. In theory, at least, their own encounter with the Bible was to give them their primary understanding of religion; words of liturgy and weekly sermons should serve only to reinforce the messages that each parishioner took from Scripture.

This model is in some ways highly appealing to a modern reader. After all, we read all kinds of books without any kind of external aid. Why should the Bible be any different? Indeed, *Understanding the Bible* is intended not to replace the work of reading and interpreting the Bible, but to whet the reader's appetite for the task. If you have a choice between reading this book and reading the Book it is about, throw this one away. This book is intended as a guide, nothing more nor less. You should read it if you find the Bible imposing and are not sure how to make sense of it. The Bible is so old and large, containing so many different books from multiple perspectives, that it is not so easy to negotiate one's way through it. The Jewish and Christian traditions saw this difficulty early on and produced new commentaries in each generation to explain the Bible's meaning in terms that people could comprehend. With the passing of time, the Bible needed to be "translated," both literally and figuratively, into the languages and ways of thinking of the people reading it. For readers today the challenge is no less than for our predecessors. Individual passages and books from the Bible are, by and large, clearly written and easy to grasp; but the overall patterns and historical background are often not apparent. Such larger trends are what it is hoped the reader can take away from this book, in a brief and accessible format.

Unlike earlier generations of biblical commentaries, this introduction is informed primarily by contemporary academic scholarship on the Bible. This scholarship need not be regarded as "secular" or "anti-religious," although it starts from a scientific and historical perspective rather than a perspective of faith. This book will not shy away from points of conflict, but it will not put those conflicts at the center of its analysis. Those conflicts are real, and it is important to learn about them in order to understand the Bible as a historical document. For people curious about what modern scholarship has to say regarding the Bible's historical accuracy, this question will be treated in Chapter 4. However, unlike the work of most biblical scholars, this book does not regard the Bible *only* as a historical document. It recognizes the Bible's timeless relevance for people of two great religious traditions. Modern scholarship has much to tell us that will enhance our understanding and increase our appreciation of the Bible, no matter where the reader is starting from.

What Kind of Book Is the Bible?

Imagine that you find yourself inside of your local mega-bookstore, one from which the category "Bibles" has been removed. Where should you look for the Bible? Almost every category of book can find its counterpoint in biblical passages.

History. The Bible primarily tells the history of a people called first Hebrews, then Israelites, and later Jews, through 1,000 years of internal and external conflict.

Classics. The Bible is one of those books "one should have read."

Self-help. Portions of the Bible, and the entire book of Proverbs, contain practical advice for living in society, being happy, and getting ahead.

Geography. There are thousands of place names in the Bible, many of which correlate to discoveries by modern archeologists.

Science. While not a work of science as we know it, the Bible reflects the scientific understanding of its time; it recounts the origin of the rainbow (Genesis 9), an application of a fertility treatment (Genesis 30), a day when the sun stood still (Joshua 10), and an episode of mouth-to-mouth resuscitation (2 Kings 4).

Law. The Bible contains several law codes that lie at the heart of its religious message; it represents a crucial development in the history of legal thought.

Poetry. Biblical poetry can be found throughout, and the major poetic books – Psalms, Job, and Song of Songs – have been translated, annotated, and printed separately like other works of poetry.

Fiction. The Bible's stories have gained increasing recognition as masterpieces of narrative art. They also have served as the inspiration for numerous novels, short stories, plays, and films.

Religion. Perhaps an obvious one – the Bible provides the direct starting point for two major religions, and indirectly for a third.

Mythology. If mythology is a collection of stories about the origins of the world and human institutions through divine agency, the early portions of the Bible certainly serve that function.

As we see, the Bible is a kind of encyclopedia of a nation's (the ancient Jews') collective knowledge, a compendium so vast and seemingly amorphous that it requires us to rethink the very concept of the book.

Thinking about the Bible: Two Models

How can a book be so large and comprehensive? The Bible both defines and defies our very notion of what a book is. When we refer to a book that is definitive of its kind we often call it "the bible of" something. But what is the bible-ness of the Bible?

In order to understand what kind of book the Bible is, one must not think of it as a "book" in the way that we assume a book to be. What do we ordinarily mean by a book? A book is a unified work, written from beginning to end (or meant to be read in that order), usually by one person. By its very name, the Bible tells us it is something else. While today we hear "the Bible" as the title of a religious document, the name originally comes from the Greek *ta biblia*, meaning the books or scrolls. (The books of the Bible were written not in the physical form of a book as we know it today – the form known as a codex – but in scrolls like ones read in synagogue.) The same root can be found in such words as bibliography and the French *bibliothèque* (library). The name of the Bible, therefore, announces that it is not *a* book but a collection of different writings assembled into one. In contemporary terms, we would call it an anthology. Another way of putting it is that the Bible contains the national library of the Jews from ancient times, winnowed down to the books deemed most worthy of preservation. This model does not suggest that the Bible lacks order and shape, only that its shape is more characteristic of a miscellany of disparate works than of a unified volume. It contains the kind of range you might find if you took, say, classics of British writing – historical tomes, imaginative literature including prose and poetry, even science writing like Darwin – and tried to assemble them all into a single collection.

Another useful model for understanding the Bible addresses not the shape of the whole but the texture of the writing itself. The Bible is not only an ancient book, it's also a book containing traditions that were passed down over centuries in different ways until they acquired the form that we have today. Each book of the Bible has its own history of composition, transmission, rewriting, and editing into its current shape. Although those histories were never written down, modern scholars have studied the texture of the Bible like the layers of an archeological dig, trying to assign dates to different strata and to reconstruct the histories behind the final product. An analogue to this process is the ancient artifact known as a palimpsest. A palimpsest is a piece of papyrus or parchment upon which something was written, then erased; something else was written, then perhaps it too was erased, before it reached its current form. Crucially, the previous writings are not entirely removed, and using new technologies such as infrared, scholars are sometimes able to retrieve ancient texts that were written over through this process. Similarly, biblical texts nearly always contain several layers of writing behind the latest manifestation, and scholars perform a sort of detective work, trying to go backward in time to uncover the putative stages of their history.

How Do Jews and Christians Read the Bible?

Most people who were raised in a Jewish or Christian community are probably accustomed to the phrase, "The Bible [or Torah] says" or "teaches." Of course, it's perfectly natural and legitimate for religious groups to harness the Bible to particular moral and theological teachings; the Bible, as God's word to humanity, is the ultimate source of divine instruction for Jews and Christians. The wide spectrum of messages preached by a multiplicity of religious factions within Christianity and Judaism, however, indicates that the Bible does not necessarily say one "thing," and that it says different things to different people and traditions. One Jewish saying captures this variety as follows: "Every word of God [given at Mount Sinai] turned into 70 languages.... Like a man who strikes an anvil and sparks fly here and there." This expression suggests two kinds of variety: that the Bible can be understood by people throughout the world through their own languages and cultures; and that each person receives a different "spark" of God's word, understanding it in a distinct way.

9

There is yet another sense of the Bible's diversity: it speaks to each person differently, not only because he or she possesses unique experiences and expectations, but also because there is more than one "Bible" in the Bible. The Bible changes faces entirely as one passes from Deuteronomy to Isaiah to Job to Daniel – not surprising in a collection of works spanning 1,000 years. The effort required to see the unity among such differences can be as challenging as to imagine that Shakespeare and Stephen King form part of a single oeuvre. Even within a single biblical book, from one story to the next, the progression of events frequently astonishes us with its unpredictability. In Exodus 3, for example, God appoints Moses to represent the Israelites to Pharaoh, king of Egypt; in Exodus 4:24 "the Lord encountered him [Moses] and sought to kill him"!

A quick way to grasp the idea that the Bible speaks in various ways is to contrast the ways that Jews and Christians comprehend it. Leaving aside the Apocrypha – books included in the Catholic and Eastern Orthodox Bibles but dropped from Jewish and, later, Protestant Bibles – the Jewish Bible and the Christian Old Testament consist of exactly the same books, arranged in different order. This seemingly minor distinction reveals the crucial dissimilarity in the ways Jews and Christians understand the Bible. Jews organize the Bible into three sections, identified by the acronym TaNaKh: Torah, the five books of Moses (often called the Pentateuch in English); Nevi'im, the Prophets; and Ketuvim, the Writings. These divisions represent the religious significance accorded to the material: Torah is the most important of the three parts, Ketuvim the least. The Torah is read in order, in its entirety, every year, in portions divided relatively evenly week by week. Nevi'im serves as the source for Haftarot, additional weekly readings paired with the Torah portion, usually with a thematic connection that expands upon its meaning. Books of the Ketuvim traditionally are read either on one's own (Psalms, Proverbs, Job [during periods of mourning]), in synagogue during holidays (Song of Songs, Ruth, Lamentations, Ecclesiastes, Esther), or only rarely (Chronicles, Ezra–Nehemiah, Daniel).

The three sections of TaNaKh exhibit as well a diminishing level of internal coherence. The Torah hangs together by its story, focusing on Moses and the rise of the Israelites, as well as by its emphasis on law. The name of the last section, Writings, accurately points to the mixed nature of the material in it; there is slight organization, with the first books being the most poetic and aphoristic, the next group containing the five scrolls read on holidays, and the final selections returning to historical writing. The middle section, Prophets, falls somewhere in the middle. Initially, there seems little relation between the first books of this section, Joshua through Kings, which continue the story of the Israelites after the life of Moses and are referred to as the Former Prophets, and the subsequent teachings of individual prophets, referred to as the Latter Prophets. Indeed, might not the editors have just as well named the section "Israelite History" as "Prophets"? However, closer inspection does reveal overlap between the Former and Latter Prophets: the "historical" books devote much attention to the early prophets, such as Elijah and Elisha, and the prophetic material contains many references to historical people, times, and places. Putting it more strongly, the prophets cannot be properly understood without reference to the historical circumstances in which they found themselves (unlike, say, the psalms and proverbs). One of the prophets, Isaiah, even is mentioned in the book of Kings; a large passage from Kings (2 Kings 18:13–20:21) is repeated virtually verbatim in Isaiah 36–38. Another passage (2 Kings 24:18–25:21) appears with slight variations in Jeremiah 52, and much of Jeremiah chronicles his concern for the fate of contemporary kings and empires.

In the Christian Bible, the books of the Old Testament are not divided into smaller units; rather, the entire TaNaKH is now subsumed as the "Old Testament" into a larger whole. This lack of segmentation indicates that the material in the Hebrew Bible is now viewed, collectively, as a prelude leading up to the main event for Christianity, the life of Jesus as depicted in the Gospels. Although the Old Testament is about four times as large as the New, its significance for Christianity is considerably less. Some early Christian leaders debated whether to include this material at all in their sacred Scripture. They did so, in part, because the New Testament assumes a knowledge of the Old in so many ways. The theological concepts and historical framework of Christianity are rooted in Judaism, and the editors of the Christian Bible recognized that their Scripture would be less comprehensible and meaningful without the books that provide its foundation.

They arranged the books of the Old Testament in a manner that reflected its new significance: historical books, in chronological order (Chronicles here coming before Ezra–Nehemiah and Daniel, unlike in the TaNaKh); miscellaneous (poetry-aphorisms); prophets (with Lamentations coming after Jeremiah, who is traditionally considered its author). The historical books now represent the prehistory of Christianity, the early development of religion from Creation through Judaism. By contrast, the prophets come at the end of the Old Testament because of their great importance for the New. Christians consider them as anticipating Jesus' mission and as proof that Jesus is the messiah. Malachi, the last book of the prophets, ends with God promising to send "Elijah the prophet before the great and terrible day of the Lord comes." In Jewish tradition, Elijah is the herald of the messiah. Hence, when Christian readers turn the page to the book of Matthew, starting, "The book of the genealogy of Jesus Christ" – Christ being a Greek translation of Messiah – the two parts come together as a seamless whole. In this order, the Old Testament becomes a history of the world from the beginning to the eve of Christianity; the Jewish people are relegated to a stage in that history – a crucial stage, but one whose role has passed. Nevertheless, by retaining the Old Testament, Christianity remains perpetually locked in an ambivalent relationship with Judaism: forever anchored in the old, forever pushing away.

Not surprisingly, the order of the TaNaKh tells a very different story. It starts in the same place, with the creation of the world in Genesis, but ends in 2 Chronicles as follows:

> And in the first year of Cyrus, king of Persia, in order to fulfill the word of the Lord according to Jeremiah, the Lord aroused the spirit of Cyrus, king of Persia, and he spread a proclamation throughout his kingdom, even in writing, saying, "Thus said Cyrus, king of Persia: 'The Lord, God of the heavens, has given me all kingdoms of the earth, and He has appointed me to build Him a House in Jerusalem, which is in Judah. Whoever among you, from all His people, who has the Lord his God with him – let him go up!'" (2 Chronicles 36:22–23)

In this passage, which narrates an event in about 530 B.C.E.,[1] Cyrus grants the Jews his permission to build the Second Temple in Jerusalem, at the location where the First Temple had been destroyed a few decades earlier. Chronicles does not narrate the latest events in the Bible; the Books of Ezra and Nehemiah recount the beginnings of the Second Temple period, and the story of Esther takes place at some point later on under Persian rule. Why, then, would the rabbis have chosen to end the TaNaKh here? These concluding lines suggest an answer. The rabbis who edited the Bible into its final shape lived in Yavneh, in Roman Palestine, shortly after the destruction of the Second Temple in 70 C.E. With that tragedy so fresh in their minds, the rabbis did not foresee the cessation of Temple sacrifices as a permanent condition. The final lines of Chronicles, for them, strike the perfect note of hope for the Temple's future restoration. Just as King Cyrus allowed the Second Temple to be built a mere seventy years after the destruction of the First Temple, so, too, the Jews should have faith that a Third Temple will arise from the ashes of the Second. The optimistic note for national revival struck at the end of Chronicles contrasts with Nehemiah's despairing plea to God at the end of Ezra–Nehemiah – hence the rabbis' decision to arrange these works out of chronological order.

Two further differences between the TaNaKh and the Old Testament speak volumes about the divergences between Jewish and Christian biblical interpretation. The form in which the books are written down have a crucial impact in determining the way they are read. In the synagogue, Jews still read the Torah and some of the other books in the form in which they were originally written, as a scroll. Torah scrolls can be quite beautiful; they are arduous to produce, requiring a year's work by a qualified scribe, and consequently are quite expensive. The words are written with quail feather and ink on pieces of parchment made of animal skin woven

---

1. This book uses the terms B.C.E. and C.E., "Before the Common Era" and "in the Common Era," to avoid the theological implications of B.C., Before Christ, and A.D. for Anno Domini, in the year of our Lord. The former terms are now employed widely by historians and scholars.

together. No mistakes are tolerated; if even one letter is misshapen or unclear, the entire Torah is considered invalid for recitation. In its completed form, the Torah scroll is esteemed as a holy object, requiring the utmost respect and care. It is clothed in crowns and sumptuous cloth coverings; if it falls, the assembled are required to fast; when it becomes too old to use, it must be buried in a cemetery.

The names that Jews assign the five books derive from their origin as scrolls: each takes its name from the first significant word in the text, making it easy to identify the scroll when it is opened. The book of Leviticus in Hebrew is called Vayikra, "And He called," the first word of the scroll; Numbers is Bemidbar, "In the wilderness," the fifth word in the opening sentence. These titles reveal nothing of their contents; they are purely bibliographic aids. Most important, a scroll must be read straight through in the order in which it is rolled. It is difficult to jump around in a scroll as one can do in a book. For one thing, it takes two people to wind it. By reading the Torah portion by portion, week by week, Jews gain a sense of divine history unfolding in a constant motion from the beginnings of time.

By contrast, the Christian Old Testament was written down in a codex, an ancient form of the book as we know it, complete with pages and a cover. Old Testament titles correspond to our conception of the names of books – accurate summations of the contents. Genesis: the beginning of the world; Exodus: the going out from Egypt; Leviticus: the book of the priests; Numbers: the census taking (there are two of these in the book, besides other forms of reckoning); Deuteronomy: the second law (a restatement of the Mosaic code laid down at Sinai). The codex form fits perfectly the uses that Christianity accorded this body of writings. People might first read the Old Testament in sequence, gaining a sense of how it leads from Old to New. Once they reached the New, however, they could now flip the pages backward and forward to see how the New builds upon the foundation of the Old. Many modern Christian Bibles aid this process of cross-referencing by providing footnotes, in the Old Testament to passages in the New, and in the New Testament to passages in the Old. Even without these footnotes, many readers from previous generations would have heard these cross-references chime in their ears because they had often memorized large portions of the Bible. The codex thus freed up the reader to approach the Bible more selectively. For Christians, it was less important to read the Old Testament in its order than to gather up the clues seeded therein for the future.

Finally, we should take note of the Jewish and Christian names of the Bible, for these names are indeed the keys to how Jews and Christians read their books. The term "Old Testament" is a misleading translation of the Latin *Vetus Testamentum*, since a "testament" in English means a will, a division of property. *Testamentum* was the Latin translation of "covenant" (*brit* in Hebrew). Hence, "old testament" means the old terms of the relationship between humanity and God. The Jewish covenant, according to Christianity, has been replaced, in whole or in part, by a new relationship that God has established through the person of Jesus. Paul, the chief architect of this new, separate religion that broke away from Judaism, envisioned the difference between the two covenants as based in the distinction between law and faith:

> Now before faith came, we were confined under the law, kept under restraint until faith should be revealed. So that the law was our custodian until Christ came, that we might be justified by faith. (Galatians 3:23–24)

Paul regards the Jewish covenant as one founded upon a law that was burdensome and constricting. It was a necessary corrective to the sinfulness of human nature, especially after the "fall of man," according to the Christian reading of Genesis 3; but the new covenant with Jesus freed people from law's enslavement and opened the promise of God's redemption to the entire world.

Obviously, Jews have a very different relationship to their TaNaKh. The key term encapsulating the Jewish vision of the book is Torah. "Torah" has many meanings, all of which play a role in the Jewish understanding of Scripture. It can be compared to waves that billow out in ever larger concentric circles, from their initial source at Sinai. In its narrowist, most common use, "Torah" designates the "five books of Moses." In biblical Hebrew, the word *torah* can refer to individual laws, groups of laws, the law as a whole, or a book containing laws. Jews call the first five books "Torah" because those books are considered to contain all of the commandments in the TaNaKh. But the meaning of Torah extends well beyond these senses. Another, larger meaning is "instruction"; a teacher in Hebrew is *moreh* (feminine *morah*), which comes from the same root. Not just laws, but biblical stories, poems, and history as well are prized as eternal and inexhaustible sources of edification. Considering the entire TaNaKh as God's word to humanity, the Bible in its entirety was given to teach and inspire, so it is all Torah. The earliest rabbis called it the "Written Torah," to distinguish it from the "Oral Torah," which included ancient teachings passed down from teacher to student until they were assembled into the vast compendiums of law and wisdom, the Mishnah and Talmud. In its largest sense, the Torah's unending revelation includes the teachings inspired by it to this very day.

How Should You Read the Bible?

When we sit down to read the Bible today, in our homes, libraries, on bus, subway, or plane, we don't unwind it in a scroll but open a book, that handy modern-day codex. Since the Bible is an anthology and not a large novel composed to be perused in order like, say, *War and Peace*, there is no particular reason to read it straight through from page 1 to page 1624 (in the JPS translation). A famous saying of the ancient rabbis holds that "there is no early or late in the Torah," meaning that the Bible is not a book that has to be read linearly. In other words, to be faithful to the Bible's own logic means to read it with a different kind of logic, the logic of one's own temperament and inspiration. The traditional Jewish educational system initiated children into the Bible with Leviticus, thus reinforcing this very point. In the religious view, God's Truth is not historically conditioned; the books of Genesis, Proverbs and Daniel are, under the light of eternity, simultaneous.

Whether you approach the Bible with a profound religious awe or merely out of a sense of curiosity, there are an infinite number of ways to enjoy and appreciate this majestic anthology. Like Julio Cortazar's post-modern novel *Hopscotch*,[2] the sections of the Bible can legitimately be read in different orders, and the meaning of the whole may change with each approach. Embarking upon a first reading, you may wish to get the story first, by going through many of the books, especially the historical ones, from cover to cover; you might skip over the laws of Leviticus and jump straight from 2 Kings to Ezra, where the historical thread picks up again. The book of Ruth poses a challenge: does one read it between Judges and 1 Samuel, where it appears in the Christian Bible, because Ruth takes place "in the days when the judges ruled," according to its opening sentence? Or instead does one hold off and read it as one of the short books, known as the "five scrolls," according to its late placement in the Jewish sequence? You might even prefer the approach of the Talmud, which places Ruth before Psalms (Ruth being the ancestor of David, traditionally considered the Psalms' author).

For another approach, try a literary reading. A poet could start with the obvious classics of the Psalms and Song of Songs, Lamentations and Job, move on to the prophets, and then scour the rest for poems nestled into prose narratives, like David's woeful dirge upon the death of Jonathan and Saul in 2 Samuel 1. A novelist may wish to concentrate on the recurrent power struggles throughout the Bible: Cain and Abel, Sarah and Hagar, Jacob and Esau, Moses and Pharaoh, Jael and Sisera, Samuel and Saul, Saul and David, Adonijah and Solomon, Elijah and Ahab, Job and God. A lawyer can find great interest in the legal passages of the Bible where others yawn and skip. The prophets may appeal to unlikely

---

2. Here are the "Table of Instructions" from *Hopscotch*:

In its own way, this book consists of many books, but two books above all.

The first can be read in a normal fashion and it ends with Chapter 56, at the close of which there are three garish little stars which stand for the words *The End*. Consequently, the reader may ignore what follows with a clear conscience.

The second should be read by beginning with Chapter 73 and then following the sequence indicated at the end of each chapter. In case of confusion or forgetfulness, one need only consult the following list:

73 – 1 – 2 – 116 – 3 – 84 – 4 – 71 – 5 – 81 – 74 – 6 – 7 – 8 – 93 – 68 –
9 – 104 – 10 – 65 – 11 – 136 – 12 – 106 – 13 – 115 – 14 – 114 – 117 – 15 –
120 – 16 – 137 – 17 – 97 – 18 – 153 – 19 – 90 – 20 – 126 – 21...

bedfellows: to religious preachers, seeking inspiration for their sermons; to social activists, moved by the prophets' fearless championing of the poor and their denunciation of corruption by the powerful; to people hunting for clues of the future in ancient sayings. Seekers of guidance will find much to ponder in the teaching of the Proverbs or, if they are of a more cynical cast, in Ecclesiastes. Politicos and war buffs may delight in the clash of armies, personalities, and ideologies recounted in Kings (and retold in 2 Chronicles), while diary readers may be transported by the immediacy of the first-person accounts and letters from Persian kings inserted in Ezra–Nehemiah. Another famous rabbinic expression claims, "Turn it [the Torah] and turn it again, for everything is in it." Although most modern readers would not go that far, it is surely true that the more you look in the Bible, the more you will find.

CHAPTER 2

Storytelling

Suggested reading: Genesis 1–Exodus 15

The Bible begins with stories and ends with stories. Many of the world's best-known stories can be found in the Bible, along with quite a few that are extremely strange and rarely taught in religious school. Most important, the Bible has a characteristic way of *telling* stories, a highly recognizable storytelling style. Some of its hallmarks come from distinctive expressions widely considered as "biblical" in a quaint, archaic way: "And Abraham knew his wife Sarah," "And it came to pass, in the days of…" "Behold,…." Starting most sentences with "and" is a characteristic of biblical storytelling, suggesting continuity of action. Other expressions have become familiar as "biblical" through the cadences of the most important English translation, the King James Bible: x "begat" y. "Who told thee that thou wast naked?" "And Lamech took unto him two wives…." "I wot not who hath done this thing."

A work of literature may not be most people's main impression of the Bible. Some biblical scholars would beg to differ. In recent years, scholars trained in literary analysis have mined biblical stories and poetry for their literary characteristics. They have demonstrated that biblical stories reveal a remarkable literary sophistication. Most unexpectedly, the Bible's verbal art rewards multiple rereadings the same way that the *Canterbury Tales* or *Madame Bovary* does. Another way of putting it: the Bible is as fascinating a literary document for literary scholars as it is a religious document for religious scholars. Its stories are rich in ambiguity, allusion, irony, narrative patterns, and openness to multiple interpretation, all values highly prized in works of imaginative writing. The eminent literary scholar Harold Bloom, for one, considers the author of the major strand of stories in the Pentateuch to be "the greatest of all ironists." What follows is a description of some features of biblical storytelling that lend it a distinctive style and rhythm, contributing to its power as one of the exemplary models of literary art.

Microcosm: Mind the Gaps

Biblical stories contain all the psychological tension and conflict of a great potboiler. One characteristic that makes the Bible unique, however, is that it covers in a couple verses as much action as a novel would present in one chapter, if not several. Biblical stories are told in such compressed, rapid form that they inevitably leave out a great deal; when examined closely, they appear as full of holes as Swiss cheese. These stories preserve only the barest essentials necessary to hold the narrative thread together and keep it moving at a breakneck pace.

The passage narrating Moses' transition into manhood provides a textbook of the kinds of gaps commonly found in biblical stories:

> [11]And in those days, Moses grew up and went out to his brothers, and he saw their burdens. He saw an Egyptian man striking a Hebrew man, one of his brothers. [12]He turned this way and that, and saw there was no one; and he struck down the Egyptian and buried him in the sand. [13]He went out the next day, and, behold, two Hebrew men were struggling with each other; and he said to the guilty one, "Why do you strike your fellow?" [14]And he said, "Who made you ruler and judge over us? Do you mean to kill me as you killed the Egyptian?" Moses was frightened, and he said, "Indeed, the matter is known!" [15]Pharaoh heard of this matter, and he sought to kill Moses. But Moses fled from Pharaoh, and he dwelt in the land of Midian and sat down beside a well. (Exodus 2:11–15)

The verse preceding this passage describes how Pharaoh's daughter raised and named Moses; here, Moses is already acting as an adult. In a mere five verses Moses passes from boyhood to manhood! There are at least three separate discernible "events" narrated in these spare lines. The density is extraordinary even by biblical standards, giving the impression of breathless rapidity. A sudden whirr of activity transported Moses from dandy in the royal court to public enemy number one.

So much information is left out of this passage, it is astonishing how smoothly it reads. "And in those days" – what days exactly? Verse 10 said that when "the boy grew up" he was brought to Pharaoh's daughter; by verse 11 he "grew up" some more. How much more? Is Moses a teenager? In his twenties? Or even older? And what happened during Moses' childhood? Why did the Bible skip over that period of his life entirely, especially if Moses is such an important character? After all, the Bible reveals plenty about the childhood of Jacob and of Joseph and his brothers. Moses is a kind of mirror image of Joseph: Joseph is born as an Israelite and becomes a ruler in Egypt; Moses is born as an Egyptian (his name means "son" in Egyptian) and becomes the ruler of the Israelites. Is Moses' childhood any less worthy of recounting?

That question becomes more urgent in light of the next gap. Moses "went out to his brothers, and he saw their burdens." Is the word "brothers" a reflection of Moses' consciousness, or merely the narrator's observation? Assuming the former – he went to observe their labors *because* he knew he was their kin – how did Moses know that the Hebrews were his brothers? Did Pharaoh's daughter raise Moses to receive a full awareness of his ethnic identity? (How very modern of her if she did!) Or did Moses' mother do considerably more than nurse him (verse 9)? Did she in fact raise him herself for many years and educate him to be a Hebrew before handing him back over to Pharaoh's daughter? What is Moses' status in his society? Do the members of Pharaoh's palace regard him as an insider or an outsider? How do other Egyptians regard him? As a nobleman? An interloper? And Moses himself – does he think of himself as an Egyptian, or perhaps a Hebrew-Egyptian, like the hyphenated identities of many Americans today? A few choice words from the Bible would have avoided such a chain of questions: any novice editor would have had the author correct the omissions. But the biblical narrator decided that such details were not worth the time for the story he needed to tell.

Next question: was this the first time that Moses learned of the

Hebrews' enslavement? Was it possible for him not to have known such a fact, given his awareness of his "brothers"? Did he know that other Hebrew boys were drowned in the Nile and that his very existence was miraculous? If so, how did he feel about that; did he wait a long time for a chance to meet his fellow Hebrews firsthand? If not, how could that policy have been hidden from him? In short, what does Moses really know at this point about the Hebrews, other than the fact that he is somehow one of them? And how does he feel about his Hebrew brethren before going out to observe their hardships? Was his sense of Hebrew identity active? Did he, for example, observe their holidays and socialize with them, or had he been isolated from them for years, his Hebrewness become vestigial? Most crucially, does he believe in one God or many?

And another: What is it that pushes Moses over the edge to make him kill the Egyptian? Assuming for the moment that this is the first time Moses has learned about Hebrew enslavement, does this scene then reveal Moses to be rash and impetuous, or on the contrary, is the haste with which he decides to kill the Egyptian admirable? An alternative scenario: Did Moses go out to his brothers and witness their burdens over an extended period of time? If that is the case, then did the repetition of witnessing suffering, over and over, accumulate in Moses' mind until he snapped? In other words, is this the first time Moses "going out to see his brothers" is mentioned because it is the first time he goes out, or it is the first time he acts – or both?

Four paragraphs of questions, and just on the first verse. Verse 12, though shorter, is equally puzzling. One wonders how there could have been "no one about" when he is in the middle of the mass of slaves performing their labors, surrounded by taskmasters. Was there really no one about, or was that merely Moses' perception in the heat of anger? How did Moses strike down the Egyptian? Was Moses extremely strong and brave, or did he sneak up from behind when the Egyptian wasn't paying attention? Was there a struggle? Did the Egyptian assume Moses was on his side because he was dressed like an Egyptian? Was Moses a famous person in Egypt, as a special ward of Pharaoh, and thus above suspicion of harboring sympathies for the slaves? Was it known that Moses was Hebrew-born? And why did Moses hide the body in the sand? To protect himself? Or was he also ashamed of his action? Does the biblical prohibition against murder apply to Moses, or was his act justifiable homicide? Is Moses here a second Cain? Both characters appear foolish in their attempts to hide or deny their killing. Will the Egyptian's blood, like Abel's, cry out from the ground (Genesis 4:10)? The narrator is reticent to issue an explicit judgment upon Moses' violent deed.

Verses 13–14: What made Moses go out again the next day among the Hebrews? Was he looking to kill another Egyptian? Did he have a plan of action that day, perhaps seeking to organize a rebellion? Or perhaps, in a more general sense, he hoped to solidify his feeling of kinship with the Hebrews? If so, he must have felt gravely disappointed, as he suffers a stinging rebuke, accused of arrogance by the people he means to help. Two questions immediately arise from the dialogue here: First, how did Moses determine which of the two Hebrews fighting was the "guilty one"? Was it obvious from the situation, or did Moses tell purely by his nose for injustice? Second, how did the Hebrews find out that Moses had killed the Egyptian? Do these Hebrew men even know who Moses is? Do they resent him for the life of privilege he has led, as the only Hebrew to escape slavery? And what did Moses feel upon hearing these words? Did he expect gratitude for saving a Hebrew slave from punishment? How did he have the strength and confidence to continue, not only to identify as a Hebrew, but on his path to leadership of the Israelites? (Another possible scenario: Was the slave merely feigning resentment as a way to tell Moses, "Everyone knows what happened. Flee for your life!")

We are not told whether such potentially devastating thoughts crossed Moses' mind. Rather, Moses faces the more practical issue that if the Hebrew slaves know, the rumor will quickly spread elsewhere, and he must flee. His ignorance of how the story got out might well have increased his sense of fear, even inducing a moment of paranoia. In that split second, Moses realized that there was no going back; he had unwittingly crossed over from being an Egyptian to a Hebrew. Verse 15 confirms Moses' logic: Pharaoh seeks to kill Moses, but Moses is already a step ahead of him.

The gaps in the biblical narrative thus awaken a hive of questions around the narrated action. Most of the questions concern issues of characters' motivation, but sometimes there are gaps in the story itself (e.g., how did people find out about the murder?). Why does the Bible typically leave so much information out? In part, one can generalize that ancient storytelling largely does not portray interior thoughts and feelings. Contemporary storytelling, at least since the rise of the novel in the eighteenth and nineteenth centuries, dwells primarily upon such personal concerns, so that we are trained as readers to look for them. To a degree, then, the gaps we perceive derive from our own assumptions projected upon the biblical story. This is not at all to suggest that the interior world of the characters is left entirely opaque in the Bible. In verse 14 we are explicitly told that Moses was frightened, and we are given Moses' thought in the form of interior monologue: "And he [Moses] *said*, 'Indeed, the matter is known!'" Thought in the Bible is typically conveyed in this form, showing a character "saying" something to himself or herself. In verses 11 and 12 the narrator stays close to Moses' perspective without going inside of his head, whereas in verse 15 the narrator reports events in a more detached manner. Thus this passage incorporates the range of relations between the biblical storyteller and the characters. The narrator moves freely and rapidly between closeup and long shot, only rarely and briefly putting the lens directly within the character's head.

Most of the gaps described above, however, cannot be ascribed to the difference between contemporary and ancient norms of storytelling. Contrasting the storytelling styles of the Bible and Homer's *Odyssey*, two books from roughly the same time, Erich Auerbach demonstrates that Homer leaves nothing out in his description of place, characters, and action, whereas the Bible is "fraught with background," tracing the action concisely and sharply while leaving much of the narrated world suggestively unexpressed. Another way of describing biblical storytelling is that it places a great deal of the work in the hands of the reader. Biblical narrative is the reading equivalent of Connect the Dots; what's given on the page resembles dots more than a full picture, and it's up to the reader to connect them in a way that fleshes out the image. The Bible's remarkable openness to an enormous range of interpretations derives mostly from the laconic quality of biblical prose.

With so much left out of the story, what guiding principles determined what was to remain? In bold strokes, this passage describes Moses' qualities as a leader. His chief characteristic is decisiveness: he sums up a situation quickly and determines a course of action. Striking the Egyptian, hiding him, moderating between the Hebrews, fleeing Pharaoh – Moses shows no hesitation before any challenge put to him. Later on there will be occasion for self-doubt. In Exodus 3–4, for example, at the burning bush, Moses accepts his divinely appointed role with great reluctance, and not as a brash young courtier of Pharaoh's house. Another quality revealed in this incident is his keen sense of justice. Moses cannot abide oppression, whether performed by Egyptian taskmasters or by one Hebrew against another. Although quick to take charge, Moses is not reckless; when he senses that his life is in danger, he decides to flee rather than remain to face punishment and sure death. As described here, Moses is innately qualified to be a leader. The narrative connections – the who-what-where-when-whys certifying that the story makes sense in all its details – were not important and could easily be sacrificed. The picture of Moses comes across like the work of a portraitist whose care at depicting his subject contrasts with his dismissal of the setting in a few perfunctory waves of the brush. (Quick: where does the story take place? What does the location look like? Is it even possible to visualize it? Our one clue: sand.)

These rapid-fire occurrences prefigure later conflicts in Moses' life. His fight with the Egyptian slave driver and Pharaoh's anger against him initiate the full-scale showdown between Pharaoh and Moses, the Egyptians and the Israelites. But while Moses leaves the life of privilege he enjoyed in Egypt, he never is able to identify completely with the people he is called to lead, the Israelites. He remains a distant and uncomfortable ruler, concerned from the beginning that they would not accept him; and time and again the Israelites chafe under his rule, just as the Hebrew slaves here reject his authority. (The tension between Moses and the Israelites led Sigmund Freud to conjecture that the Israelites actually killed him!)

Moses' distance from his people comes across in both positive and negative terms. On the one hand, the fact that he did not grow up a slave gives Moses the habits of freedom and responsibility necessary to be a leader. No other Israelite could possibly be as qualified to act with such courage, wisdom, and decisiveness. On the other hand, the feeling that he is not "one of us," mutual to him and to his followers, shadows him his entire life and leads him to outbursts of unhappiness, whether by shattering the first tablets with the Ten Commandments, or in his bitter complaint found at the beginning of Deuteronomy. With Moses being a transitional figure not at home in one culture or another, his choice of a Midianite wife makes good sense, reinforcing his status as an outsider.

Turning back to the passage in Exodus 2, where we might have expected a glorification of the hero, instead the Bible shows Moses as flawed, despite his noble qualities. Besides his troubled relations with his "brothers," Moses' quickness to act with violence is not depicted entirely in positive terms, as the suggested parallel with Cain makes clear. This same character flaw is revealed in the enigmatic episode where Moses strikes the rock and causes water to pour forth, rather than speaking to the rock as God had commanded (Numbers 20), thereby drawing God's punishment forbidding Moses from entering the land of Israel. Moses, the embodiment of the biblical hero, clearly stands above his fellows while at the same time, all too human, presents no challenge to the kingship and unity of God. The Bible leaves no chance for Moses to be confused with a deity. Despite its numerous narrative gaps, this passage draws a remarkably rich and subtle picture of Moses' complex personality.

Traditional Jewish commentary is extremely sensitive to these gaps in the story. It attempts to fill them from other clues in the Bible, and relies upon interpretations handed down from previous generations of commentators. The most important Jewish commentator throughout the ages has been Rashi (an acronym deriving from the initials of his full name, Rabbi Shlomo Yitzhaki; 1040–1105 c.e., France). His notes are typically brief, lucid, often commonsensical, and filled with helpful linguistic insight. Examination of a few of his glosses demonstrates that Rashi's activity as a commentator was, to a large extent, occupied with filling in the Bible's narrative gaps. On Exodus 2:11, "And he saw their burdens." Rashi: *He cast his eyes and heart to feel their distress.* "Saw" is such a neutral word; Rashi seeks to explain Moses' emotions: seeing is feeling, empathizing, not just looking. "He saw an Egyptian man." Rashi: *He was one of the slave drivers.* This detail, not made explicit in the Bible, clarifies that the cruelty was an ongoing pattern. "Beating a Hebrew." Rashi here recounts a legend that this Egyptian had in fact raped this Hebrew slave's wife and was beating the man because he knew that the Hebrew had found out. Usually Rashi makes use of the vast store of Jewish legends sparingly; when he does cite one of them, it provides an explanation he senses is badly needed in the story. Here Rashi needs a justification for Moses' killing of the Egyptian. The fact that the Egyptian was a bad guy, and even that he was beating the Hebrew slave, didn't justify Moses' vigilante justice in Rashi's mind. By expanding upon the wickedness of the Egyptian slave driver, the legend leaves no doubt that Moses did the right thing.

The Midrash, classical collections of Jewish legends and interpretations accumulated over centuries, similarly seeks to clarify the material perceived as missing in biblical verses, often through creative elaborations. In verse 11, how old was Moses? *Moses was twenty at the time; some say forty.* Midrashic collections cite conflicting opinions, and in this case the uncertainty over Moses' age reflects the obscurity in the story. The repetition of the expression "and he grew up" in verses 10 and 11 might justify the opinion that Moses had grown up twice, and if "growing up" means reaching adulthood in about twenty years, then growing up twice means Moses is forty. In explanation of the clause "And he saw their burdens," the Midrash creates a moving story of Moses' great concern for his people:

> Rabbi Eleazar, son of Rabbi Jose the Galilean, said: He saw great burdens put upon small people and light burdens upon big people, and a man's burden upon a woman and a woman's burden upon a man, and the burden which an old man could carry on a youth, and of a youth on an old man. So he left his suite and rearranged their burdens, pretending all the time to be helping Pharaoh. God then said to him: "Thou hast put aside thy work and hast gone to share the sorrow of Israel, behaving to them like a brother; well, I will also leave those on high and below and only speak with thee."

This story portrays Moses' greatness more explicitly than the biblical text that inspired it. The Midrash not only explains what Moses was doing when he "saw their burdens," it also answers another puzzler: How was Moses permitted to wander among the Hebrews? According to Rabbi

Eleazar, Moses invented a pretext of helping Pharaoh; the exact nature of that pretext is left to the imagination of the next interpreter. At the end of this Midrash, God rewards Moses by promising to speak directly only to him. Rabbi Eleazar recognizes that the passage in Exodus 2 establishes Moses' worthiness to receive the divine communication at the burning bush, where God calls Moses to lead the Jewish people. The passage as we have it only hints at Moses' merit; the Midrash tries to fill in the picture.

Macrocosm: Moving Forward, Layering Backward

As a long, ongoing story spanning many centuries, the Bible had to find a way to give shape and meaning to the book overall. Like other large collections of diverse materials culled from different sources and eras — whether the compendium of mythological tales in Ovid's *Metamorphoses* or the epic historical sweep of Gibbon's *Decline and Fall of the Roman Empire* — biblical stories share common themes, patterns, and structures that lend to the whole an identifiable narrative arc. The combination of an uninterrupted history with a strong, overarching narrative creates certain characteristic tensions. There is a tension between the continuous nature of history, generation following generation, ruler succeeding ruler, versus a sense of progression, development, significant change, building to a climax. In history, all climaxes must be followed by anticlimaxes; no high point of civilization lasts forever. Biblical stories build upward to a defining moment, then come crashing downward, only to build up again to a different height. Creation starts as a barren waste and progresses up to the pinnacle of humankind, who, given sufficient opportunity in the Garden of Eden, eat from the forbidden fruit. After years of bitter struggle and recriminations, Joseph and his brothers achieve reconciliation and prosperity in Egypt, only to have their descendants suffer brutal slavery. Moses leads the people from slavery to freedom, then onward to receiving the commandments on Mount Sinai, where his followers grow impatient in his absence and create a golden calf to worship. Joshua takes the next generation into the land of Israel, followed by countless tales of betrayal and apostasy. History never stands still; no climax is final, but no low is without hope for future ascent. The very length of history, its relentless duration, ensures that there can be no happily-ever-after.

Another tension stretching beneath the surface of biblical history lies in the conflict between the forward movement of time versus the repetition of events and character traits. The very repetitions that can forge a sense of unity and pattern within the grand sweep of history can also lend a gloomier cast to events, an impression that characters are doomed to reenact historical scenarios beyond their control. These two aspects may be called the linear versus the cyclical views of time. Ecclesiastes, one of the latest books of the Bible, expresses the cyclical view as follows: "What was, that will be; and what was done, that will be done; there is nothing new under the sun!" (1:9) The jaundiced imagination of Ecclesiastes did not originate this cynical view of history as a web of folly; it is woven into the fabric of biblical history as it was written. One of the more ominous repetitions comes at the end of many of the stories in the Book of Kings. For the kings of the northern kingdom of Israel, their accomplishments are routinely summarized thus: "He did what was displeasing to the Lord; he followed in the ways of Jeroboam and the sins which he caused Israel to commit." The Book of Kings calls to mind the famous quotation of the philosopher George Santayana: "Those who cannot remember the past are condemned to repeat it," a dire view of history, whose repetition is a kind of curse. However, in the Bible's eyes history is not so uniformly negative. Just as often, the past represents a model of glory to which present actors aspire, whether in the form of an idyllic place (Eden) or leader (Moses) or building (the Tabernacle) or administration (Solomon).

These two dominant tensions throughout biblical narrative establish the rhythms through which the music of the stories flows. The first rhythm – call it topsy-turvy – moves the drama up and down, through peaks and valleys, cresting and falling like the waves of the ocean. The second rhythm – call it ebb-and-flow – brushes the reader forward and backward, like the movement of the sea's undercurrent. Up and down, back and forth – biblical stories always train one eye on the future and the other on what came before.

Repetitions: Marking a Heritage

In Genesis and Exodus, too, there are numerous repeated elements, from small phrases – e.g., "And God saw that it was good" in Genesis 1 – to actions and whole scenes. Many of these repetitions reinforce the impression that the nation's ancestral founders resemble each other as spiritually gifted members of a family chosen by God to bear His message to the world. We find an explicit statement that Isaac follows in his father's footsteps in Genesis 26:18:

> And Isaac returned and dug the wells that were dug in the days
> of Abraham his father, wells that the Philistines stopped up after
> Abraham's death. And he named them after the names that his father
> called them.

Here Isaac consciously reenacts his father's actions in order to claim them as his own. On other occasions the characters repeat the actions of their predecessors without any express awareness on the part of the narrator or characters. It is up to the reader to weave the similarities between the patriarchs into a larger narrative, historical, or theological pattern. According to a famous rabbinic saying, "The deeds of the fathers are a sign for the sons," an observation that early rabbis no doubt derived not just from "human nature" but from their close reading of these biblical stories.

Since Abraham and his descendants have a religious mission from God, some of the most salient repetitions concern their roles as religious leaders:

God's Promises and Blessings. At key points in their lives, the patriarchs all receive direct statements from God promising them blessings of various kinds. Abraham receives his first blessing when he is singled out as a central character in the story (he had been mentioned a few verses before as the son of Terah):

> And I will make you into a great nation, and I will bless you and
> magnify your name to be a blessing. And I will bless those who bless
> you, and those who slight you I shall curse; and through you all the
> families of the earth shall be blessed. (Genesis 12:2–3)

This blessing immediately establishes Abraham's importance for the rest of biblical history. Abraham will become the father of a large nation, which will achieve particular fame through the special care it will receive from God. Other nations will share in God's blessing to the extent that they acknowledge God's relationship with Abraham's descendants. Subsequently, Abraham continues to receive promises, blessings, and direct communications from God at every turn of his life. God promises him the land of Israel, offspring – both a single heir, Isaac, and progeny as numerous as the sand on the shore – and future conquest of enemies: "your offspring shall possess the gates of their foes" (22:17).

Although Isaac lives the longest of the three patriarchs (180 years, versus 175 for Abraham and 147 for Jacob), the Bible accords to Isaac's life the fewest pages and adventures. No matter how long he lives, he remains in his father's shadow and seems to accept his lesser role as the transmitter of Abraham's legacy. God does bless Isaac, but only on account of His promises to Abraham:

> For to you and your offspring I shall give all these lands, establishing the oath I swore to Abraham your father. And I will multiply your offspring like the stars of heaven, and I will give your offspring all of these lands, and through your offspring the nations of the earth shall be blessed – because Abraham obeyed Me… (26:3–5).
>
> I am the God of Abraham, your father. Fear not, for I am with you, and I will bless you and multiply your offspring for the sake of Abraham My servant. (26:24)

Isaac's wife Rebekah fares at least as well as her husband in obtaining blessings. When her father and brother send her off to get married, they offer her the same blessing that God has granted Abraham:

> Our sister! May you become a vast multitude; may your offspring possess the gates of those who hate them. (24:60)

This parallel with Abraham confirms Rebekah as the appropriate choice for Isaac. The fact that her blessing speaks of triumph over enemies, unlike the more benign promises to Isaac, aptly reflects her dominance over him. She receives an additional prophecy from God explaining the fate of the two sons struggling in her womb (25:23).

As the second in the chain of blessing, Isaac bears the responsibility to pass along his blessing just as he received one. He proves as clumsy in this task as he is weak in his other endeavors. Despite Isaac's preference for Esau, Rebekah deceives him into giving the primary blessing to her favorite, Jacob, clad in goatskin to appear hairy like his brother. Jacob has given his father plenty to eat and drink to help further befog his mind (27:25).

> May God give you the dew of heaven and the fat of the earth, plentiful grain and new wine. Peoples shall serve you, nations shall bow down to you; take charge over your brothers, so that your mother's sons bow down to you. Those who curse you are cursed, and those who bless you are blessed. (27:28–29)

Thinking that he is blessing Esau, Isaac's words fit as roughly upon Jacob as his hairy gloves. Isaac begins by recalling the good food and wine he has just ingested; his blessing anticipates the benefits that Moses will promise the Israelites when they enter the land of Israel (e.g., Deuteronomy 11:14) but speaks little to the condition of Jacob himself, a shepherd. Next he envisions Jacob's glorious superiority over other nations. Promising that Jacob's brothers would bow down to Jacob fits better with Noah's son Shem (9:26–27) or with Jacob's own son Joseph than with Jacob's situation. He has only one brother, who is physically more powerful; later on it is Jacob who bows down to Esau, seven times (33:3)! The final blessing succeeds in designating Jacob as Abraham's heir, but in contrast to God's promise to Abraham in 12:3, Isaac mentions the cursers ahead of the blessers. This upside-down blessing portends the troubled life that Jacob will lead. In the Bible a blessing, like a curse or vow, contains its own potent force that, once released, can scarcely be revoked. Isaac's confused utterance provides both a blessing and an underhanded slap at his trickster son. By contrast, Isaac's later blessing to Esau more accurately targets Esau's character: "By your sword shall you live" (27:40).

The Patriarchs' Shrines. Abraham and Jacob are like religious Johnny Appleseeds; both establish shrines – prayer centers, future temple locations – wherever they go. The shrines usually mark places where they have encountered God, though sometimes these places are significant in their lives for other reasons. Immediately after Abraham's initial blessing, he builds two altars, one at Shechem, the other between Bethel and Ai. When he moves to Hebron, he builds an altar there; onward to Beer-Sheba, where he "invokes God's name" at the place he plants a tamarisk tree. At the mountain where Abraham sacrifices a ram in place of his son Isaac, Abraham names the place "the Lord will see" (Adonai Yireh), presumably indicating yet another religious center. (According to Jewish tradition, this site was the location of the future Temple in Jerusalem.)

Not surprisingly, Isaac founds only one altar, and that at Beer-Sheba, where Abraham had already prayed. Jacob resumes Abraham's wanderlust and zeal for spreading God's name. At the location where he dreams of angels ascending and descending a ladder, he sets up the stones into a pillar and names the shrine Bethel (presumably at a different place than Abraham's shrine). After a long sojourn with Laban, his brother-in-law, Jacob offers sacrifices on "the Height" at Mizpah. The next morning Jacob encounters two angels along his way and names the place Mahanayim. Later on, when he wrestles with an angel, Jacob names the place Peniel. This pattern of shrine-naming connects the biographies of the patriarchs with the religious, historical, and geographical landscape of their descendants. The significance of the patriarchs' actions vastly exceeds the moments in which they took place. They establish models of divine–human encounter memorialized forever through names, temples, and stories.

Here are some of the other notable repetitions in Genesis:

+ Barren wives: Sarah, Rebekah, and Rachel (later, Hannah in 1 Samuel 1).
+ Favored/rejected wife: Sarah/Hagar; Rachel/Leah (note that the rejected wife is the fertile one).
+ Wife-sister tales, wherein the patriarch passes his wife off as his sister to save himself: Abraham twice (Genesis 12, 20), Isaac (Genesis 26).
+ Bride discovered at well: Abraham's servant finds Rebekah (Genesis

24), Jacob finds Rachel (Genesis 29), Moses finds Zipporah (Exodus 2).[1]

+ Younger son inherits birthright: Isaac over Ishmael, Jacob over Esau, Joseph over brothers, Ephraim over Manasseh (Genesis 48).
+ Material success: Abraham (13:2), Isaac (26:12–14), Jacob (30:43), Joseph in Egypt.
+ Blindness in old age: Isaac (27:1), Jacob (48:10) (mentioned, in both cases, when they are in the act of giving a blessing; Isaac's blindness explains how he was deceived into blessing the younger son rather than the older, Jacob's, how he was *not* confused, despite his blindness, when he gave the blessing to the younger son).

These repetitions create a sense of design to history, superimposing larger patterns upon the individual tales surrounding the Israelites' ancestors. Because of the uniquely open nature of biblical storytelling, readers throughout the centuries have read the stories from different perspectives and on different levels: narrative, psychological, theological, literary, historical. What is particularly remarkable about the biblical patriarchs is that, at the same time that they are meant to serve as legendary prototypes representing the Israelites as a whole – God names Abraham to indicate he is the "father of a multitude" (17:5); Jacob is renamed Israel (32:29; also 35:10), hence "the children of Israel" are literally his descendants – and despite these numerous repetitions emphasizing their similarity one to another, they nevertheless remain in the mind of the reader as fully formed, memorable characters with entirely distinct personalities.

1. Robert Alter cites these story patterns (wife-sister tales, betrothal at well) as examples of "type-scenes," repeated stories containing many of the same details, whose differences are crucial in defining the particular features of characters. Alter regards biblical type-scenes as comparable to certain archetypal moments in a Western – the hero's entrance into a bad town, the duel on main street, etc. – which the audience enjoys both because it expects certain standard features to be present (e.g., the creaky saloon doors, hitching posts, ten-gallon hats, boots with spurs) and it relishes the clever innovations that the great Westerns bring to the form.

Moses as Archpatriarch

The narrative vectors winding through the patriarchs reach a culmination in the character of Moses. By sharing characteristics with his predecessors – all except Isaac, who, as we have seen, is the most passive and the least remarked upon patriarch – Moses appears as a kind of archpatriarch, the perfect inheritor of God's promise to Abraham and his family. These narrative connections underline Moses' legitimacy as a ruler, which he needs in order to fulfill his greater and more difficult task of leading a large nation rather than a small family-tribe. By "digging the wells" of the patriarchs, that is, displaying some of their characteristics and repeating some of their actions, Moses ensures the continuity of their line through the crucial period of national liberation and formation.

The first time Moses speaks to God, he reminds us of Abraham. Moses and Abraham share a profound intimacy with God, combining reverence and faith with the courage to express their deepest thoughts to God, even to challenge and disagree with Him. Their intimacy with God qualifies both men as leaders. Abraham hears God speak to him at every turn in his life. Whereas at first the conversation is one-directional, God promising future blessings to Abraham and his descendants, Abraham rapidly comes to feel close enough to God to be able to speak back to Him. God promises Abraham,

> "Fear not, Abram. I am a shield for you; your reward is very great." But Abram said, "O Lord God, what can You give me, while I remain childless, and the heir of my household is Dammesek Eliezer?" (15:1–2)

With this surprising rejoinder, Abraham jumps off the page to become a three-dimensional character. Momentarily he refuses to remain the perfect role model, silently obedient to God, carrying out His will in complete trust. God has piled on promise after promise, yet Abraham and Sarah continue to be without a child. Who will inherit God's blessings or transmit the message that Abraham has brought into the world? How can there be a "great reward" if it will die with the receiver? From where will come the heirs, let alone the nation, that God has guaranteed to Abraham? Abraham acts as if he cannot listen to another promise couched in vague generalities. He addresses God with the raw emotional directness characteristic of their intimate relationship. God responds with an even greater promise, reassuring Abraham that he will indeed have an heir and that his offspring will be as numerous as the stars in heaven. Abraham has found a way to confront God that brings him even closer to God, by expressing his deepest concerns, fears, and hopes. Abraham being utterly guileless and uninhibited, his willingness to pit his own sense of morality against God's reaches its culmination in the verbal wrestling between God and Abraham over Sodom and Gomorrah's imminent destruction (18:16–33).

Similarly, Moses does not hesitate to talk back to God when he demurs at God's decisions. When God commissions Moses at the burning bush to lead the Israelites out of Egypt (Exodus 3–4), Moses is full of questions and objections. "Who am I that I should go to Pharaoh and bring the Israelites out of Egypt?" "Suppose they do not believe me and do not listen to me, but say, 'The Lord did not appear to you'?" "Please, O Lord, dispatch whom You would dispatch" (the implication: someone else). Moses' sharp rejection by the Israelite slaves who were fighting in Exodus 2 may explain his extreme reluctance to accept his new divinely appointed role. However, his willingness to argue with God, even bargain with Him – wringing the concession that Aaron will be his spokesman – demonstrates that intimacy with God characteristic of a great leader. Moses continues to consult with God, alone, "face-to-face," in the Tent of Meeting throughout his reign.

Later on, Moses, like Abraham, argues with God over a threatened destruction, this time, of the Israelites (Numbers 14). When the people hear that the land of Israel is filled with giants, they become angry at Moses and Aaron for taking them out of Egypt, and they are about to pelt them with stones when God intervenes. Zealous for Moses' sake and enraged at the people's stubbornness, God says that He will wipe out the people, starting anew with Moses as the father of the nation. Moses' response contains a complex argument that takes God's anger down several notches; he appeals to God's reputation among the nations, to God's history of care for the Israelites, and finally, to God's great mercy and ability to forgive. Here Moses seems to be reminding God of His own better nature. Although Moses succeeds in averting total destruction, unlike the case with Abraham, his victory is only partial, as God promises to kill off this generation before they reach the Promised Land: "In this very wilderness [their] corpses will fall."

The Bible draws an even closer parallel between the two figures in Genesis 12:10–20. When Moses argues with God, Moses reminds us of Abraham; in Genesis 12, Abraham reminds us of Moses. This passage briefly forebodes events that will be climactic episodes for Moses and the Israelites. Abraham and Sarah descend to Egypt because "the famine was heavy in the land." Pharaoh's courtiers find Sarah to be very beautiful, so, having been told that she is Abraham's sister, they take her into the palace and reward Abraham with livestock. God punishes Pharaoh and his household "with mighty plagues," at which point Pharaoh sends the pair off with their possessions. In a nutshell, this scene is a very close summation of the Israelites' descent to and exodus from Egypt, the major difference being that this Pharaoh is a good guy. (The deceived monarch as good guy is a convention of the wife-sister tales.) Even the detail that they left with their possessions has a parallel in the "vessels of silver, vessels of gold, and clothing" which the Israelites "borrowed from the Egyptians" as they fled (Exodus 12:35). The main purpose of this story is to solidify the connection between Israel's two great early leaders, Abraham and Moses. The fact that Abraham, unlike the other patriarchs, acts as a military leader (Genesis 14) further enhances Moses' stature as a second Abraham (compare Exodus 17:8–13).

The outline of Moses' early life conforms in certain ways with Jacob's. Both of them flee for their life – Jacob from Esau, Moses from Pharaoh. Significantly, Jacob's flight takes place at the behest of his mother, Rebekah, whereas Moses flees on the basis of his own intelligence. Jacob spends much of his life struggling with the designs of parental figures (Isaac and Rebekah, his uncle Laban, God's angel); Moses' lack of parents, who disappear from the story early on, enables him to come into his own much more quickly. Both Jacob and Moses spend many years living with their fathers-in-law (Jacob lives with Laban for twenty years; Moses stays with Jethro – also called Reuel and Hobab – for "a long time" [Exodus 2:23] until the Pharaoh dies). And both seek to learn the name of God during an episode of divine revelation. Jacob, after triumphing over the angel, is not granted his wish: "You must not ask my name!" (Genesis 32:30). By contrast, Moses at the burning bush receives the full account of God's name:

> Moses said to God, "Behold, when I come to the children of Israel and say to them, 'The God of your fathers sent me to you,' and they say to me, 'What is His name?' what do I say to them?" And God said to Moses, "I-Shall-Be-Who-I-Shall-Be.²" And He said, "Thus you shall say to the children of Israel, 'I-Shall-Be' sent me to you." And Gold spoke again to Moses, "Thus you shall say to the children of Israel: 'The Lord – God of your fathers: God of Abraham, God of Isaac, and God of Jacob – sent me to you.' This is My name forever, thus I am remembered throughout the generations." (Exodus 3:13–15)

This passage depicts Moses as the inheritor of the patriarchs' special relationship with God, and its culmination. Only Moses is allowed to know God's Name; the Names by which God was known to the patriarchs were somehow incomplete. Moses continues the line of the patriarchs but exceeds them in his greatness as a leader and in his intimacy with God. He is the archpatriarch.

Moses and Joseph resemble each other as figures in a mirror. Joseph starts out as an Israelite and becomes an Egyptian, rising from the depths of prison to the heights of Pharaoh's trusted adviser, thus paving the transition for his family and their descendants. Moses emerges from the inner sanctum of Pharaoh's palace to become an outlaw, leading the Israelites back to Israel, back to the ways of their ancestors, united now by new traditions. The passage both ways – for Joseph to Egypt, for Moses

---

2. This version of God's name explains the meaning of the new name of God given here. That new name, generally translated "The Lord," is known as the Tetragrammaton, the four-letter name (spelled in English as Y-H-W-H). According to Jewish tradition, this name should not be pronounced, because the original pronunciation has been forgotten. Some scholars spell the name as "Yahweh"; German translators originated the pronunciation of "Jehovah."

and the Israelites to Israel – is fraught with peril, but both are guided on their journeys by God's providence. Suffering from famine in the land of Canaan, Joseph discovers a land of plenty in Egypt and establishes rules, through dreams from God, for preserving the food. The Israelites are threatened with starvation in the desert, and God appoints a special food to rain down for them, manna, with specific instructions given to Moses telling how the food shall be gathered and measured (Exodus 16). Joseph and Moses both have Egyptian names (Pharaoh renames Joseph Zaphenath-paneah in Genesis 41:45). Both have foreign wives – Joseph marries the daughter of an Egyptian priest, Moses the daughter of a Midianite priest – despite the importance of marrying within the group for Isaac and Jacob. Both are taken by others to be Egyptian – Joseph by his brothers (e.g., Genesis 42:6), Moses by Midianite shepherds (Exodus 2:19). Both demonstrate their familiarity with Egyptian customs – Joseph serving his brothers apart from the Egyptians "for the Egyptians could not break bread with the Hebrews, since that would be an abomination to the Egyptians" (Genesis 43:32), Moses, in response to Pharaoh's command that the Israelites sacrifice "within the land," replying that "what we sacrifice to the Lord our God is an abomination to the Egyptians" so they must offer sacrifices in the wilderness (Exodus 8:22). Joseph and Moses are both leaders at pivotal moments of transition. The long sojourn in Egypt, for all the trauma of slavery and the drama of breakneck escape, covers the crucial historical shift from small tribal origins to the growth of an incipient nation. The leaders' expertise with Egyptian customs and access to royal power prove decisive in enabling that transition to take place.

The Genesis Triangle: Favoritism–Jealousy–Reconciliation

The largest pattern, spanning all of the family stories in Genesis, might be called the Genesis triangle. There is a rivalry, usually between siblings, over the affection of a third party, usually God or God's surrogate. One of the rivals is chosen above the other; the nonchosen rival envies and seeks to harm the other. Usually the characters reach a settlement enabling them to live in peace, if at a distance, allowing the story to move on to the next generation. From the beginning to the end of Genesis, this pattern unfolds like a fugue, starting with a statement of the theme, through a series of increasingly complex variations, culminating in a grand finale tying the threads together.

Authority (God or surrogate)

/ \

Rival 1: favored – Rival 2: less favored (usually siblings)

The pattern first emerges with stark simplicity in the story of Cain and Abel (Genesis 4:1–10). Cain and Abel, brothers, both present offerings to God. God "paid heed" to Abel's offering, not to Cain's. No reason is given. In distress, Cain kills Abel; the fact that he kills him "in the field" and then denies knowledge of Abel's whereabouts to God, indicates some awareness of guilt and an attempt to hide the deed. God curses Cain, but also protects him with a mark that warns off others from attacking him. Although God favors Abel above Cain, God maintains a relationship with Cain as well throughout the story, trying to direct him to act justly after his offering was rejected, reproving him after the murder, protecting him thereafter despite his sin. This story demonstrates two elements crucial to the Genesis Triangle: the danger of violence inherent in the rivalry for affection and blessing; the close relationship that God preserves with the less favored rival. Indeed, in this story the favored child dies in his youth, while the less favored child is blessed with a long line of descendants. Clearly favoritism, from God or parents, carries great risks.

The next two examples, although not fully fleshed out, still form part of the overall design of Genesis. Noah's sons, Shem, Ham, and Japhet, come forth from the ark as equals. Shortly thereafter, an enigmatic event distinguishes them and their offspring forever (9:18–27). Noah invents wine and becomes drunk from it. Ham enters Noah's tent, sees his father's nakedness, and tells his two brothers; they go into the tent backwards and put a cloth over Noah, taking care not to see him. When Noah awakens and discovers what happened, he blesses Shem and Japhet and curses Ham. Even though Shem and Japhet cover their father together, Japhet receives a slightly lesser blessing than Shem: "May God enlarge Japhet, and may he dwell in the tents of Shem." Shem is the favored son. This story explains the branches of human anthropology as the Bible understands them. Shem, Ham and Japhet are the forebears of the three groups of human civilizations, enumerated in Genesis 10. The story jumps from the particulars of an individual family to a universal chart of "clans and nations." At this point the story abandons the brothers without allowing them a chance to reconcile. Shem is the ancestor of Abraham, chosen by God to inaugurate a new period of history. Ham gives birth to Canaan, father of the tribes that Abraham's descendants are commanded to fight and dispossess. The story ends here, then, because no compromise is envisioned between the sons of Ham and Shem.

Similarly, Abraham and his nephew Lot share unequally in the blessing (13:5–13). Abraham receives God's special favor, but Lot, as part of Abraham's family and in Abraham's charge, cannot be left out entirely. The rivalry between them occurs at a low level – ostensibly between their herdsmen, though the fact that "the land could not support them living together" strongly suggests a clash of personalities besides an overabundance of possessions. Like Jacob and Esau later, Abraham and Lot agree to split up, Lot moving to Sodom in the fertile plain of the Jordan River, Abraham staying in Canaan, which has already suffered a famine (12:10). There the competition ends. Afterwards Abraham will have to save Lot from his neighbors' cruelty, shortly before God destroys the cities of Sodom and Gomorrah. Abraham is perhaps too great a figure to endure a rival. His relations with Lot provide an alternative to the story of Noah's sons, informing us that, even though the line of blessing descends through one son in each generation, nevertheless other relatives may not be excluded from the family fortunes and from God's care.

The rivalry between Sarah and Hagar extends the Genesis triangle to new territory. For the first time, the rivals are women; they are not blood relations; they fight not over God's blessing but over a husband's favor. Moreover, the contest is completely one-sided: Sarah is the full wife while Hagar, her slave, is given to Abraham as a concubine upon Sarah's urging. Further, Sarah singlehandedly turns their relationship into a rivalry, appearing jealous and competitive, insisting that Abraham choose between herself and Hagar, treating Hagar harshly, and ultimately expelling her; Hagar's sole offense against Sarah is that "her mistress grew slight in her eyes" (16:4) after Hagar gave birth to Ishmael. But as in other cases, the less-favored wife enjoys an advantage by being endowed with natural fertility. Hagar, and later Leah, have no difficulty getting pregnant; Sarah and Leah's sister Rachel require miraculous help to bear children. The favoritism of Sarah, Abraham, and by extension, the Jewish people, does not bring with it an easy life. Where others might thrive on the bounties of nature, all too often it is only by throwing themselves on God's mercy that they are able to survive.

Isaac and Ishmael's rivalry is carried out by their mothers; the story doesn't talk about their feelings toward each other, let alone recount personal interactions. Isaac is the favored son because Sarah is the favored wife. In the triangular model, this rivalry would be depicted as extensions of the Abraham–Sarah–Hagar triangle. Abraham is again the authority deciding between them, but he does not want to make the choice; God's intervention, promising Ishmael his own nation, is needed to allay Abraham's concern (21:11–13). True to form, God endows Ishmael with natural fertility. He fathers twelve sons, the chieftains of tribes, anticipating the pattern for the Israelite nation. Isaac's wife Rebekah is, of course, barren and manages to conceive twin sons only through Isaac's prayers to God. After Sarah dies, Isaac and Ishmael reunite at the burial of their father, Abraham: "His sons Isaac and Ishmael buried him in the cave of Machpelah" (25:9). This is the first instance of reconciliation in Genesis; remarkably, no reconciliation is mentioned. Presumably, none was required, the brothers bearing no bad will against each other. Once their mothers' feud had passed, Isaac and Ishmael could resume being brothers.

At first blush, Rebekah is the only ancestral figure not bound up in a triangle. She has no siblings and no other wives to contend with. However, upon closer examination, Rebekah is the crucial figure in the rivalry of her sons, Jacob and Esau. Rebekah is the God-surrogate who favors Jacob and arranges for him to win the blessing. If Jacob is a trickster, he has learned all his tricks from his mother. Rebekah is forced to rely upon deception because Isaac favors Esau. The spouses are in effect rivals at the top of the triangle, competing over which son inherits the blessing of Abrahamic descent. Rebekah is more perceptive than Isaac in evaluating the relative merits of her sons, stronger than Isaac in her determination to establish her choice of heir, and cleverer than Isaac in employing her own and Jacob's wits to vanquish Esau's brawn and Isaac's will. In the contest between the spouses, Isaac does not stand a chance.

As with Sarah and Hagar, the tension between Rebekah and Isaac spills over into the second generation, this time with much more hostility between the rivals. Cheated out of both his birthright and blessing by Jacob, Esau not unreasonably threatens to kill his brother. Rebekah again intervenes, saving Jacob's life by sending him off to the home of her brother Laban, where, she hopes, he will settle down and marry until Esau's anger subsides. A great deal of water must pass under the bridge before the two brothers rejoin each other's company: Jacob laboring for Laban twenty years, fathering twelve sons and one daughter with two wives and two concubines; Esau marrying three wives, whose five sons and numerous grandsons inaugurate the Edomite nation. Like Ishmael and Cain before him, less-favored Esau does not seem to suffer much from losing the main blessing.

Upon returning to Canaan, Jacob approaches his brother with great trepidation. Even before facing Esau, Jacob makes elaborate preparations for the encounter. He sends messengers to herald his return and is startled to find that Esau is arriving accompanied by 400 men. He selects hundreds of animals to offer as presents. The night before the reunion, occurs the famous scene of Jacob wrestling with an angel; in context, this event suggests Jacob's inner struggle with his fear of his brother, the angel often being interpreted as a stand-in for Esau. Jacob needs to draw upon all of his mother's cleverness in handling his brother. He showers Esau with wave upon wave of gifts and bowing people, hoping to overwhelm him so that he forgets his fraternal grudge. Fearful Jacob does not mind groveling if necessary: "I have seen your face like one sees the face of God, and you have accepted me" (33:10). The brothers achieve reconciliation, but a limited one, more a permanent cease-fire than a Most Favored Nation treaty. Patently, Jacob remains quite wary of Esau's intentions, even after Esau runs to greet him and kiss him. Jacob rejects Esau's entreaties to travel together or to be accompanied by Esau's men. After they part, the narrator tells us that "Jacob came safe to the city of Shechem" (33:18); the implied message is: unharmed by Esau.

The struggle between Rachel and Leah is the most poignant, the most evenly matched, and the deepest in Genesis. When Rachel cries out to Jacob, "Give me children or else I will die!" (30:1) after Leah has borne four children in a row, we know that the rivalry consumes her entirely. The contrast between them marks them as rivals in their very being: "The eyes of Leah were weak; Rachel was beautiful in shape and appearance" (29:17). "Weak eyes" appears, in contrast to Rachel's beauty, to be a euphemism for "unattractive." We are told nothing about Rachel and Leah before the moment that Jacob arrives, but the sharpness of this contrast, and the bitterness of their rivalry, suggests that there had always been a vein of jealousy and resentment between them.

Jacob naturally falls in love with the beauty – and has to pay for his choice. Laban, Rachel and Leah's father and Jacob's uncle, makes Jacob work for him seven years before he can marry Rachel, then secretly switches Leah for Rachel on his wedding night because "It is not done, in our place, to marry off the younger daughter before the older" (29:26). Jacob has to work another seven years for Rachel, and an additional six to build up his own possessions. As with several of their predecessors, Rachel and Leah's opposition is framed by another rivalry. Rachel and Leah's struggles take place in the open, whereas Jacob and Laban compete through trickery and deception, Jacob besting his uncle later when he negotiates terms for leaving (30:25–43). God again supports the less favored as much or more than the favored one: "The Lord saw that Leah was despised and He opened her womb. Rachel was barren" (29:31). Not only does Leah have more children than Rachel, but in this case her children are just as much heirs of Abraham's promise, "children of Israel," as the sons of the more favored wife, Rachel. Jacob's two concubines' children are likewise not rejected, unlike Ishmael; they become equal members of the fraternal alliance. Rachel and Leah achieve a détente, which, while not perfect, is warmer than Jacob and Esau's truce. Rachel agrees to let Leah sleep with Jacob in exchange for some mandrakes, presumably a root known in the ancient world for enhancing fertility. It was only after this reconciliation that "God remembered Rachel…and opened her womb" (30:22). In their last encounter, the sisters speak with one voice as equals in Jacob's household; they urge Jacob not to settle with Laban for less than he owes them (31:14–16).

In the story of Joseph and his brothers, one of the most elaborate narratives in the Bible and one of the most beloved in all of literature, the triangular pattern of favoritism and contention achieves a satisfying resolution. The story lays out the triangle right away:

> Now Israel [Jacob] loved Joseph most of all his sons, for he was the child of his old age; and he made him a fine linen tunic. His brothers saw that their father loved him most of all his brothers; they hated him so much that they could not even greet him. (37:3–4)

Of course, Jacob favors Joseph because he was not only a late son, but also, along with Benjamin, a son of Rachel. Joseph well deserves his brothers' enmity: on top of the fancy clothes, he flaunts his special relationship with Jacob by bringing "bad reports of them [his brothers] to their father" (37:2). He stokes their anger further by boasting to his brothers of two dreams he had, interpreting them to mean that his brothers and parents will in the future bow down to him. As obnoxious as Joseph is, his dreams indicate that God, as well as his father, has favored him, since dreams and the ability to interpret them correctly were considered God-given visionary powers.

The story's sense of culmination derives in part from its recapitulation of earlier motifs. For example, Jacob sends Joseph away to his brothers, and Joseph gets lost in the fields. The reader may get a shudder of recognition, recalling another resented brother who goes out alone in the field: Abel. Indeed, in the next scene the brothers see Joseph coming and "conspired to kill him." When they decide instead to sell him to traders heading to Egypt, they dip his tunic, the symbol of Jacob's favor, in the blood of a goat they slaughter. Surely, this gesture serves more than to exculpate the brothers; by desecrating the tunic, and telling their father that Joseph has died, they avenge themselves against their father for holding them in lesser esteem than their coddled brother.

The process of reconciliation is long and intricate. It involves some of the economic wrangling of Jacob and Laban, as well as the elaborate gift-giving and groveling of Jacob and Esau. Joseph's experiences in servitude and prison break his arrogant belief in his own power. His brothers endure their own remorseful transformation through a series of tests that Joseph devises. Finally, when the poignancy of Joseph's hiding his identity from his brothers becomes too great for him to bear any longer, he reveals himself to them, full of forgiveness and humility. They have come to accept their father's – and God's – will in favoring Rachel's sons, Joseph and Benjamin; Joseph sees the hand of God in his passage to Egypt and subsequent rise in Pharaoh's court.

For reasons not always obvious, God favors some over others in their human destiny. Inner contentment and peace between rivals come only from accepting the hand that one is dealt and from acknowledging the Dealer. Of course, the brothers are not only individual characters in a story; they also represent twelve tribal territories in a future state of Israel. Hence, the story's message carries a political dimension to it. The story admonishes the tribes to accept the different resources allotted to each rather than to fight among themselves. In this light, the brothers' reconciliation after bitter strife presents an idealized image of unity for a country that, for much of its history, engages in various forms of internal and external warfare.

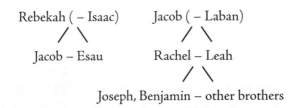

Conclusion

It is hard to really sink into the Bible as one can a novel. The actions and stories move too quickly, jumping from scene to scene in one or two verses without dwelling upon details of description and psychology that we usually associate with the style of realistic prose. Yet in other ways the Bible is extremely realistic. For a book filled with a character named God, biblical stories generally remain on the human plane of action. God may comment upon the action, offer promises, blessings, or curses, but rarely does God interfere with human affairs. Almost never does God so overwhelm the action as to distort the story beyond what seems humanly plausible.

For all the gaps, the Bible's stories retain their extraordinary power because of their incisive style. In a few words, they construct a scenario that is immediate, graspable, emotionally resonant. The Bible portrays the difficult love between husband and wife, parent and child, sisters or brothers that we can all relate to in our own complicated family relationships. It warns of the dangers inherent in such relationships and offers hope that the thorns of contention can be overcome. It is up to the reader to find the gaps and to fill them, discover patterns and elucidate them. Biblical stories are a pleasure and challenge, enlisting all the reader's powers of attention and imagination to interpret them faithfully, freshly, creatively. They continue to inspire us not only to read them in their historical context as products of an ancient culture, but to bring the characters into our lives by making the stories our own as well.

CHAPTER 3

Law

Suggested reading: Exodus 19–24; Leviticus 10–11, 18, 21

The legal sections of the Bible are not easy to read. The Bible's lists of legal injunctions often appear random and highly repetitive. While the Ten Commandments (Exodus 20) are inspiring, even necessary, moral instructions, how useful are the subsequent laws in Exodus 21, which begin, "When you acquire a Hebrew slave, he shall serve six years; in the seventh year he shall go free, without payment"? To people living in a modern democracy, this law and hundreds of others can seem irrelevant or worse, sanctioning forms of behavior, including slavery, women's subservience, and animal sacrifice, that our society happily has moved beyond.

Yet, the law in the Bible is not so easily dismissed; it is absolutely central to the message of the Torah, the first five books of the Bible, and of the historical and prophetic books that follow. If you want to understand the Bible, you cannot afford to ignore the law. Biblical stories are inseparable from legal passages. The two are interwoven throughout the five books of Moses, because the Bible considers them as equal products of God's word. The stories explain the origins of the laws; the laws encapsulate the lessons of the stories. The account of creation in Genesis 1:1–2:4 concludes with God ceasing from work on the seventh day, the paradigm for the human Sabbath; the commandment to observe the Sabbath (Exodus 20:8–11, part of the Ten Commandments) harkens back to the story of creation: "For six days did the Lord make the heavens and the earth…and He rested on the seventh day." Similarly, at the climax of the Exodus from Egypt, right before the Egyptian firstborn males are killed and the Israelites flee, the story is interrupted in Exodus 12 by the laws of the Passover celebration. According to the Bible's vision, the law arises from particular historical circumstances; when people carry out the law, they should be conscious of the reasons why the law was given. The law establishes a connection between its present practitioner and the ancestors who received it and first carried it out. Simultaneously, it transcends time by asserting an eternal bond between man and God.

This chapter aims to encourage the reader to give biblical law a second look. The key to its appreciation lies in understanding the general concepts and principles that give life to the legal system. To comprehend the relevance of particular laws requires a grasp of the idea of a covenant that provides a framework for those laws. The notion of covenant, in turn, leads to a discussion of its roots in the cultures surrounding biblical Israel, known to scholars as the Ancient Near East. Comparison of some of the laws in the Bible with their counterparts in other Ancient Near Eastern law codes gives a sense of the ways that biblical laws resemble and differ from the laws of those societies. Finally, an examination of the system of laws given in Leviticus helps to unravel the mystery of the rituals elaborated for the priests in the ancient Temple.

A proper understanding of biblical law can render the most obscure and strange laws more comprehensible, and even, when considered from the right perspective, inspiring. For biblical law does not consist of a dry enumeration of individual statutes. It provides the key to a profound, revolutionary vision of human morality and history. The law is what makes the Bible such a unique and timeless work in the history of human thought.

Promises

The Hebrew word *brit* means treaty, that is, an agreement between two parties, whether individuals or larger groups, in which one or both parties promise to give something to the other party. The word is perhaps most familiar in its alternate pronunciation, *bris*. Many people think that the word *bris* means circumcision, but *bris* is actually a shortening of the term *brit milah*, meaning the *covenant* of circumcision. There are nearly 300 uses of *brit* in the Bible, many of them representing a mundane legal pact between two people. In Genesis 21, for example, Abraham and Abimelech overcome their mutual suspicion by making a *brit*: Abraham claims ownership of a well at Beer-Sheba, he gives Abimelech seven ewes, they swear an oath, and the pact is binding. The word *brit* signifies other kinds of legal agreements as well, including a work assignment (2 Kings 11:4), military alliances (in Genesis 14:13, Abraham's "allies" are in Hebrew his *ba'alei-brit*, literally treaty-bearers), and a peace treaty between nations (Judges 2:2). Typically, the Hebrew expression is "cut a *brit*," referring to an original ceremony common in the ancient world in which animals were cut in half to signify the agreement between the parties (discussed further below). In the English Bible, a *brit* with God was translated as covenant (from the Latin *con* + *venire*, coming together, making an agreement), not treaty or pact, presumably because a rarer, more elevated term was desired to express the formal relationship between man and God.

The covenant at Mount Sinai recounted in Exodus 19–24 is without doubt the most important covenant between man and God in the Bible. Nevertheless, there are numerous other such covenants. Following the patterns discussed in the last chapter, the covenants in Genesis introduce several instances of a theme, building up to a climactic instance in Exodus. Scholars regard the biblical covenants between man and God as consisting of two basic kinds: the covenant of grant, and the covenant of obligation. Prior to Sinai, the most common one is the covenant of grant. As its name suggests, in this covenant God promises something to a person with no strings attached. The grantee has no obligations toward the grantor; he (the biblical examples are all male) is the beneficiary of the covenant solely because the grantor, God, feels kindly toward him. Sometimes there is a small condition at first, before the grant kicks in; but that condition is for one time only, whereas the benefits hugely outweigh the grantee's action. In other words, the covenant of grant is a kind of gift that the grantor is legally binding himself to give, for a long period of time and in some cases forever.

In these types of covenants in Genesis, the grant usually comes with an explanation of why it is given. After nearly sacrificing his son Isaac, Abraham receives the following covenant:

> By Myself I swear, the Lord declares: Because you have done this
> thing – not sparing your son, your only one – I will bless you abun-
> dantly and make your descendants as numerous as the stars of heaven
> and the sand on the seashore; and your descendants shall possess the
> gates of their enemies. All the nations of the earth shall bless them-
> selves by your descendants, because you have obeyed Me. (Genesis
> 22:16–18)

This covenant culminates a series of God's promises to Abraham. The
occasion for the covenant is clearly spelled out: it is a reward to Abraham
for passing this most difficult test of faith, obeying God's command to
sacrifice his heir, Isaac. No terms are set for Abraham and his descendants
to receive God's promise; whatever had to be done, Abraham has already
accomplished. Likewise, God sets no expiration date. Will the promise be
fulfilled once and then expire? Or instead, does it represent an idealized
end of time that, once arrived, will last forever? The promise is so grand
and sweeping that it is hard to reconcile with tangible historical aims. For
that reason, God's concrete promise to give Abraham's descendants the
land of Israel is not included here. That may appear too limited a gift for
Abraham's boundless sacrifice.

In the covenant with Isaac discussed in the last chapter, Isaac receives
the covenant largely by virtue of his father:

> The Lord appeared to him and said, "Do not go down to Egypt. Dwell
> within the land that I will tell you. Reside in this land, and I will be
> with you and bless you; for I will give all these lands to you and your
> descendants, and I will fulfill the oath I took with Abraham your
> father. I will multiply your descendants like the stars of heaven, and
> I will give your descendants all these lands, and all the nations of
> the earth will bless themselves through your descendants, because
> Abraham obeyed Me, carrying out My charge, My commandments,
> statutes, and laws." (Genesis 26:2–5)

The repeated language from Abraham's covenant (seed as numerous as the stars, the nations will be blessed by your seed) emphasizes Isaac's indebtedness to his father. This passage deviates from the pattern in explaining why Abraham received his covenant: God has granted it to him not because he "listened to My voice" but rather because he "kept...My commandments." Abraham is made out to be a proto-Jew, demonstrating his fidelity to God through observing God's laws. Though Isaac's merit pales in comparison to his father's, he nonetheless makes his own modest contribution. Despite a famine, God commands him to stay within the land rather than descend to Egypt. As a country with an abundant source of irrigation, the Nile River, Egypt lacks the persistent droughts that trouble the land of Israel, which is dependent upon the vagaries of annual rainfall. For Isaac to stay within the land, he must undergo his own trial of faith, trusting that God will provide his family with rain and food to survive. Thus Isaac's covenant does imply some reciprocity: "If you reside in the land, then...." However, this condition is one that Isaac has already fulfilled; 26:1 informs us that Isaac went to Gerar, not to Egypt, to escape the famine. At the point where the reader learns of the covenant, Isaac has no further requirement to fulfill before receiving the blessing.

A similarly small condition is attached to a great blessing in Abraham's first covenant:

> Go forth from your land and from your birthplace and from your father's house to the land that I will show you. I will make you a great nation. (Genesis 12:1–2)

Again, the promise is conditioned upon the fulfillment of God's command: "If you go forth...." But since that fulfillment is so little in doubt, and is immediately accomplished in verse 4, this covenant is considered one of grant. Here, unlike the covenant given after Abraham almost sacrifices Isaac, Abraham has done nothing yet to merit so great a reward. God's first covenant with Abraham demonstrates God's great faith in Abraham, therefore, just as the binding of Isaac reveals Abraham's faith in God. Up to this point, the Bible is utterly silent regarding the reasons why God saw such potential in His chosen protagonist.

God grants Noah a far more ambiguous covenant after the flood:

> Noah built an altar to God. He took from every pure beast and from
> every pure bird and made sacrifices upon the altar. And God smelled
> the soothing odor, and God said in His heart, "I will not continue
> to curse the earth any more on man's account, for the inclination of
> man's heart is bad from his youth, and I will not continue to strike
> all living beings any more as I have done. For the remaining days of
> the earth, sowing and harvest, cold and heat, summer and winter, day
> and night shall not cease." (Genesis 8:20–22)

In the next chapter (9:1–17) God offers a much more positive covenant
directly to Noah, to his offspring, and "with every living creature that is
with you." This initial version of Noah's covenant, however, is rather disturbing, provoking a chain of unsettling questions. First, the rationale for
the covenant is unclear: is it given because God likes Noah's sacrifice, or
because "the inclination of man's heart is bad from youth"? If as reward
for Noah's merit, the quotation gives no indication of it. But what kind
of explanation is the latter? Aren't covenants granted because of extraordinary merit, not incorrigible wickedness? Isn't this wickedness the explanation for the flood in the first place – and now it explains the cessation
of floods?! If man's nature is evil, whose fault is that? What causes God's
cynicism toward man, and does God hold this view permanently or is it
a passing mood? Is God's message, in effect, "I'm fed up with the human
race; let Me leave people to their own devices"?

Second, with whom is the covenant made? Why does God speak to
Himself alone? Aren't covenants made between two parties, with both
fully aware of the process? Does God not trust Noah the way He will
trust the patriarchs? Or does this passage reveal a darker strain of God's
reflections that do not usually emerge so candidly from the pen of the
biblical narrator? Is God admitting that the flood was a mistake, that since
people will never be good, there was no point in wiping out a generation?
Even worse, was it a mistake to destroy all living things for the faults of
human beings? In context, God appears to be rehearsing, expressing hesitation about the world He recently created, before making another official

statement upon the stage of history. As this example shows, variations from the standard pattern are often the most interesting.

One other peculiar covenant of grant found in Genesis contains strong parallels with Ancient Near Eastern ritual:

> [God] said to him [Abram]: "Take for Me a three-year-old heifer, a three-year-old goat, and a three-year-old ram, a turtledove, and a pigeon." And he took all these things for Him, halving them in the middle, and he set each half opposite the other, but he did not halve the birds. Vultures descended upon the carcasses, and Abram drove them away. As the sun was going down, a heavy slumber fell upon Abram; and behold, a fear dark and great came over him. And He said to Abram, "Know for a certainty that your descendants will be sojourners in a land not their own, and they will be enslaved and op-pressed, for four hundred years."…And when the sun had set, there was thick darkness, and behold, there were a smoking furnace and a flaming torch passing through these parts. On that day God cut a treaty with Abram, saying, "To your descendants I have given this land, from the river of Egypt to the great river, the Euphrates River." (Genesis 15:9–13, 17–18)

Other than the circumcision of Abraham's family in Genesis 17, this is the only time when the Bible uses the word "covenant" to describe God's promise to Abraham. Here the term recalls the legal background of this ritual. Throughout the Ancient Near East, people often formalized a treaty by cutting an animal into parts, literally "cutting a treaty." The symbolic significance of this action can be seen in a treaty between Ashurnirari v, king of Assyria, and Mati'ilu of Arpad:

> This spring lamb has been brought from its fold…to sanction the treaty between Ashurnirari and Mati'ilu…. This head is not the head of a lamb, it is the head of Mati'ilu, it is the head of his sons, his officials, and the people of his land. If Mati'ilu sins against this treaty, so may, just as the head of this spring lamb is torn off, and its knuckle placed in its mouth, […], the head of Mati'ilu be torn off and

his sons [...]. This shoulder is not the shoulder of a spring lamb, it is the shoulder of Mati'ilu, it is the shoulder of his sons.

Cutting the animal into pieces represents a curse threatening the parties if they break their side of the bargain. To cite a particularly colorful example of this widespread practice, the Amorite expression for making a treaty is "to kill a young donkey." Another detail of Abraham's covenant has a counterpart elsewhere: the flaming torch that passes between the parts recalls a Hittite ritual in which people walk between animal halves. The flame is a potent image of God, foreshadowing Moses' encounter at the burning bush.

God's treaty with Abraham appropriates this gruesome ancient legal custom for the needs of the story in Genesis 15. The biblical version envelops the ritual in an atmosphere of fearful mystery. Instead of one animal, as in the Ancient Near East treaty, Abraham must bring five different kinds. His failure to divide the birds does not bode well; it suggests that the treaty is incomplete from its very inception. Vultures descend upon the animal pieces, threatening to scuttle the covenant before it is made. Abraham falls into a heavy slumber and feels "a fear dark and great." A dire prophecy of Israel's enslavement intrudes upon the covenant. Then God enacts the ritual, taking on the eerie appearance of a smoking furnace with a flaming torch. Details of sunset and darkness further darken the mood before the promise of land finally arrives. This strange and powerful section transforms a common legal procedure into a story of dreadful foreboding about the future of Abraham's descendants. It opposes the sunny promise of Abraham's other covenants with an intuition of the nightmare of history.

Our knowledge of the Ancient Near Eastern parallels to Abraham's covenant between the parts helps us to understand the ritual significance of Genesis 15, but the explanation raises its own set of questions. Why is this legal form used at all in the Bible? Not every ancient practice is found in the Bible; ancient Israel in many ways attempted to distance itself from the surrounding cultures. An answer might be that this practice was the international norm for sealing a treaty, just as, say, different Indian tribes recognized the mutual smoking of a pipe as a formal procedure signifying peace. One problem with this theory is that no other biblical treaty,

whether between two human parties or between man and God, concludes
with this ritual; if the practice were standard in ancient Israel, surely other
biblical covenants would have employed it. However, there is one other
suggestive reference in the Bible to this kind of covenant:

> I will make the men who have transgressed My covenant, who did
> not carry out the words of the covenant that they cut in My presence,
> like the calf that they cut in two, whose parts they walked between.
> Officials of Judah and Jerusalem, the officers and priests and all the
> people of the land who have passed through the calf's parts – I shall
> deliver them to their enemies, to those who seek to destroy them.
> (Jeremiah 34:18–20)

Jeremiah invokes the implied curse of the covenant between the parts
upon the people of Judah for breaking the commandment to release all
Hebrew slaves in the sabbatical (seventh) year. By doing so, he merges
Abraham's covenant with the covenant of Sinai: the covenant at Sinai
requires the release of Hebrew slaves, whereas only Abraham's covenant
consists of cutting animal parts. Jeremiah may reflect a later trend to
regard all of the ancient covenants with God as essentially one covenant;
alternatively, there may have been a ritual reenactment of the Sinai covenant at which people would confirm their obligation by walking between
the parts. Whatever the historical reality, Jeremiah's curse, even if it refers
to no actual ritual that took place, assumes an audience familiar with this
covenantal mechanism.

One final covenant of grant, that between God and King David, has
had the largest impact on Jewish history through the ages:

> When your days are completed and you lie down with your fathers,
> I will raise up your seed, who will come forth from your loins, after
> you, and I will firmly establish his kingdom. He will build a house
> in My name, and I will establish the throne of his kingdom forever.
> (2 Samuel 7:12–13)

God promises David that his descendants will rule over Israel eternally.

This covenant has always been in the minds of Jews as they lived dispersed throughout the world, reliant upon the mercy of foreign rulers. It gave rise to the belief in a messiah, a great leader who would take the Jews back to their ancestral homeland, establish Jewish self-rule and rebuild God's Temple. The words of a popular Hebrew children's song, "David, king of Israel, lives and exists!" express the longing for the restoration of Jewish sovereignty, symbolized by King David. As will be seen in the next chapter, at one time this promise led to a crisis in religious worldview, when the certainty in the eternal rule of the House of David gave way to conquest by foreign powers, the sacking of Jerusalem, the destruction of the First Temple, and the exile of the community's leaders.

Obligations

The second type of covenant found in the Bible is called the covenant of obligation. As its name suggests, this covenant places demands upon both parties to carry out the terms of the agreement. The covenant of obligation thus entails a degree of mutuality lacking in the covenant of grant. One early example is the covenant of circumcision in Genesis 17. After promising Abraham the land of Israel as "an everlasting holding," God continues:

> As for you, maintain My covenant, you and your descendants to fol-
> low, for generations. This is My covenant for you to observe, between
> Me and you and your descendants after you: circumcise every male….
> An uncircumcised male, who has not been circumcised in his fore-
> skin, that person shall be cut off from his people; he has broken My
> covenant. (17:9–10, 14)

For the other covenants between God and Abraham, Abraham's descendants receive God's gifts without any responsibilities, solely by virtue of God's special love for their ancestor. Only in the covenant of circumcision does a duty precede the blessing. Yes, the people overall will inherit the land, but any individuals who refuse to undergo circumcision will be expelled from the community, cut off from God. For the first time, the Bible says that a covenant can be broken. As opposed to later versions of the covenant, the responsibility and punishment here devolve entirely upon the individual: the individual must obey the command, or else he and he alone will face the consequences.

The idea of a covenant that bestows obligations as well as blessings, that can be upheld or broken, becomes the central paradigm for Israelite law with the revelation of God at Mount Sinai. The laws conveyed in Exodus 20 and the succeeding chapters serve to guide the individual on the path to a moral life, pleasing to God. As part of a pact between God and Israel, these laws are also addressed to the people as a collective entity. They lay down the rules for all of Israelite society; the society as a whole is responsible for ensuring that the law is carried out. These laws, then, are a mechanism for both individuals and the community to enter into an ongoing relationship with God:

> "Now, if you carefully listen to My voice and observe My covenant, you shall become for Me a treasured possession among all peoples, for all the land is Mine. You shall be to Me a kingdom of priests and a holy nation." (Exodus 19:5–6)

God speaks the words from Sinai to the entire people of Israel. Each person has an obligation to God and to the collective to obey the law. When people break God's covenant, not only do they open up themselves as individuals to punishment, their harmful actions also endanger the fabric of their society and, if undiscovered and unpunished, threaten the relationship between God and the people.

People respond to God's command; God pays attention in kind to human response. God judges the people according to the law, "visiting the sin of fathers upon sons to the third and fourth generation of My enemies, but acting with lovingkindness for thousands of generations to those who love Me and observe My commandments" (Exodus 20:5–6). Breaking the law is so serious because it entails a rejection of God. Although punishment is necessary to enforce an agreement, the quotation above suggests that God's motive in giving the law is a desire to love rather than to punish: Israel will become God's "treasured possession" when they obey their side of the covenant. Indeed, in Jewish retellings of the Sinai story, the covenant is compared to a marriage contract between God and the Jewish people. The law gives an opportunity for people to come close to God.

In the conception of Sinai, the Bible brings together three different kinds of experiences generally conveyed elsewhere as separate phenomena: the revelation of God, a covenant, and a code of law. The combination of these renders the Sinai passage as a tremendous climax to the stories, themes, and motifs that come before, trumpeting the centrality of the law in Jewish history. God's revelation at Sinai is described in far more awe-inspiring terms than revelations elsewhere in the Bible:

> On the third day, in the morning, there were thunder and lightning and a heavy cloud upon the mountain, and the sound of the ram's horn was very strong; and all the people in the camp trembled.... Mount Sinai was entirely in smoke, because God descended upon it in fire. The smoke rose up like the smoke from a kiln. The whole mountain trembled greatly. The sound of the ram's horn grew stronger and stronger. Moses spoke, and God answered in thunder. (Exodus 19:16, 18–19)

Whereas God appeared earlier to Moses as a modest flame in a bush, calling out to Moses only after he turned to look at the flame (Exodus 3:2–4), at Mount Sinai the sights and sounds create an overpowering impression. Here God comes also in fire, but of a scale reminiscent of a volcano in its size, setting, and energy. The scene overwhelms the senses of the Israelite spectators: sight (lightning, cloud, smoke, fire, mountain), sound (thunder, horn), smell (smoke), touch (trembling mountain). In the covenants to the patriarchs, God communicated to them directly – there is nothing problematic about divine–human conversation. At Sinai, all of the people, not just Moses, hear God, yet the Bible emphasizes the disparity between the parties. The people must be "pure," washing their clothes and abstaining from sex; still, they cower when God approaches them, and they must keep away from the mountain or else they will die. Moses alone is permitted to come closer. The revelation at Sinai is uniquely democratic in taking place before the entire people; however, only the spiritually gifted leader is capable of speaking to God at a level approaching intimacy.

God's revelation takes the form of a covenant. As with the covenant of grant, the covenant of obligation at Sinai shares many basic features with a widespread treaty format discovered in many documents from the Ancient Near East. Scholars call this a suzerain–vassal treaty, borrowing medieval terms for a powerful ruler and a lesser landholder. The ruler extends protection to the vassal, guaranteeing him control of his property, in exchange for the vassal's loyalty and tribute to the suzerain. In one of the most impressive such treaties, Esarhaddon, king of Assyria, lays out terms for a subordinate ruler. Here are some excerpts from a document containing over 650 legal clauses:

> This is the treaty of Esarhaddon, king of the world, king of Assyria, son of Sennacherib, likewise king of the world, king of Assyria, with Ramataya, city-ruler of Urakazabanu,
>
> With his sons, grandsons, with all the people of Urakazabanu,...
>
> [with] all those who will live in the future after this treaty;
>
> the treaty which he has made binding with you before Jupiter, Venus, Saturn, Mercury, Mars and Sirius; before Ashur, Anu, Enlil, and Ea, Sin, Shamash, Adad and Marduk....
>
> When Esarhaddon, king of Assyria, departs from the living, you will seat the crown prince designate Ashurbanipal upon the royal throne, he will exercise the kingship and overlordship of Assyria over you. If you do not serve him in the open country and in the city, do not fight and even die on his behalf, do not always speak the full truth to him, do not always advise him well in full loyalty, do not smooth his way in every respect; if you remove him, and seat in his stead one of his brothers....
>
> [Then] just as a honeycomb is pierced through and through with holes, so may holes be pierced through and through in your flesh, the flesh of your women, your brothers, your sons and daughters while you are alive.

> May they [the gods] let lice, caterpillars, and other field pests
> eat up your land and your district as if locusts....
>
> Just as this bedbug stinks, so may your breath stink before god,
> king, and men.

The sheer verbosity of this document, whose conditions and curses accumulate at considerable length, creates a devastating impression of its absolute importance. Resistance to the treaty is pointless; the whole world, both human and divine, ensures that it must be carried out.

This document contains some, though not all, of the basic features found in a suzerain–vassal treaty. It starts with an identification of the suzerain – here, Esarhaddon, who proclaims himself modestly as "king of the world." There follows a historical review, legitimizing the king's rule and his relationship to the vassal. In this case, the treaty tells us only that Esarhaddon's father was Sennacherib, likewise "king of the world." Next we find an identification of the vassal, Ramataya the "city-ruler of Urakazabanu." The treaty obligates Ramataya, along with all of his family, descendants, and subjects. Following these announcements come the witnesses: the gods. Esarhaddon displays great liberality toward the denizens of heaven: he invites all the gods of the region to witness this treaty. The gods guarantee the validity of the agreement, certifying that the vassal will suffer the curses if he breaks it (each god is mentioned separately as inflicting his or her own curse). Then come the stipulations. Despite the great number of them, nearly 400 in this treaty, they all essentially say the same thing: be loyal to Ashurbanipal, my heir, after I die. The remaining 250 clauses detail the curses, devised with ingenuity and sadistic glee. Presumably, the Assyrians believed the stick to be far more efficacious than the carrot.

The numerous parallels between the suzerain–vassal treaty and the biblical covenant suggest that the Israelites were familiar with this important Ancient Near Eastern legal form and to a large extent modeled their covenant with God after it. The covenant begins with an identification of the suzerain, or greater power, followed by a statement about His role in history: "I am the Lord your God, who brought you forth from the land of Egypt, from the house of slavery" (Exodus 20:2). God's rescue of the Israelites from Egypt obligates them to accept the covenant. Next come stipulations, commonly called the Ten Commandments. In Hebrew the term for them is *aseret ha-dibrot* (or *ha-devarim* in Deuteronomy 4:13), which translates literally as the Ten Sayings. These terms reveal the different way that Jews and Christians understand the significance of these commandments. For Christians these ten are the most important of the commandments in the Old Testament; they remain valid, even as most of the other biblical laws are no longer in force after Jesus. Jews regard these as ten supremely important principles; as commandments, however, they are not necessarily greater than the other commandments in the Bible. According to the traditional count, there are 613 laws in the Bible, all of which are equally binding because all come from God. By calling these the Ten Sayings, Jews acknowledge their supremacy as guiding ethical rules but deny their priority in the system of commandments.

Other common features of suzerain–vassal treaties are scattered throughout the Torah. Invoking the pantheon of gods may not have been possible, but Moses does the next best thing in Deuternomy 30:19:

> I call the heavens and the earth today as witnesses against you. Life and death I place before you, blessing and curse. Choose life, so that you and your descendants might live. (Moses invokes these witnesses again in Deuteronomy 32:1)

Just as Esarhaddon establishes his treaty not with Ramataya alone but with "his sons, grandsons, [and] with all the people of Urakazabanu," so, too, in the Bible God makes a covenant with "you and your son and your son's son" (Deuteronomy 6:2). The list of curses enumerated in Esarhaddon's treaty finds its counterpart in Leviticus 26 and Deuteronomy 27–28. The biblical curses are less fanciful than those in Esarhaddon's treaty; it is considerably harder to smile while reading them. Perhaps that is indeed their point. They threaten all aspects of the Israelites' agricultural, physical, and political existence: land, produce, food, livestock; bodily illnesses; defeat in battle and exile. Their directness, the lack of extravagant metaphor, makes these curses much more real and terrifying than Esarhaddon's longer tirade.

Two other features of the Ancient Near Eastern covenant are present in the Bible: the deposition of a copy of the covenant in a holy sanctuary (Exodus 25:16), and a public reading of the covenant reaffirming its validity (Exodus 24:7), mandated at regular intervals (Deuteronomy 31:10–13).

A Covenant Unlike Any Other

Despite the numerous formal similarities between Israel's covenant and Ancient Near Eastern treaties, it is the uniqueness of the former that makes it such a radically original document in human history. Biblical laws are not merely a list of enactments decreed by a ruler; they form part of a treaty between two parties. The power issuing these laws is not a human king, but God. These two aspects of biblical law, unique in ancient times, carry several important implications. First, the covenant reconstitutes the relationship between humanity and divine forces. No longer are people subject to the whim of their gods, made to suffer from their displeasure and thought of as solely their servants. Contrast the biblical vision with mankind's role as spelled out in the Babylonian Epic of Creation (often called *Enuma Elish*, its first words):

> [The god Marduk says:] I will establish a savage, "man" shall be his name. Verily, savage-man I will create. He shall be charged with the service of the gods that they might be at ease!

After Sinai, both man and God accept a system of mutual obligations spelled out in the covenant. Naturally, this is not a treaty between equals: God will always be the more powerful party, the "suzerain," and man must rely upon God's guidance and blessing, not vice-versa. God nevertheless agrees to bind Himself according to clearly defined terms, rewarding people when they uphold their obligations and punishing them when they break the covenant. The law becomes the chief vehicle for communication between man and God. Previously, sacrifices served that function. For sure, Israelite law does not dispense with sacrifices, since dozens of biblical laws describe the proper method for each kind of sacrifice appropriate to a variety of circumstances. Nevertheless, these sacrificial laws now are subsumed under a larger legal system, and all of the commandments together affect the relationship between man and God. The covenant thus provides the foundation for later rabbinic Judaism, which emphasizes the importance of study over sacrifices and replaces sacrifices altogether with synagogue prayer after the destruction of the Second Temple.

The second major implication of the biblical covenant, a code of laws given by God, is that morality no longer consists of an arbitrary contractual agreement between two human parties, nor is law the imposition of a human sovereign's will over his subjects. With Sinai, justice becomes an essential part of the fabric of the universe. In the Hebrew Bible, God's justice reigns supreme in this world, not in the next life; indeed, heaven and hell, later creations of the religious imagination, are nowhere to be found in these books. God's essential nature now is bound up with His concern for earthly justice, unlike the beliefs in the surrounding cultures in the Ancient Near East, which considered divinity primarily active within agriculture, war, or local guardianship. In Israel, these functions never entirely disappear, since God controls everything; yet God's main task is to ensure that good deeds will be rewarded and bad deeds punished. This faith is given poetic expression in the Psalms:

> Let the sea and its fullness thunder, the world and those who dwell
> in it; let the rivers clap hands, the mountains ring out together in the
> presence of God, for He has come to judge the earth; He shall judge
> the world with justice, and the peoples with equity. (Psalm 98:7–9)

God's justice applies to the entire world. In the Bible's vision, the covenant in all its details is given to Israel; nevertheless, God will judge all the people of the earth according to universal principles of moral behavior. The covenant imparts a profound belief that people can control their own destiny through the morality of their actions. The corollary to this faith – why, then, do bad things sometimes happen to good people? – is a question that the Bible has difficulty answering; the book of Job, as will be seen in chapter 7, tries out many possible solutions to monotheism's quintessential conundrum without finding one that is entirely satisfactory. However, at root this faith is an optimistic one, empowering people to believe in their own ability to improve the world and achieve good relations with God and other people.

A third implication is that the law looks very different when it is given by God rather than composed by people. God, by definition, does not make mistakes. Consequently, biblical law can never be changed. People, on the other hand, do change greatly from one historical era to the next. Each era brings its own ethical outlook, which often differs fundamentally from its predecessor. Biblical laws that may have appeared absolute at the time of Sinai came to look otherwise centuries later. In practice, teachers and judges found that, while they were not free to erase unpopular laws from the "books," they could reinterpret them to suit their own ethical beliefs, in effect, reading those beliefs back into the "original intent" of the Bible. A classic example is the discussion of *lex talionis*, "an eye for an eye" (Exodus 21:22–24; Leviticus 24:19–20; Deuteronomy 19:19–21). In the Talmud (Bava Kamma, 83b-84a), the rabbis interpret these biblical laws to mean not an actual eye but monetary damages. Most scholars believe that during the biblical period, justice did actually demand a literal punishment equal to the physical damage that the perpetrator inflicted on the victim. By the time of the Talmudic rabbis, in the postbiblical period, "an eye for an eye" no longer seemed to be a proper exercise of justice. This process of reinterpretation characteristic of rabbinic Judaism can even be found within the Bible itself. One well-known example concerns the location of sacrifices. In Exodus 20:21 God permits the Israelites to offer sacrifices in a plethora of locations:

> An altar of earth shall you make for Me and sacrifice upon it your burnt offerings and peace offerings, your sheep and cattle. In every place where I put the memory of My name I will come to you and bless you.

Later on, when Moses prepares the people to inhabit the land of Israel, he indicates only one place of sacrifice:

You will cross the Jordan and dwell in the land that the Lord your God causes you to inherit.... And the place where the Lord your God will choose for His name to dwell, there shall you bring all that I command you: your burnt offerings and your sacrifices. (Deuteronomy 12:10–11)

This centralized location becomes the Temple in Jerusalem, constructed more than two hundred years after Moses' death. The change in the law – one of many in the Bible – clearly represents a development in ritual practice over history.

Fourth, if God has authored all of the laws, then there is no distinction between a crime, which is a transgression against another person, and a sin, which is a transgression against God. All crimes are also sins. God enacts and enforces behavior between man and God – "religious" law – as well as between people – "civil" law. Civil law, the law regulating social interactions at every level, now becomes a subset of religious law. This combination of the two kinds of law into one is a creation of the Bible, not found in any Ancient Near Eastern counterparts. If God cares so deeply about justice on earth, then people are obligated to emulate God through ethical conduct in all spheres of life. According to the covenant, there can be no distinction between private and public morality, behavior in the Temple and behavior in the marketplace. King, priest, and commoner alike have one set of rules that they must follow.

The covenant at Sinai plays a crucial role in the political and historical understanding of the Israelites. Like the Declaration of Independence, it sets forth national principles; like the Constitution, it establishes the foundations of the law. The Bible portrays the establishment of the law as the true beginning of Israelite history. The stories about the ancestral family in Genesis are rendered as prehistory, as background to the creation of the nation with the revelation at Sinai. Now the Israelites can function as a state, with a sovereign, a legal system, and rules regulating war, commerce, and property. All that is missing is land. The biblical covenant thus serves as the paradigm for all documents that seek to create a society through principles of legal justice, whether the Magna Carta, the Constitution, or the *Déclaration des droits de l'Homme et du citoyen*.

God's authorship of biblical law gives the covenant another dimension, beyond being a political, legal, and historical document. As developed throughout the Bible's historical writings, the law comes to be regarded as the key to the Israelites' national destiny. When the Israelites obey God's law, God rewards them with success: triumph over enemies, continued residence on the land, material plenty. When they fail to uphold the covenant, the nation suffers. This theological premise, read backwards, becomes the guiding idea for interpreting the past. During periods when the Israelites' collective fortunes waxed, they must have been led by a pious ruler; when their fortunes waned, they surely broke the covenant. Morality and destiny, individual fate and national history all are woven tightly together by the logic of God's covenant with people.

The Laws: A Closer Look

An examination of some of the individual laws can reveal the governing trends and concerns behind them. The examples below are from the Covenant Code of Exodus 21–23, so-called because these laws follow immediately upon the giving of the Ten Commandments, forming part of God's covenant at Mount Sinai. One of the most striking aspects of biblical law is how diverse it is in comparison with other legal codes. As was discussed above, there is no biblical distinction between religious and civil law, and indeed those two kinds of laws are brought together in the Covenant Code, just as they are in the Ten Commandments. For example, smack in the middle of laws concerning property and lending we find, "He who sacrifices to gods, except for God alone, shall be banned" (Exodus 22:19). While many of the laws resemble those found in ancient secular law codes, others assign a role to God in the legal process:

> In all cases of breach of trust, concerning an ox, a donkey, a sheep or garment, all losses of property for which one might say, "This is it," the dispute shall go before God; whoever God convicts shall pay double to his fellow. (22:8)

Assuming that God's agents in dispensing the law are human judges, still, laws such as this emphasize God's attention to human justice. According to the ideal vision of the covenant, no form of abuse or deceit will go unpunished. God protects the weakest members of society: the poor, orphans, and widows:

> Neither mistreat nor oppress the stranger, for you were strangers in the land of Egypt. Do not afflict the widow and orphan. Should you dare afflict them – if they should cry aloud to Me – I shall surely heed their cry. I will grow angry; I shall slay you by the sword; your wives will become widows, your sons, orphans. If you lend money to My people, the poor among you, do not act toward them like a lender: do not impose interest upon them. If you take your fellow's garment in pledge, you shall return it when the sun sets. For it is his only clothing, a covering for his skin; in what else can he sleep? When he cries out to Me I will listen, for I am merciful. (22:21–26)

This passage magnificently demonstrates that the Covenant Code is much more than a legal compendium. Beyond an enumeration of transgressions and punishments, biblical law includes stirring exhortations to moral behavior, and a depiction of God's active intervention on behalf of victims. People who take advantage of society's weakest members, God warns, will in turn find themselves in their number. Strikingly, God uses the expression "My people," elsewhere referring to all the Israelites (e.g., "Let My people go!"), specifically for the poor. Such passages portray God somewhat differently than the narrative portions of the Bible, showing God's intimate care for every human being, not just the rulers, priests, and prophets. In other laws, Israelite history is invoked to project a similar ethical message: "Do not oppress the stranger, for you know the life of a stranger, since you were strangers in the land of Egypt" (23:9). To lead a lawful, moral life, in the Bible's vision, requires internalizing the lessons of history and theology to guide one's actions toward others.

A comparison of a couple of biblical laws with similar laws from Hammurabi's Code, the most important law code before the Bible, written circa 1700 B.C.E., brings dramatically to the fore the Bible's moral vision. Here are laws concerning theft:

> If anyone steals cattle or sheep, or an ass, or a pig or a goat, if it belongs to a god or to the court, the thief shall pay thirtyfold; if they belonged to a freed man of the king he shall pay tenfold; if the thief has nothing with which to pay, he shall be put to death. (Hammurabi, law 8)

> If a man steals an ox or sheep, and slaughters it or sells it, five cattle he shall pay for the ox, and four sheep for the sheep. If the thief is discovered tunneling and is struck and dies, there is no bloodguilt. If the sun is shining upon him, there is bloodguilt. He must pay; if he cannot, he is sold for his theft. If the theft is found in his hand, whether an ox or donkey or sheep, alive, he shall pay double. (Exodus 21:37–22:3)

And others concerning negligent homicide:

> If an ox is a goring ox, and it is shown that he is a gorer, and he does not bind his horns, or fasten the ox up, and the ox gores a freeborn man and kills him, the owner shall pay one-half a mina in money.

> If he kills a man's slave, he shall pay one-third of a mina. (Hammurabi, laws 251–52)

> If an ox gores a man or woman, who dies, the ox shall surely be stoned and its flesh remain uneaten, but the ox's owner is guiltless. But if the ox was a gorer previously, and its owner was admonished but did not guard it, and it kills a man or woman, the ox shall be stoned, and its owner also put to death…. Should the ox gore a manservant or maidservant, he shall give thirty shekels to its master and the ox shall be stoned. (Exodus 21:28–29, 32)

There are many striking similarities between the ancient Babylonian and Israelite law codes. They treat comparable situations, such as the case of a goring ox, likely a widespread problem in societies dependent upon livestock. Both codes consider capital punishment appropriate in certain circumstances, so it would be wrong to say that one society is more lenient than the other. Since Hammurabi established his legal system centuries before the Bible, it presumably exercised a significant influence on the Israelites as they set out to create their own law.

Yet the sharp discrepancies between the punishments prescribed for specific crimes suggest a profound difference between these two ancient societies. In the case of theft, both codes hold the crime to be significant enough to warrant a punishment sufficient for deterrence. Nevertheless, Babylonian property law goes far beyond Israelite law in its severity. Convicted Babylonian thieves who cannot pay the exorbitant restitution are put to death, whereas poor Israelite thieves make good their crime through enslavement. (Keep in mind that imprisonment as a widespread legal practice for punishment is a modern phenomenon.)

In the case of homicide, the situation is reversed. Courts in ancient Israel immediately have an ox stoned if it has killed someone. An ox known to have violent tendencies toward people must be restrained by its owner. If that ox proceeds to kill someone through the owner's carelessness, the owner is held responsible for the murder and is himself put to death. Babylonian law does not treat negligent homicide as seriously; the careless owner of an ox that gores suffers monetary damages only. (Both codes reckon the value of slaves at less than that of free citizens.) This contrast demonstrates that Babylonian law places property as the greatest value, whereas the Bible values life above all else, and to such an extent that there can be no monetary equivalent for shedding blood:

> But I shall avenge your life-blood; from every beast I will avenge it. And from man, from each man's brother, I will avenge a man's life. He who spills the blood of man, by man his blood shall be spilled; for in the image of God He made man. (Genesis 9:5–6)

Because man is created in God's image, homicide constitutes an attack against God. Possessions, by contrast, contain no such theological stigma.

Levitical Laws: The Power of Holiness

Holiness is one of the Bible's central concepts, the word "holy" appearing in different forms over 750 times. Its most important application involves Israel's relation to the law. When God prepares Israel to receive the covenant at Sinai, He tells them, "You shall be to Me a kingdom of priests and a holy nation" (Exodus 19:6). Israel *becomes* a holy nation by receiving the covenant. It is holy not by nature, only by its acceptance and fulfillment of God's law.* The Hebrew word for holy, *kadosh*, literally means "separated, apart." Something holy is separated from ordinary reality, from everything else that exists, by being dedicated to God's service. Israel is a "holy nation" insofar as it is committed to worshipping and obeying God. It is a "kingdom of priests," however, only metaphorically. Priests are people selected to serve God; they have been separated off from everyone else, made holy. Just as the priests are a holy group among the Israelites, so the Israelites are considered holy, according to the Bible, among all the nations through their devotion to God.

Not surprisingly, the concept of holiness is paramount in Leviticus, the law code of the priests. As God says amid the laws of keeping kosher, "You shall be holy, for I am holy" (Leviticus 11:45). In the vision of Leviticus, the purpose of the law is for people to become holy by emulating God's holiness. Just as God is separate from the world, the Temple is apart from other buildings, sacrifices are kept apart from other food, and priests remove themselves from society in certain ways. Leviticus holds the sanctity of ritual as so essential because it is a necessary means to approach God. All of the priests' activities revolve around holy things, generally produce or animals that people have designated for God. These holy things must be treated with the exacting attention required by their awesome purpose. Through their role in facilitating sacrifices, the priests ensure that the people's prayers are heard. Their mistakes carry dire consequences for themselves, for the supplicant, and potentially for all of Israel.

In the words of anthropologist Mary Douglas, the laws of Leviticus revolve around the notions of "purity and danger." The priests must execute the Temple rituals in a state of purity; any defilement carries great

---

* Deuteronomy 7:6–11 presents the opposite perspective: Israel is holy because God has chosen it—therefore Israel should observe God's law, in gratitude for a status already confirmed.

danger. This message emerges from one of the few stories told in Leviticus, an enigmatic and disturbing episode about Aaron's sons:

> Aaron's sons, Nadav and Avihu, each took his fire-pan and put fire in it, laying incense over it; and they offered strange fire before the Lord, which He had not commanded. And fire went forth from the Lord and consumed them, and they died in the presence of the Lord. (10:1–2)

Jewish interpreters have offered a wide range of explanations in grappling with the harshness of God's decree in this passage: Were Aaron's sons drunk? Did they try to give an offering that had not been commanded? Whatever the correct explanation, this story presents a clear warning to priests that they must carry out their responsibilities in the Temple exactly. A good contemporary analogy is a nuclear plant: workers there must fulfill their tasks with great meticulousness and seriousness. One minor slipup can bring disaster.

Biblical priests regard their own roles in precisely the same way. They are required to follow the rules that apply to all of Israel, as well as specific laws just for them (see Leviticus 21). Priests are forbidden from having any contact with the dead, except for the closest of kin. Even today, cohens, descendants of the priests in the ancient Temple, will not attend a funeral or enter a cemetery. The high priest may not attend the funeral even of his parents. Priests may marry only a virgin. A variety of physical deformities renders one unfit to serve in the Temple. The priests must carry out the law with the highest degree of stringency: "They shall be holy to their God and not profane the name of their God, for the Lord's offerings by fire, their God's bread, they bring forth, so they shall be holy" (21:6).

Many of the laws of Leviticus aim to achieve holiness by imposing a certain order upon the undifferentiated flow of nature. The laws of keeping kosher in Leviticus 11, for example, establish categories that separate animals, birds, fish, and insects into clean and unclean, permissible to be eaten versus impermissible. Animals that have cleft hoofs and chew their cud can be eaten; fish must have fins and scales to be edible; for birds, the Bible gives no anatomical specifications but lists a number of forbidden birds, all of which are predatory; locusts, crickets, grasshoppers, and catydids alone are acceptable among the insects. Only certain foods are allowed; by eating those foods and avoiding others, the Israelites are conscious of fulfilling the will of God. Similarly, the Bible's sexual laws, spelled out in Leviticus 18, create a certain order among the welter of possible relations, regulating the social sphere and endowing the most intimate relationships with religious meaning. The Bible reaches into all aspects of people's lives, from the personal to the social, the economic, and the political, from the mundane to the exalted, establishing a system of distinctions to instill awareness of God at all times.

Thus the Bible imposes a structure that encompasses all aspects of society. Its legal code determines basic rights and protections for all inhabitants of the land. Although the Bible acknowledges the ancient practice of slavery, it emphasizes the rights of slaves during their servitude and mandates the release of slaves every seven years. The Bible imposes the same responsibilities upon rich and poor, the powerful and the weak, demanding that the weakest members of society receive the same justice as the strongest, while insisting that they not be favored either: "You shall not follow the majority in wrong.... Nor shall you favor the poor in his dispute." (Exodus 23:2–3). Biblical law requires the formation of a legal system, with courts, judges, and proper witnesses, ensuring that justice is carried out as fairly and impartially as humanly possible. Simultaneously, the law formulates rules for holiday and ritual observance that provide the means of communication between God and people. Distinctions between the holy and the secular, between permissible and forbidden acts, allow people to lead lives of quiet dignity, conscious every day that they are striving to emulate God through the fulfillment of God's will. Hence, biblical law properly understood lays down a religious and moral path for living. No wonder that Judaism considers the study of the law to be the most rewarding spiritual activity on earth.

CHAPTER 4

History in the Bible

Suggested reading: 1 Samuel 8–17, 23–24; 2 Samuel 3–5, 11–12; 1 Kings 1–11; 2 Kings 22–23; Ezra 1, 6–7; Nehemiah 8

There are several kinds of history pertinent to our understanding of the Bible. First, there's the history *in* the Bible, the history that the Bible relates from the creation of the world through the triumphs and misfortunes of the ancient Israelite people. Second, there's history *behind* the Bible: archeological discoveries from the Ancient Near East which open up questions regarding the relationship of biblical history to the actual events and circumstances of the past. Third, there's the history *of* the Bible, namely, the process of composition, transmission, and collection of the traditions united into one large volume. A fourth kind of history describes the influence of the Bible after it was written, its interpretation by religious thinkers and denominations for the past 2,000 years – a fascinating and immense subject that is beyond the scope of this guide. This chapter covers the history in the Bible and summarizes the archeological findings; the next chapter discusses theories of the Bible's formation.

The Bible is shaped as a work of history: it starts at one point in time, ends at a later point in time, and moves chronologically forward between those points. This simple characterization, however, does not tell the whole story. Biblical history does not move smoothly and evenly through time. Rather, it concentrates on selected periods that are significant for historical or theological reasons. For example, the Bible devotes almost no space to describing the generations of enslavement in Egypt, because, from the narrator's perspective, nothing happened during that time. The

Bible strongly distinguishes periods of history with particular overarching themes, historical trends, and major personages that make them highly memorable and dramatically different one from another.

History holds great importance in the Bible for two main reasons: it relates the origins of a people, the Israelites; and it recounts the role that God has played in human affairs. Yet despite the great emphasis placed upon history in the Bible, and despite the fact that the Bible is written in a chronological manner similar to how books of history are written, scholars today are not at all in agreement about whether the Bible should rightly be considered a work of history. Ira Gershwin was prescient when he wrote in *Porgy and Bess*, "The things that you're liable to read in the Bible / They ain't necessarily so." Over the past several decades, the accuracy of more and more of the Bible has come under question, leading some scholars to assert that no statement in the Bible should be taken at face value as a reflection of historical reality. Relatively few accounts in the Bible can be independently verified through ancient documents or archeological research. This lack of verification has led some to consider the Bible a collection of ancient tales of origin united by a theological perspective, rather than a work of history. Other scholars insist that the Bible retains a core of reliable historical information, or at the very least, it *may* contain accurate information even if no independent support has been found thus far. These scholars are not willing to dismiss the Bible as a source of historical understanding, especially since it is by far the largest and most significant document from the Ancient Near East. And most scholars still hold that the later the events that are described in the Bible, the more historically accurate they are. This dispute has implications far beyond academia and will no doubt continue for years to come.

The timeline on the following page represents the standard dating for the major periods in the Bible. It includes reference to the postbiblical period, during which the Bible reached its final form.

The account of biblical history in this chapter alternates summaries of the Bible's version (*The Story*) with the version reconstructed by biblical scholarship. For the latter, I have adapted the term "backstory." In the theater, a backstory consists of stories that actors make up about their characters before the action in the play takes place. The backstory helps

Biblical Timeline of History

			First Temple			
2000–1500 B.C.E.	1300	1200	1030	930	722	586
Patriarchs	Moses Conquest	Judges	United Monarchy	Divided Monarchy	Fall of Israel	fall of Judah – Babylonian exile

	Second Temple				
539	516	332	164 B.C.E.	63 C.E.	70 C.E.
Return: Persian rule	Temple rebuilt	Greek rule	Maccabees – self-rule	Roman rule	Second Temple destroyed

Rabbinic Judaism	
90	132
Yavneh	Bar Kochbah revolt

the actors immerse themselves more fully in their portrayal but is entirely hidden from the audience. Similarly, the backstory in this chapter relates the story that modern scholars assert lies behind the story presented in the Bible. By just reading the Bible, one would have little idea of the historical "drama" that gave rise to its writing. An awareness of the historical backstory may inspire renewed interest in the Bible's final cut.

Beginnings: Primeval and Patriarchal Eras
Genesis
The Story
In the beginning, God created heaven and earth; five days later, God created man. According to the Bible, history is the story of human beings. Humanity is created last of all creatures, as the culmination of God's creation. However, while man is the main story, he is not the whole story. Genesis 1 reminds us that God's perspective is greater than man's perspective, that man is just one, albeit a highly significant, part of the cosmos, and that all other beings and entities that exist in the world are likewise the handiwork of God. The Bible's opening both reinforces and restrains humanity's narcissistic tendencies. It elevates people to beings created "in the image of God," endowed with the power to dominate and exploit all other species. At the same time, we find a universe established with abundant variety and order, teeming with life before the first *homo sapiens* enters the scene. Man completes the arrangement of creation, but also disrupts it. He cannot accept its perfect symmetry; he must try out his powers even at the cost of challenging God and incurring God's wrath. A ball combining dust and God's breath (Genesis 2:7), the Bible's

initial portrait of human nature is a compelling mixture of supremacy and insignificance, ambition and venality.

The early chapters of Genesis (1–11) are often called the "primeval" history because they take place in the ancient mists of time, at the beginning of the world. They form a backdrop to the main history that begins with Abraham, explaining how the earth and human society took shape. Humanity begins with God's creation of a single couple, Adam and Eve. Two sexes are created as a cure for human loneliness. The creatures of the earth receive names from Adam when he goes searching for companionship. God intends for the couple to live comfortably forever in a protected garden named Eden, but because they rebel by eating forbidden fruit, humanity comes to suffer harsh conditions, including mortality, the pain of childbirth, and the toil of agriculture. Adam and Eve's son Cain invents murder when he kills his brother, Abel. Another son, Seth, establishes a line that extends several generations to Noah. In the time of Noah, humanity becomes so wicked that God decides to destroy the Earth and start again with one family. Noah survives a great flood in an ark he built, large enough to accommodate representatives of all creatures. After the flood subsides, God creates the rainbow as a sign of God's covenant that never again shall a flood destroy the entire earth. Noah's three sons and their descendants spread out upon the earth to establish the "family of nations." The plethora of human languages crop up when people unite to challenge God by building a tower reaching up to the sky; God disperses people far and wide and makes them unable to understand each other.

From these broad strokes, biblical history switches to the intimate account of four generations within a single family. The patriarchal history similarly provides explanations of origins, focusing on the national, geographic, and religious contours of ancient Israel and environs. Unlike in the earlier material, these characters are suddenly much more realistic, more fully developed, as their lives are told within a biographical frame from birth to marriage, procreation, and death. Abraham, the first Israelite, moves with his wife, Sarah, his father, Terah, and his nephew Lot from Ur, a major city in Mesopotamia, to Haran in Syria, then to Canaan after his father's death. The Bible shows Abraham and his family to be semi-nomadic pasturalists; that is, they raise livestock, move from place to place as weather conditions permit, and dwell in tents. The stories present Abraham's family as largely self-contained, isolated from other inhabitants of the land. Encounters with others tend to reveal outsiders as violent and untrustworthy. Abraham does battle with five local kings to rescue Lot; Lot again needs to be rescued, this time by messengers of God, when the people of Sodom attempt to rape him. Abraham fears for his life in the presence of the Egyptian king and, later, of Abimelech, king of Gerar in the Negev. Abraham's son Isaac is characterized by his fidelity to his father, accompanying Abraham to Mount Moriah, where Abraham places Isaac on the altar to be sacrificed, accepting the bride Abraham chooses for him, remaining in the land of Canaan. Both Isaac and his son Jacob establish the importance of marriage within the family (and by extension later on, the nation) as a way to preserve Abraham's religious heritage. Jacob expands the family into a nation by fathering sons who are the ancestors of Israel's tribal groups. Jealousy and disagreements among the brothers foreshadow the relationships between the tribes; the reunion of the brothers in mutual forgiveness and love betokens an ideal of harmony and unity achieved rarely if ever in subsequent biblical history.

The Backstory

While there may be kernels of historical memories in stories such as the Flood and the Tower of Babel, the primeval history generally is regarded as a series of legends adapted from similar material in the surrounding societies and transformed to convey the unique national and theological message of the Bible. Scholars have long noted parallels between these early chapters in the Bible and mythological writings from the Ancient Near East. The creation story, for example, is frequently compared with the Babylonian epic called *Enuma Elish*. Even stronger parallels exist between the biblical description of the Flood and the Mesopotamian epic of Gilgamesh, a popular story that exists in various ancient forms and languages. Ancient Israel is a dry land with little seafaring expertise; additionally, there is no archeological record of a devastating flood in the region. Consequently, the biblical story of Noah's Flood likely originated in the Mesopotamian tale and was retold as "an expression of the biblical polemic against paganism," in the view of Nahum Sarna, by transforming the familiar polytheistic account into a story of God's absolute control of nature. Sarna sees this same polemic operating in the Babel story, which he regards as a satire against the ziggurat of Babylon, a tower thought to serve as a meeting point between people and the gods. Whatever the accuracy of such theories, Ancient Near Eastern myth has provided the most convincing explanation for the origins of the opening stories of Genesis.

There is considerable uncertainty whether the patriarchs in the Bible actually lived or are instead legends of ancestral founders. No evidence for their existence has been found independent of the Bible. Of course, we have records of very few people from ancient history, though we might have expected some independent record considering the importance the Bible attributes to the patriarchs. Biblical historians have invested significant efforts into locating the plausible period during which the patriarchs might have lived, attempting to correlate the details from the biblical stories with data known from archeological evidence. The dominant position in the mid-twentieth century, proposed by William F. Albright, held that Abraham lived around the year 2000 B.C.E. That was a period when the urban culture in the area of Syria and Canaan went into decline. Albright posited a theory called "the Amorite hypothesis," which claimed that nomads from the desert invaded and sacked cities in the late third millennium, settled in Canaan, and later led the rebuilding of urban centers. Abraham, then, may have been an Amorite leader. However, in the past thirty years the scholarly consensus has turned against this dating, and most scholars today believe that it is impossible to affirm the existence of the patriarchs within a given historical context. Genesis tells us both too little and too much about the patriarchs: too little in that no recognizable historical figures are explicitly mentioned; too much because details mentioned often cannot be made to fit into the historical timeline given in the Bible. One of the pieces of evidence that helped sink the Amorite hypothesis, for example, is the fact that several cities that are mentioned in the Abraham stories were not found to exist in the early second millennium, according to the archeological record.

On the other hand, it is not at all impossible that the biblical stories include elements of genuine historical memories. One such element is the patriarchs' names: Abra(ha)m, Isaac, Jacob, Joseph, and Israel all are attested, in variant forms, independently of the Bible in ancient records or are historically plausible on the basis of known name types. For example, Jacob was a common personal name in the mid-second millennium B.C.E. In the form "Jacob-El," which probably means "Let El protect," the name appears in a list of cities and groups conquered by the Egyptian ruler Tuthmosis III in the fifteenth century. Jacob may have been the name attributed to the founder of this group. Another historical detail with independent affirmation is the rise of a non-Egyptian to a position of power within an Egyptian government, a fairly common occurrence according to Egyptian annals. Joseph's ascent within the administration of an unnamed pharaoh parallels the career of Irsu, who gained power, probably during a period of famine, around 1200 B.C.E., and most likely came from Canaan.

Despite such ancient threads, anachronistic details in the biblical stories suggest a late date for the Bible's final composition. Two such details are given after Joseph's brothers have cast him in the pit (Genesis 37:25): "Looking up, they saw a caravan of Ishmaelites coming from Gilead, their camels bearing gum, balm, and ladanum to be taken to Egypt." Archeologists have found that camels were not widely used as beasts of burden until after 1000 B.C.E., and that the Arabian trade in spices first flourished under the Assyrian empire in the eighth to seventh century. Another anachronism commonly cited is found in Genesis 26:1: "There was a famine in the land…and Isaac went to Abimelech, king of the Philistines, in Gerar." The Philistines were among several groups collectively called the "Sea Peoples" who came from the Mediterranean and Aegean Seas and landed in Canaan after 1200 B.C.E. The city of Gerar, according to modern archeologists, was insignificant until the eighth to seventh century. These and other discoveries suggest that the traditions of Israel's origins were written down long after the time in which they were thought to take place.

The Moses Years: Egypt and Wilderness
Exodus, Numbers, Deuteronomy
The Story

Joseph, who rises to prominence under the Egyptian pharoah, arranges for his family to move to Egypt and settle in an area called Goshen, where they can prosper during a period of drought in Canaan. During the family's stay, which lasts several generations, they multiply enormously, changing from a small clan to a sizable nation. The Egyptians grow concerned that these Israelites might become powerful in their land. A later pharaoh chooses to subjugate these foreign dwellers, enforcing a harsh form of slavery while requiring them to work on massive building projects. He decrees that first-born Israelite boys be cast into the river.

At this time, Moses is born. After three months his parents can no longer hide him; they prepare a special floating basket, put him in it, and place it in the reeds along the shore. Pharaoh's daughter happens to discover him there; she takes pity on him and arranges for him to be raised within the Egyptian court. As a young man, Moses flees from Egypt after killing an Egyptian taskmaster. He encounters God at the burning bush, where God informs Moses that he will lead the people. With help from his brother, Aaron, Moses confronts pharaoh and demands that the Israelites be allowed to leave and worship God. Pharaoh denies their request time and again, provoking God's wrath in ten plagues of increasing severity against the Egyptians. When God kills the Egyptian firstborn, including Pharaoh's son, pharaoh finally relents and permits the Israelites to leave Egypt. But again he has a change of heart, unleashing his chariots to pursue the Israelites as they escape. Putting their faith in God, the Israelites step into the Sea of Reeds, which parts, enabling them to walk through it. As the Egyptian charioteers enter the sea behind them, the waters fold back upon them and they drown.

Moses leads the people for forty years in the wilderness. Their first destination is Mount Sinai, where the people receive a covenant from God, including two tablets with commandments. While Moses ascends the mountain in order to receive these tablets, the people grow restless and demand that Aaron make them a golden calf to worship. Upon Moses' descent, he becomes furious at the people's infidelity and smashes the tablets, then pulverizes the calf and forces the people to drink water with its dust. He subsequently reascends to receive a second pair of tablets. Meanwhile, on God's instructions, the Israelites build a highly elaborate and portable Tabernacle in the desert as a place for them to worship God. They receive a detailed code of instruction for sacrifices to be conducted by priests, which will serve as a manual centuries later when they have an opportunity to build a Temple in the land of Israel. Aaron is installed as the first high priest, overseeing a legion of priests performing sacred rituals.

Even though the direct route between Egypt and Israel would take no more than two weeks by foot, God takes the people the long way so that they avoid violent confrontation with the Philistines along the coastal road. God leads the people with a pillar of cloud by day and a pillar of fire by night, supplying them with special food called manna. But the long travail through the desert wearies the people of their resolve; they complain repeatedly against God and Moses, wishing at times that they had stayed in Egypt rather than strive for an elusive, unknown Promised Land. Korah, a Levite (a kind of priest), leads a rebellion against Moses, attracting 250 followers before God causes the earth to open and swallow them up. When Moses appoints spies from the twelve tribes to scout out the land of Israel, only two of them bring back a good report. The rest complain that the inhabitants are giants who can never be defeated. At times God tells Moses that He plans on wiping out the entire nation and starting anew with Moses; only Moses' pleading can assuage God's wrath. Nevertheless, Moses, too, grows impatient with the people's grumbling. When the people protest to Moses that they are dying of thirst, Moses rashly taunts them, "Listen up, rebels: from this crag shall we bring forth water for you?" (Numbers 20:10) before striking the rock to yield water. God criticizes Moses and punishes him by denying him entry into the land. On the eve of entry into Israel, therefore, the triangular relationship between the people, Moses, and God appears very shaky.

Hence, on his final day, Moses rallies the new generation to strengthen their hearts for the challenges ahead. Knowing that he will not enter the land with them, Moses reveals all-too-human bitterness: "God also grew angry at me on your account, saying, 'You too shall not go there'" (Deuteronomy 1:37). But despite his anger, Moses urges the people on toward their own improvement and the realization of God's promise. His oration, occupying nearly the entire book of Deuteronomy, reminds the people of God's special relationship and history with them. Moses sings the land's praises, waxing poetic over a land he has never seen:

> For the Lord your God is bringing you to a good land: a land of
> fast-flowing streams, of fountains and deep waters, emerging from
> valley and mountain; a land of wheat and barley, vine and fig tree
> and pomegranate; a land of olive oil and honey; a land where you
> shall not eat bread in poverty, you shall not lack for anything; a land
> whose stones are iron, and from whose hills you shall quarry copper.
> (Deuteronomy 8:7–9)

Moses encourages the people to follow God's commandments in the land of Israel in order to be worthy to retain its possession. Frequently he warns them to distance themselves from the idolatrous practices of the land's current inhabitants. In a prophetic poem, Moses foresees that Israel's troubled fidelity to God will continue to blot their history for centuries once they settle into their homeland. After Moses issues a final blessing for each tribe, God leads him to a mountaintop, where he can see the entire land that the people will inherit, although he, poignantly, will not enter it with them. Having been granted these supreme visions in time and space, Moses dies "at the command of the Lord."

The Backstory

From a historical perspective, the transition between Joseph and Moses covers over a host of difficult questions regarding the origins of the Israelite people. The details are hard to reconcile: Jacob's family descends to Egypt seventy-strong, and the Israelites, now a nation, leave Egypt some time later as "about six hundred thousand men on foot, aside from children" (Exodus 12:37; and what about women?). The duration in Egypt is also unclear, varying from 430 years to four generations. Further, when, where, and how did this family decide it was a nation? What is the origin of "Israel"? At what point did Israel become a distinct ethnic and national group? Moreover, when and how did this group develop its strong religious perspective? The Bible treats such developments as natural occurrences needing no explanation.

The difficulty that scholars have in finding any record of the sojourn in Egypt, the exodus, and wandering in the desert is more unsettling than the gaps in the historical record concerning the patriarchs. One can understand not finding traces of individuals or families, but the accounts of events in Exodus and Numbers give the impression that these are world-shaking occurrences with a major impact for the entire region:

> Nations hear, they quake,
> Dwellers of Philistia writhe in anguish.
> Then chiefs of Edom take fright,
> Moabite captains tremble,
> All the Canaanites melt away. (Exodus 15:14–15)

The Egyptian government kept very good records, and their libraries have been discovered by archeologists over the past two hundred years; yet they contain no indication of a large nation called the Hebrews inhabiting a section of Egypt, being forced as slaves to build cities, or fleeing the country after confronting the Egyptian king, nor of a battalion of Egyptian charioteers chasing this group and drowning in the Sea of Reeds.

Nonetheless, numerous details from the Exodus story find striking confirmation in ancient writings and archeological discoveries. We know that the Egyptians allowed tribes to cross their border in times of famine. Here's an ancient report from a border official: "We have finished letting the Bedouin tribes of Edom pass the Fortress of Mer-ne-Ptah Hotep-hir-Maat...which is in Tjeku, to the pools of Per-Atum...to keep them alive and to keep their cattle alive." Between the eighteenth and sixteenth centuries B.C.E., a significant number of people from Canaan crossed into Egypt and formed a colony in the eastern Nile Delta, the same area called "Goshen" in the Bible. This group, known as "Hyksos" meaning "rulers of foreign lands," actually took control of Egypt for more than a hundred years, before another Egyptian king drove the Hyksos out of Egypt and back to Canaan. The broad agreement between this story and the basic outline of the Exodus led some scholars to posit the Hyksos as the ancient Israelites.

This theory conflicted with other details from the Bible, and scholars gradually abandoned the Hyksos hypothesis for a later date in the thirteenth century B.C.E. Most telling is the name Raamses for one of the cities the Israelites were consigned to build (Exodus 1:11). The Egyptian king Raamses II ruled for a long period in the thirteenth century. He built a new capital and named it after himself, conscripting large numbers of civilians and foreigners as forced laborers. Also there are records of laborers under Raamses II being allowed time off from work to worship their gods. Undermining the hypothesis of a thirteenth-century exodus, however, are discoveries that at this time the Egyptians had established a series of strong border fortifications, besides exercising significant control over Canaan. Scholars find it unlikely that a large group of escaping slaves could have gotten past the military forces of the region's dominant power.

An additional problem with the Bible's version lies in the names of places visited by the Israelites in the desert. Most of the them have never been attested by archeologists. Only two locations have been identified with archeological sites: Kadesh-barnea and Etzion-geber. However, both of those sites contain no evidence of habitation until hundreds of years after the thirteenth century. The thirteenth-century hypothesis, just like the Hyksos hypothesis, has lost much of its credibility. Again, the biblical account seems to contain a wealth of genuine historical memories, even as they have been woven together into a larger pattern that does not accord with independent accounts of the region's history.

Conquest, then Anarchy
Joshua, Judges
The Story

Driven on by Moses' stirring exhortation to unite under God's law, the Israelites reach one of the high points in their history with the conquest of the land under Moses' appointed heir, Joshua. Joshua faithfully follows in Moses' footsteps, dutifully obeying God's commandments and maintaining an intimate relationship with God. Under Joshua, the Bible says nothing about the people's grumblings or stiff-necked opposition to their destiny. Their success in conquering the land and defeating the Canaanite inhabitants derives in part from their newfound unity of purpose.

The other main cause for the Israelites' overwhelming victory is Joshua's brilliance as a military tactician. Battle after battle, the Bible portrays Joshua outsmarting his Canaanite opponents. He shows consummate preparation for each encounter. Before attacking Jericho, he sends spies into the city to discover the mood of the population. They report back that the people are terrified, having heard of Israel's triumph against other tribes. Joshua capitalizes on the inhabitants' fear by staging a march around the city walls for seven days with priests blowing horns. (In the lingo of contemporary warfare, Joshua invented psy-ops.) This boisterous, drawn-out siege of the city has enhanced the impression of the Israelites' fearsome might. On the seventh day, Joshua's minions circle the city seven times and then shout, reaching a fevered frenzy that causes the city walls to collapse. Israelite soldiers proceed to kill all the inhabitants except for the family that helped the spies.

In subsequent battles, Joshua displays the same piety, ingenuity, and ruthlessness. Local tribal leaders learn of his exploits and try to band together in opposition, but with God's aid Joshua is unbeatable. Joshua even orders the sun not to rise for one day while he attacks his enemies under cover of darkness; Joshua is so close to God that God ensures the sun's obedience: "Such a day never existed before or since, when God obeyed the voice of a man" (Joshua 10:14). After the conquest is complete, the Bible lists in great detail the boundaries for each tribe allotted within the new land. Reuben, Gad, and the half-tribe of Manasseh had already taken territory outside of Canaan during the time of Moses, in exchange for agreeing to fight with the other tribes. The Levites receive land within the portions of the other tribes. Before his death, Joshua gathers the people together just as Moses did on his final day. Joshua too delivers a final oration, attempting to instill obedience to God within the people, reminding them of God's continued presence and sustenance.

As the book of Judges demonstrates, Joshua's speech exerts no lasting impact upon history. "Judges" might more accurately be translated as "tribal chieftains," a title referring to a period of chaotic disunity among the various tribes. Whereas during the conquest Israel seems to be entirely unified under Joshua, in the period of Judges there is no discernible national entity or leader. Instead various tribes put forth their own separate leading figures, who, for good or ill, strut their hour upon the stage of history. The effect is something like the dissolution of Yugoslavia after the death of Marshall Tito.

Over the course of the Book of Judges, the characters tend to become more grotesque, their actions more horrific. Even when things go well, as they do in some of the early stories, something is not quite right. The first chieftain, Othniel the Kenizzite, is from a non-Israelite tribe allied with the Israelites. The second hero, Ehud the Benjaminite, kills Eglon, king of Moab, by stabbing the king while he is sitting on the toilet. Eglon is so fat that Ehud is able to hide the blade hilt in his belly, helping facilitate his escape. The next heroic figures are Deborah the prophetess and Jael the Kenite. Deborah summons the general Barak to do battle against Sisera, a Canaanite general. Barak routs the enemy army, and Sisera flees to the tent of Jael, who drives a tent pin in his head while Sisera is sleeping. Though Deborah and Jael are depicted heroically, the story makes clear that the lack of Israelite leadership requires the army to rely on the initiative of women. A later chieftain, Jephthah the Gileadite, vows to sacrifice whatever comes out of his house if he returns victorious from battle – a vow he must bitterly fulfill when his daughter, his only child, runs to greet him. Several chapters are devoted to the well-known story of Samson the Danite, the supernaturally strong warrior who allows himself to be seduced and blinded by Delilah, a spy for the Philistine enemy. Judges ends with its most gruesome tale, an incident of rape, murder, and mutilation casting shame upon the tribe of Benjamin. The last sentence famously summarizes the Bible's perspective on this era: "In those days there was no king in Israel; everyone did what was right in his own eyes."

The Backstory

As with the previous biblical eras, initial archeological finds broadly confirmed the conquest described in Joshua, but later discoveries and analysis raised questions concerning the Bible's history. Researchers looked at the mounds, called *tels* in Hebrew, containing deposits of pottery shards, ruins of buildings, bones, tools, inscriptions, even food and other detritus piled up over thousands of years. Since the Book of Joshua mentions dozens of Canaanite cities conquered, scholars might have expected to find evidence of widespread, simultaneous devastation from about the year 1200 B.C.E., when the conquest is thought to have occurred. Indeed, a number of sites excavated show signs that they were sacked just around that time, including Lachish, Debir, Bethel, and Hazor. Yet for some of the major cities whose battles are described in Joshua, no trace of thirteenth- or twelfth-century destruction can be found. At Jericho, the world's oldest city with ruins going back some 11,000 years, archeologists revealed a city wall that was destroyed around 1560 B.C.E., but almost no trace of human habitation, let alone a walled city, for centuries thereafter. The city of Ai, another major battle site in Joshua, presents similar problems: a walled city there was destroyed in 2400 B.C.E., with little subsequent settlement until a small unwalled village took root between 1200 and 1050 B.C.E. Several other towns listed in Joshua show no evidence of residency during the estimated period for the conquest.

These discrepancies with the archeological record have directed biblical historians toward different theories about Israelite origins. For cities destroyed around this time, current thinking points to other culprits: the Egyptians, who dominated Canaan for much of the second millennium B.C.E., or the "Sea Peoples," including the Philistines, who inhabited parts of the coastal area about 1200 B.C.E. In the wake of the conquest theory, how do scholars believe the Israelites originated and came to occupy the land of Canaan? The leading alternate theory, first penned by German scholar Albrecht Alt and still championed in modified form to this day, claims a peaceful, gradual settlement of nomads crossing over into Israel from beyond the Jordan who eventually established settlements in the central highlands, where most of the biblical cities are located. Largely empty in the fourteenth century, these highlands were suddenly dotted with dozens of small settlements by the end of the thirteenth century. One drawback to this theory, according to recent archeology, is the fact that the new settlers were farmers and herders rather than nomads. Another theory sees Israel arising as a revolt of rural farmers, peasants, and nomadic brigands against corrupt urban Canaanite lords. This romantic scenario is largely discredited as owing more to Marxism than to the reality of ancient times. Recent studies indicate that the land of Canaan during this period exhibited no great cultural upheaval (for example, a marked change in pottery styles), concluding that whatever changes occurred within the land resulted from a mostly indigenous population rather than groups outside of the land.

The earliest reference discovered to a group named "Israel" can be found in the Merneptah Stele, a large stone monument commemorating a victory of the Egyptian king Merneptah in the late thirteenth century B.C.E.:

> Plundered is the Canaan with every evil;
> Carried off is Ashkelon; seized upon is Gezer;
> Yanoam is made as that which does not exist;
> Israel is laid waste, his seed is not;
> Hurru is become a widow for Egypt!

How delightfully appropriate that Israel's first mention on the plain of history announces its destruction! The Merneptah Stele seems emblematic of subsequent Jewish history, its continuous cycles of devastation and rebirth. But who is the "Israel" referred to in this monument? The poem itself gives little clue, since "Israel" is merely one group mentioned among many in the region. The Book of Judges may offer insight into the development of this Israel group. Most of the action centers on the tribe of Benjamin and its neighboring areas, including the tribes of Ephraim, Gad, and Manasseh. This may have been the nucleus of the original Israel. A next stage may be represented in the song of Deborah in Judges 5:14–18; ten tribes are mentioned there, including Ephraim, Benjamin, Machir, Zebulun, Issachar, Reuben, Gilead, Dan, Asher, and Naphtali, two of which – Machir and Gilead – are not mentioned in subsequent lists. At some later point, possibly under King Solomon, the final twelve-tribe pattern emerged.

Although the Book of Joshua gives the impression that the conquest of Israel was total, with the indigenous population entirely destroyed or subjugated, close attention to the Book of Judges yields a surprisingly different picture. The book opens, "After the death of Joshua, the Israelites inquired of the Lord, 'Who will lead us in going up against the Canaanites and fighting them?'" After the Book of Joshua, one would think there were no Canaanites left to attack. The author of Judges appears ignorant of the conquest of Israel under Joshua. Judges tells of repeated conflicts between Israelites who already inhabit the land and Canaanites who never entirely leave. Judges 1 mentions numerous places where the Canaanites continued to dwell side by side with Israelites. The portrait in Judges is likely closer to historical reality than Joshua, which presents a simplified, absolute, and highly ideological depiction of events.

A question that remains mired in scholarly disagreement is, when did the consciousness arise among a group of Israelites that they possessed a separate religious identity in opposition to the people around them? Answers range from the beginning of the period of Judges to relatively late in biblical history. Archeology has, if anything, made this issue more murky. As an example: there is evidence that throughout the First Temple period, worship of the Lord, the biblical God of Israel, and other gods, including Canaanite deities El, Baal, and Asherah, did exist, often side by side. Does this practice reflect an original Israelite-Canaanite religion, out of which biblical monotheism emerged only later, or instead, was there a conflict between monotheistic purists and religious syncretists (combining elements of different religions) over the centuries, as the Bible indicates?

One final difficulty concerns the ethnic origins of the Israelites. No independent proof survives from before the Merneptah Stele for the existence of an ancient group named Israel. The Bible gives abundant clues for the origins of the Israelites – so many that it is difficult to piece them together into a consistent picture. Before the word "Israel" first appears in the Bible, as a name God awards to Jacob after he wrestled with the angel, Abraham is called "the Hebrew," and Joseph receives the same ethnic marker among the Egyptians. No ancient people with that name has been found. The Amarna letters, a trove of fourteenth-century documents discovered in Egypt, contains reports from officials in the land of Canaan that mention a menacing group of rebels called Apiru. It is tantalizing to draw a connection between the Apiru and Hebrews (*Ivrim* in the Hebrew language), but scholars are uncertain about this derivation, primarily because the Apiru represent not a distinct ethnic group but a social class of outcasts and marauders widespread in the Ancient Near East over several centuries.

The diverse origins of the patriarchs suggest that the Israelites may have begun as an alliance of parties from different backgrounds. According to the Bible, Abraham's family comes from Ur in Mesopotamia, as well as Haran in Syria. Isaac may once have represented a distinct northern group, as is suggested by Amos 7:9: "The high places of Isaac shall become desolate, and the altars of Israel laid waste." Jacob, as is mentioned above, is the name of a tribe or city listed in an Egyptian document. Moses' name, as was discussed in chapter 2, is Egyptian in form, and he may embody an Egyptian remnant among the Israelites. A further suggestion of this Egyptian component exists in the "mixed multitude" said to take part in the Exodus (Exodus 12:38). The names of some Levites in the Bible, including Hophni and Phineas (Pinchas), are Egyptian in origin, suggesting that the Egyptians who fled their land and formed part of the new Israelite nation were a group of priests who brought with them worship of a God named Yahweh. Moses' father-in-law (called by three different names) is a Midianite priest, and his decision to join with Moses and his followers may point to another Israelite segment. Furthermore, the tribe of Dan may derive from one of the Sea Peoples named the Danai, who, like the Philistines, landed on the coast in about 1200 b.c.e. Thus it is possible that the Israelites took shape as a league consisting of native and foreign groups. One theory has called this alliance an "amphictyony," that is, a federation of different groups under religious rather than political unity. (Amphictyony is the name of this kind of federation among different tribes in ancient Greece.) The covenant in Joshua 24 might contain the formula for such an alliance of groups from diverse backgrounds:

> Joshua said to all the people, "Thus said the Lord, the God of Israel, 'Beyond the Euphrates, your forefathers dwelled of old, Terah, father of Abraham and Nahor, and they served other gods. But I took your father, Abraham, from beyond the Euphrates and led him through all the land of Canaan. I multiplied his descendants and gave him Isaac. (Joshua 24:2–3)

The foreign-born, idol-worshipping Terah may symbolize a panoply of different tribes, nationalities, and ethnic groups subsumed under an Israelite league.

The Glory of Monarchy
1 Samuel–1 Kings 11
The Story

The period commonly called the United Monarchy, when the kings ruled over both the northern and southern parts of the country, looms by and large in the Bible as a golden age in Israel. The books of Samuel through 1 Kings 11 resemble the Book of Joshua in their depiction of a time when Israel is endowed with strength and leadership, despite considerably more struggle, both internally and externally. The United Monarchy justifies the aching need for a king expressed in Judges. Conversely, the Bible portrays the subsequent era, known as the Divided Monarchy, as a prolonged time of trouble and strife, a return to the chaotic egotism and eccentricity of the era of Judges. The Bible thus exhibits a deep ambivalence over the institution of kingship. On the one hand, the rule of David and Solomon constitutes the high point of Israelite history; on the other, all kings, even these exemplars, possess too much power and are prone to abusing the people and abandoning God. As God tells the prophet Samuel, when the Israelites demand that Samuel appoint a king to lead them, "It is Me they have rejected from being king over them" (1 Samuel 8:7).

The anarchy during the rule of tribal chieftains leads the people to install a king "like all the other nations." A crucial additional factor is the rise of the Philistines. One of a group of "Sea Peoples," the Philistines came east from the sea in the early twelfth century to settle along the shore. The Bible describes the Philistines as a belligerent people, technologically advanced, seeking to expand their territory through conquest. In order to defend themselves, the Israelites require unity under a commander-in-chief, a king who can marshal the economic and human resources of the disparate tribes together as one entity. God accedes to this demand, instructing Samuel to choose Saul as the first king. Saul initially fulfills his promise by leading the Israelite forces to defeat the Philistines. Of towering height, Saul is first and last a warrior, successful on the battlefield but out of his league as a civilian ruler or religious leader – and, as Moses' example demonstrates, Israelite sovereigns are expected to be all three. Rash in his judgment, Saul falls out of favor with God and descends into paranoia.

Recognizing Saul's growing inadequacy, God has Samuel secretly appoint his successor, David. The story of David and Saul is a web of entanglement and hostility. Like Saul, David distinguishes himself as a warrior. David starts out as Saul's protégé, serving the king as an arms-bearer and a musician whose skill on the lyre can soothe Saul when an "evil spirit" descends upon him. David proves his mettle by slaying Goliath, the champion warrior of the Philistines, in a duel with one perfectly aimed stone hurled from a slingshot. He goes on to lead his own army in various victories over the Philistines. As David grows more powerful, however, Saul waxes ever more jealous. Saul offers David his daughter's hand in marriage if he can bring back 100 Philistine foreskins, thinking that David will die in battle. When David returns with 200, Saul gives David his daughter Michal, but he continues to try to kill David in numerous ways. Saul's son Jonathan becomes David's close friend and warns him whenever Saul hatches a new plot. Forced to flee, David temporarily takes residence among the Philistines, becoming their ally against Saul. When the Philistines defeat Saul at Mount Gilboa in a battle at which both Saul and Jonathan die, David is anointed as the head of Judah, the southern region. He still must lead a campaign against Saul's relatives and allies until he gains control of Israel, the northern region, and becomes king of the entire country.

The Bible regards David as Israel's greatest military leader: "The Lord gave David victory wherever he went" (2 Samuel 8:6). He subdues the Philistine menace and conquers Edom, Moab, Ammon, and Aram, turning these perpetual enemies of Israel into vassal states forced to pay tribute. David captures Jerusalem from the Jebusites, bringing the ark of God up to the city and intending to build there a temple to God. His prophet Nathan, in a vision from God, tells David that one of his sons, not he, will be designated to build God's House in Jerusalem. Nathan also tells David that his descendants will rule forever, secure from their enemies.

Not long after David reaches the summit of his power, he enters a slow decline that lasts until the end of his reign. David notices a beautiful woman, Bathsheba, bathing on a rooftop; he arranges for her husband, Uriah, to be killed in battle and shortly thereafter marries her. From here on, the Bible reports a chain of struggles within the House of David, in which his sons practice deception and murder as if in unconscious imitation of their father. Amnon pretends to be sick, asks for his half-sister Tamar to serve him cakes, then rapes her. Her brother Absalom invites all the princes to a party for shearing the flock, arranges for Amnon to get drunk, and has his henchmen kill him. Posing as a sort of Robin Hood, Absalom then initiates a full-scale civil war against his father, provoking a struggle for loyalty within David's court and throughout the land. Absalom dies when his long hair gets entangled in branches, leaving him hanging and helpless. Finally, David's two remaining sons, Adonijah and Solomon, battle for succession while David is lying on his deathbed. Adonijah wins followers among David's advisers, who appoint him king. Bathsheba, like Isaac's wife Rebekah, engages in an elaborate plot to convince the king that her son Solomon should follow him. Their competition continues after David dies, until Solomon succeeds in wiping out Adonijah and his circle.

The Bible enshrines Solomon as the epitome of wisdom, although the latter part of his reign reveals significant shortcomings. Whereas Saul and David were primarily warriors, Solomon gains renown as an administrator. He establishes the twelve tribes as administrative districts in a federal system whose centralized government lies in Jerusalem. Solomon creates a massive government building project, conscripting the Israelites and remaining Canaanites into forced labor battalions while hiring professional masons and artisans from Tyre in Lebanon. Among his most notable buildings are the Temple and the palace in Jerusalem, as well as fortifications in major cities. Solomon amasses great wealth through trade and taxes, which he lavishes on his construction. For example, he builds a large ivory throne overlaid with gold. He assembles large garrisons of chariots stationed in specially built towns. To secure strong alliances with the neighboring territories, Solomon marries many foreign women: "He had seven hundred royal wives and three hundred concubines" (1 Kings 11:3). In his dotage, Solomon's wives lead him to worship foreign gods.

The Backstory

Initial archeological discoveries inspired confidence that the biblical account of the United Monarchy could be the first period positively confirmed with external evidence. Excavations at several sites that the Bible claims David destroyed, including Gezer, Megiddo, and Beth-shean, showed proof that they were sacked around the year 1000 B.C.E., during the period of David's rule. Philistine pottery found in numerous sites indicates the expansion of Philistine influence throughout ancient Israel at this time. Further, archeologists discovered large city gates, of a unique six-chambered pattern, that they speculated might be the remains of Solomon's national building project. Unfortunately, as with previous discoveries, the scholarly consensus crumbled after new discoveries cast doubt upon earlier conclusions. Improved carbon dating techniques demonstrated that the city gates were built in the ninth century B.C.E., after Solomon's death. Perhaps most damaging, Jerusalem bears no indication that it was an important city, let alone central capital, during this period. Archeological finds suggest that Jerusalem and all of Judah were quite sparsely populated until several centuries later. No evidence could be found for Solomon's massive construction or centralized bureaucracy. The meager population combined with the Philistines' known technological advantages in the art of war suggest that someone other than David caused the destruction of the Philistine cities. Recently, some have questioned whether there ever was a united monarchy at all, speculating that the image of a glorious era when the country was tied together politically and religiously through centralized leadership in Jerusalem is a later ideal projected upon the past. In this view, the land may always have been divided into a larger and more urban north and a rural, sparsely populated south. David and Solomon may have been little more than southern chieftains.

Archeology's persistent disconfirmations have led some naysayers to go so far as to conclude that David and Solomon may never have existed, except as legends in the minds of later writers. However, an inscription discovered in 1993 on a basalt monument at Tel Dan, dating from around 835 B.C.E., has given new life to those seeking faith in the Bible's historical accuracy. The inscription, written in Aramaic, recounts the triumph of Hazael, king of Damascus, over kings of both Israel and Judah:

I killed Jehoram son of Ahab king of Israel, and I killed Ahaziahu son of Jehoram king of the House of David. And I set their towns into ruins and turned their land into desolation.

A century after the end of the United Monarchy, according to the Bible, we find the first clear external evidence of David's lasting legacy. The inscription unmistakably distinguishes between Israel and Judah, the two branches of the Divided Monarchy. It also supports the Bible's report that Judah, the southern kingdom, continued to have rulers from David's line, whereas Israel had a succession of dynasties. Indeed, the Bible does describe the troubles Hazael inflicted upon the Israelites, even referring to a battle between him and the two kings mentioned in the inscription (2 Kings 8:28–29). According to the Bible, Hazael wounded Joram (a variant spelling of Jehoram) but did not kill either king; the discrepancy may result from Hazael's boastful exaggeration.

The Disgrace of Monarchy
1 Kings 12–2 Kings
The Story

If, despite obvious misgivings, the Bible recalls the period of David and Solomon as the high point of Israelite history, the next phase of the monarchy reaches lower and lower depths. The history from 1 Kings 12 until the end of 2 Kings gives an impression similar to that of the Book of Judges: a welter of leaders arise and fall, ranging, with a couple of exceptions, from mediocre to horrendous. No single king is able to lift the country out of its downward spiral. The exceptional monarchs emerge merely as "good kings" who fight, largely without success, to raise the Israelites up from the muck of too many bad leaders. Succeeding kings pull the country right back down, as if those good kings had never lived.

After the waning years of Solomon's reign, during which he falls under the increasing influence of foreign wives and their foreign religions, Jeroboam leads a rebellion against Jerusalem, founding a separate kingdom in the north. Jeroboam then becomes the king of Israel, the name adopted by the northern kingdom, and Rehoboam, Solomon's son, preserves the

Davidic line in a southern kingdom named Judah. The Bible portrays both kings as wicked, setting the pattern for the corruption of their successors, which leads to the downfall of both kingdoms. Rehoboam could have won the loyalty of Jeroboam and his followers, but he loses their support by threatening to rule with a heavy hand. Jeroboam takes over the north for himself and forces Rehoboam to flee to Jerusalem. Worried that the religious symbolism of Jerusalem will make it impossible for him to gain the people's allegiance, Jeroboam builds northern temples and installs golden calves in them to represent the people's god, an unpardonable act of idolatry. As the Bible states many times in its depiction of Israelite kings, Jeroboam starts a chain of infidelity to God throughout the history of the northern kingdom. He establishes the pattern of people seizing power for themselves: seven of the twenty Israelite kings during the kingdom's 200-year existence were murdered by their successors.

Israelite kings get progressively worse, reaching their lowest point with the house of Omri in the eighth century. The Bible holds Omri's son Ahab in unique opprobrium, devoting several chapters to a description of his and his wife Jezebel's perfidies:

> There never was anyone like Ahab, who devoted himself to doing evil in God's eyes, whose wife Jezebel led him astray. He became corrupt in pursuing the idols, just like the Amorites did whom God dispossessed before the Israelites. (1 Kings 21:25–26)

This last line clearly hints at what is in store. Ahab has married Jezebel, daughter of King Ethbaal of Phoenicia (north of Israel in modern-day Lebanon). The Bible shows her as a strong and heartless queen who dominates her husband. Ahab builds a special temple in Samaria, his capital, to her god Baal, erecting an altar with a sacred post and choosing this temple as his main place of worship. Jezebel embodies all of the Bible's warnings against foreign women. Throughout 1 and 2 Kings, the Bible describes an unavoidable connection between foreign alliances and religious betrayal; when the Israelites join forces with other nations, they are required to bend knee to their allies' gods as part of the agreement.

The Bible's message is that the Israelites should rely on God alone for protection, not upon the strength of other people.

A related message, that spiritual power is greater than political might, is a thread tying together a cycle of stories about the prophets Elijah and Elisha. King Ahab has a series of showdowns with Elijah, his nemesis. In one dramatic face-off, Elijah challenges the prophets of Baal to a contest over sacrifices. Four hundred and fifty of Ahab's Baal prophets sacrifice a bull, perform a hopping dance, shout to Baal, and mutilate themselves. Nothing happens. Elijah offers a sacrifice by himself, and God sends fire to consume the offering. The people who witness Elijah's victory proclaim that there is only one God and proceed, at Elijah's behest, to kill the prophets of Baal. In confirmation of Elijah's prophecies, Ahab himself dies in battle, and his wife and children meet a grizzly end. Following another century of corruption, intrigue, infidelity to God, and faulty military alliances, the northern kingdom of Israel falls in 722 B.C.E. to the Assyrian empire. As part of their policy, the Assyrians deport large numbers of Israelites to foreign lands and relocate people from other conquered territories into Israel. Consequently, the residents of the north become known as the "ten lost tribes," losing their national identity and vanishing from history.

The two books of Kings weave together the stories of the northern and southern kings in alternation, helping to coordinate the two distinct histories and creating a degree of excitement in an otherwise bleak progression by forcing the reader to keep track of two different stories at once. By juxtaposing the two, the Bible inevitably fosters a comparison between the north and south, which usually redounds to Judah's credit. Generally, the two histories are separate affairs, relating the goings-on within different courts and political realms. Occasionally, the two kingdoms come into direct contact, either in military conflict or alliance. The Bible considers it essential to read these dynastic chronicles side by side, because it regards these two histories and two kingdoms as really one, a tragic division that never should have happened. The folly of Israel's and Judah's histories are the sad but inevitable consequences of the civil strife caused by the Israelites' inability to remain united under one king and one God.

Judah is the better kingdom, but considering the north's rotten quarry of kings, that statement does not say much. Rehoboam's poor example sets in motion a succession of unmemorable southern rulers. Only after the destruction of Israel do Judah's rulers rise in stature and historical significance. The first king of Judah after Israel's downfall, Hezekiah, initiates a religious reform, cutting down sacred posts and pillars used to worship other gods. Hezekiah defies King Sennacherib of Assyria, refusing to allow Jerusalem to be captured by his troops. The prophet Isaiah strengthens Hezekiah's resolve to stand firm. By an act of God, the Assyrian troops laying siege to Jerusalem mysteriously die in one night. Manasseh, the next king, rules for fifty-five years, the longest of any monarch in the kingdom, despite reinstating the idolatrous practices that his father had forbidden. His sins are so great that during his reign God promises to destroy Judah.

Two years after Manasseh's death begins the reign of Josiah, Judah's greatest king. Under his rule, the high priest in Jerusalem discovers a "scroll of the Teaching" – in Hebrew, *sefer ha-Torah* – and gives it to the king. The scroll is said to contain the terms of a covenant from God, including a system of laws; when Josiah reads it, he realizes how far Judah has strayed from the fulfillment of God's word. Josiah inaugurates an era of national repentance and religious purification, eradicating the worship of all foreign gods throughout Judah, burning their temples and slaying their priests. The Bible praises Josiah in the highest terms: "His like did not exist before him, a king who returned to God with all his heart and being and strength, in accordance with all of the Torah of Moses; nor afterwards did his like arise" (2 Kings 23:25). Nonetheless, Josiah's virtue does not suffice to save him; Pharaoh Neco of Egypt kills Josiah when he tries to stop the Egyptians from crossing through Israel to attack the Assyrians. Nor does it save Judah from destruction at the hands of the Babylonians in 586 B.C.E. The Babylonians finish off the Assyrian empire and take over their lands. Unlike the Assyrians, the Babylonians succeed in sacking Jerusalem. They take Judah's elite into exile, remove the Temple's valuable vessels, and establish a puppet regime for as long as they retain control.

The Backstory

The Bible attributes the frequent change of fortune of Israelite kings primarily to political intrigue and religious infidelity. Behind the dramas of court and temple, though, the Bible outlines Israel's and Judah's position within the political geography of the Ancient Near East. This larger picture accurately reveals the Israelites' precarious situation during these centuries, buffeted between major powers surrounding them and troubled by other menacing societies in a kaleidoscopic array of variable ascendancies and alliances. They are continually at the mercy of the region's empires: to the south, Egypt, dominant in the second millennium, has been in decline since the twelfth century but is ever threatening to regain its dominance and looking to recapture its former territories; to the north, the Syrians (Arameans), Assyrians, and then Babylonians arise in succession to establish control over the region; and the Philistines, Phoenicians, Edomites, and Moabites are always present to rattle sabers with the kings of Israel and Judah. Additionally, the northern and southern kingdoms harbor no great love toward each other and are willing to do battle when the moment suits them. In this light, it is hard to envision how an independent nation in the ancient land of Canaan ever managed to exist at all, let alone create its own culture and religion. Only a relative lull in power among the various Mesopotamian and Egyptian empires, stretching from the late eleventh century until the rise of the Arameans in the ninth century and the more dominant Assyrians in the late eighth century, enables Israel to gain a foothold and make its mark upon the land.

Archeologists have found a great deal of external evidence from the period of the Divided Monarchy to support or flesh out the Bible's portrayal, including buildings, inscriptions, ostraca (writing on pottery), seals and cylinders, pottery, and numerous foreign accounts of battles and the imposition of tribute. With a wealth of dates (king *x* of Judah was born in the third year of king *y* of Israel and ruled for *z* years), along with seemingly realistic accounts of military alliances and battles, the books of Kings resemble other works of royal court history. Its authors regularly make reference to prior records called the Annals of the Kings of Israel and the Annals of the Kings of Judah. Not surprisingly, therefore, we find fewer outright gaps in the archeological record for this period of biblical history. Overall, archeologists consider the Bible's version here to be at least historically plausible in most though not in all details. Yet the highly ideological nature of the writing often overshadows an objective historical account.

One major discrepancy between archeology and the Bible lies in the relative evaluation of the two kingdoms. In the Bible, the extensive cross-cutting between northern and southern courts leaves the impression that the two kingdoms are roughly equal in size and importance. As was previously mentioned, archeology reveals an entirely different picture. The northern kingdom does in fact play a substantial historical role during its two centuries, and inscriptions from other cultures make reference to several northern kings. Archeologists find little evidence, however, to suggest that the south during this same period, was anything but a cultural and political backwater, rural, poor, and sparsely populated.

Most notably, recent archeological discoveries have led toward a reevaluation of the much maligned rule of the Omride dynasty, especially Omri and his son Ahab. At several archeological sites, construction originally thought to confirm the existence of Solomon's national building project now points to the era of the Omrides. Palaces, gates, and retaining walls at some of the most important northern sites are now believed to date to the ninth century rather than to Solomon's tenth century. Similar construction found at sites in Jordan suggests that the Omride empire may well have extended beyond the borders of ancient Israel. An inscription from the Assyrian ruler Shalmaneser III pays tribute to the strength of Israel under Ahab: in a list of Shalmaneser's opponents, Ahab contributed 2,000 chariots, more than the other ten allies combined, as well as 10,000 of 52,000 foot soldiers.

Ahab's infidelity to the Lord described in such scathing terms in the Bible most likely reflects standard practice throughout the land up to that time. Religious syncretism, the worship of gods from different cultures, was widespread throughout the Ancient Near East. The idea of monotheism so firmly emphasized in the Bible likely did not arise until the appearance of the prophets in the eighth century, and even afterwards it did not fully take root for centuries. After the conquest by the Arameans in the late ninth century, Israel again experienced a rebirth in the eighth century, with significant growth of trade, wealth, and cities, before it was finally doomed by the Assyrians in 722. The northern kingdom was an attractive target for these Mesopotamian empires because of its abundant resources, its fertile land, wealth, and educated population. Conversely, the poor resources in the south allowed it to remain unconquered for longer.

Archeologists have found in Judah little to go on before the fall of Israel. Research suggests that the population was quite small, no more than a tenth of the north; that there were no developed cities, with the possible but uncertain exception of Jerusalem, evidence of earlier periods perhaps obliterated in later building operations; that there was no large bureaucracy, the area being devoid of the inscriptions, ostraca, pottery, and seals one would expect from a major capital; and that the religious diversity in the south was quite similar to that found in the north, with worship of the Lord alongside other gods, both in rural households (attested by clay figurines, libation vessels, and offering stands) and in Jerusalem (the ritual practices described in Ezekiel 8 most likely were an accurate remembrance from the past).

With the fall of the north, the picture changes dramatically. Judah receives a significant influx of refugees, who help it develop into a state of some power. The number of settlements vastly increases throughout the territory, and Jerusalem grows into a large and important city, featuring grand public buildings constructed with masonry and stone capitals. For the first time, archeologists find numerous inscriptions, seals, and ostraca indicative of a mature state with a central bureaucracy. The economy expands into international trade, with the mass production of pottery, and the development of oil and wine as commodities for export, all controlled by the state rather than rural households or village clans.

Josiah bases his extensive religious reforms, described in 2 Kings 23, upon the discovery of a book, long thought to be Deuteronomy. The religious transformation of the southern kingdom took place after the Assyrian conquest of the north. Most likely, disciples of northern prophets such as Amos, Hosea, Elijah, and Elisha fled to Judah and established a base for their ideas in Jerusalem. Amos's most important student was Isaiah, who served as a trusted adviser to King Hezekiah, the first southern king said to purify Israelite worship (Isaiah 36–39 and 2 Kings 18:13–20:19). Later on in the seventh century, around the year 620 B.C.E., the vision of the prophets inspired a full-fledged revolution in Israelite religion. Working from the program set out in Deuteronomy, Josiah mandated the worship of only one God in only one place, Jerusalem. The Bible's portrayal of Josiah's reforms may accurately reflect events in Israel's official religious establishment. Archeological evidence for it is contested, however: numerous clay figurines representing Asherah, goddess of fertility, have been found throughout households in Judah dating from this time.

Exile and Return
Ezra–Nehemiah
The Story

The Babylonian exile is remembered as a time of national and religious catastrophe. The Temple, where Israel felt God's presence, is destroyed; its vessels are plundered, its priests deported. God abrogates His promise to David that his line will rule forever (2 Samuel 7:16). Judah does not suffer conquest well. King Jehoiachin lasts less than a year before the Babylonians imprison him in Babylon. They appoint his uncle, Mattaniah, in his place, changing his name to Zedekiah. Zedekiah too is not content to be a loyal puppet; his independence provokes a renewed Babylonian attack against Jerusalem, a lengthy siege culminating in sacking and pillaging. They kill Zedekiah's sons in his presence, then put out his eyes. Their last attempt at a puppet ruler is Gedaliah; fellow Judeans assassinate him and flee to Egypt. The Bible records a few waves of exiles: 3,023 along with Jehoiachin, 832 with the destruction of the Temple, 745 five years later (Jeremiah 52:28–30; 2 Kings 24:14–16 gives a different number). Not all Judeans go into exile; the elite, including commanders, warriors, priests, craftsmen, and smiths are taken away, whereas "some of the poorest in the land" remain to work as "vine-dressers and field hands" (Jeremiah 52:16). The Bible captures the unhappiness of exile most memorably in Psalm 137: "By the rivers of Babylon, there we sat, sat and wept, as we thought of Zion."

Fortunately for the Jews – as the Israelites/Judeans now come to be known – the Babylonian empire is short-lived, overtaken by the Persians, whose rule extends over the Ancient Near East and beyond for more than two hundred years. One of King Cyrus' first acts is to issue a proclamation permitting the Jews to return to their homeland. Just as the Jews left in waves, they now repatriate the land in waves over time. Under Cyrus, Sheshbazzar, a son of King Jehoiachin, brings back many of the Temple's vessels along with a large number of priests and their attendants. Under King Darius, Zerubbabel, a grandson of Jehoiachin, leads a contingent including the high priest Jeshua. Despite opposition from non-Jews – including people who had been deported from other lands by the Assyrians – Darius gives his imprimatur for the rebuilding of the Temple, completed in 516. Later, under King Artaxerxes (approximately 458 B.C.E.), another group of priests and Temple workers, led by Ezra the scribe, moves to Jerusalem. Artaxerxes places Ezra in charge of the Temple and religious practice generally. Ezra reads a "scroll of the Teaching of Moses" (in Hebrew, *sefer Torat Moshe*) in a public ceremony in Jerusalem, inaugurating the ritual of reading the Torah down to this very day. Also Ezra implements a strict policy of endogamous marriage (within the group), forcing Israelite men to divorce foreign wives.

One final transplant is Nehemiah, a cupbearer for King Artaxerxes who receives permission to return home and rebuild Jerusalem. He becomes the governor of Judah, administering at the behest of Persia. As before, other residents of the land complain and try to stop Nehemiah. At times the conflict turns violent; Nehemiah's followers work day and night, with half the people standing guard as the other half work to repair the city walls. Once the wall is finished, Nehemiah casts lots for people to reside in Jerusalem. He passes decrees enforcing the Law of Moses, including observance of the Sabbath, as well as ensuring that Ezra's provision against foreign marriage is carried out.

Thus ends the history related in the Bible. The final note is fairly positive: the Jews have returned to the land of Israel, rebuilt their Temple, and revived their religion. They have regained a degree of control over their own land, established their own law, founded a new administrative center in Jerusalem, and taken back many of their former cities. But despite the generous terms of the Persian empire, biblical history does not end in complete triumph. The Jews do not exert ultimate control over the land; they remain vassals to a foreign power, as they will for centuries to come.

They inhabit and govern just a small part of the land that was controlled under the United Monarchy. The House of David, representing Israel's glorious past and God's promise of national strength, peters out with the mysterious exit of Zerubbabel from the Bible's stage. Only in their religion do the Jews exercise complete autonomy. The end of the Bible thus marks a turn from Judah as a political nation to Judaism as a religion, a transition accentuated by subsequent Jewish history.

The Backstory

Although the details of the biblical record are fragmentary and sometimes self-contradictory, the Bible gives a vivid and accurate impression of life under the Persian empire. The Persians were indeed benevolent imperialists, allowing conquered populations to retain their lands, preserve their religions and ethnic identity, and rule with a degree of autonomy. Among archeological proofs of Persian beneficence, a cylinder of Cyrus proclaiming Babylonian autonomy in their own land, and thanking the Babylonian god Marduk, has been discovered; its contents resemble Cyrus's declaration to the Jews in Ezra 1 – in the name of the Lord! The Persians were expert at harnessing religion to politics in a multicultural empire. Ezra's scroll is likely a version of the Torah as we now know it; he established the Torah as the Jews' legal code and as their book of recitation and study, functions that the Torah has held ever since. In major matters, the Persians undoubtedly exerted control over their territories. Their authority extended to the government, military, economy, and taxation. The books of Ezra and Nehemiah contain drafts of numerous letters soliciting Persian help as well as the official decrees given in response, depicting an efficient bureaucratic hegemony from afar. As is stated in the Bible, the Jewish territory, named Yehud, formed part of a larger Persian province called Beyond the River.

It is uncertain how many Jews went into exile and how many returned. The Bible gives conflicting figures; archeology paints yet a different picture. On the one hand, Jeremiah's numbers (see above) represent a small percentage of the total population of Judah at that time, indicating that a significant portion of Judeans remained on the land throughout the Babylonian period. From his description, it appears that only the religious and political elites were forcibly relocated. On the other hand, archeological evidence suggests that the population of Jerusalem and Judah shrank significantly in the Persian period compared with that in the seventh century, before the exile. The Babylonians rendered Israel largely desolate; few of the exiles actually returned to the land to repopulate it. (A smaller population of exiles moved to Egypt after 586 and remained there during Persian rule.)

The fact that Ezra and Nehemiah are still living in Babylon decades after Cyrus permitted Jews to go back reveals that life in exile had its advantages. Most of the Jews are not taken away in chains, like Zedekiah and Jehoiachin; they are likely settled to manage royal estates located in undeveloped areas. Many of them clearly thrive in exile, as is demonstrated by the "silver vessels, with gold, with goods, with livestock, and with precious objects" (Ezra 1:6) that they donate to the Jews returning to Israel. In their own homeland, Jews have little more than their ruined homes and devastated Temple. The situation in 539 B.C.E. was not so different from the relationship between the Diaspora and Israel throughout much of subsequent Jewish history. The exiled community in Babylon formed the core of a thriving Diaspora population that left modern-day Iraq only with the creation of the State of Israel in the twentieth century.

Postscript: Greeks, Romans, and the Bible's Completion

Thus ends the story written in the Bible. The story of the Bible, however, continues for another half-millennium. Several books in the Bible are written during this time, including Esther, Ecclesiastes, and Daniel. The other books are copied, refined, and edited until they reach their final form as we know it today. Jews continue to write works that build upon the religious heritage of Israel. At a certain point in time – to be precise, around 90 C.E., in the town of Yavneh in Israel – Jewish leaders make a final distinction between writings they consider sacred, to be included in the final edition of the Bible, and those books that would not make the cut. The excluded books are known as the Apocrypha; they have been preserved throughout the centuries because Christians have often included them in their Bibles.

Scholars refer to this vast stretch of time as the Second Temple period. This era sees tremendous growth in the Jewish religion; the basic structures of Judaism down to this day arise during that time. Judaism develops into a religion of the book as well as of the Temple sacrifices. The Torah becomes a book to read in public and study in private, to contemplate, translate, and interpret. During the Second Temple, Judaism creates prayers to serve as a vehicle for communicating with God. Jews build synagogues – places of gathering – for local communities to come together, read and discuss the Torah, and pray together three times daily, in accord with the three sacrifices offered daily at the Temple in Jerusalem. Alongside the expansion of this alternative religious system, a new religious leadership takes root: rabbis. Rabbis are teachers whose qualifications derive not from birth but from their command of the Torah. They represent a new model of leader, achievable by all males through study of the sacred tradition.

While the Jewish religion thrives by and large during this period, politically the Jews struggle under a succession of foreign rulers who at times provoke feelings of resentment and yearning for independence. In 332 B.C.E., Alexander the Great defeats the Persians and founds a Greek empire. Greek colonial rule differs substantially from the Persian; the Greeks spread their Hellenistic culture throughout their enormous area of control. When Hellenistic influence remains limited to things like philosophy and athletic competition, the Jews happily adapt to their rulers' ways. The situation changes in the second century, when the local Greek ruler insists that the Jews alter their religion, even introducing a statue of a Greek god in the Temple and outlawing circumcision and kashrut, the Jewish dietary laws. Led by a family called the Maccabees, Jews rebel against the Greeks starting in 165 B.C.E. and succeed in removing them, purifying the Temple and winning national independence for about a century. The Maccabees' descendants become known as the Hasmonean dynasty of Jewish kings. Regrettably, the Jews fare little better under self-rule than under foreign control; the Hasmoneans on the whole prove a corrupt and divided lot, and they themselves invite the Romans to take charge of the country with little initial opposition from the populace.

Roman rule brings to the fore an array of hostile divisions among Jews that began under Greek administration. Culturally and politically, these foreign pagan empires elicit conflicting responses among their Jewish subjects. Most Jews prudently submit to their foreign rulers, supporting revolt as a last resort. Greek and Roman culture exerts different levels of influence upon Jews: some imitate their masters in all fashions and manners, others study their thought and adapt it to Jewish tradition, and a third factor zealously seeks to protect Judaism from all foreign influence. Jewish society thus comes to harbor an increasing number of schisms: politically, between those who oppose or support the foreign rulers; religiously, between the Saducees, consisting of Temple priests and their wealthy patrons, the Pharisees, consisting of the rabbis and their popular movement, and the Essenes, a much smaller group, who separate from society, at times forming celibate communities of hermits. Another small group that forms in the first century c.e., the Christians, crystalizes around the widespread contemporary belief that the end of time is at hand, and that the messiah, in the person of Jesus, has come to redeem them.

Disagreement between supporters and opponents of Roman rule comes to a head in 66 c.e. with a Jewish revolt against the Romans. Centered in Jerusalem, the revolt garners some initial success, despite incidents of brutality between different groups of Jews. Eventually Vespasian, the new Roman emperor, turns Israel into an example of Roman might: he sacks the city and Temple in 70 c.e., hauls away its vessels, and takes hundreds of Jews as slaves. With the end of the Temple ritual, the rabbis gain control over Judaism, while priests retain a residual role in synagogue life as a token of their former eminence. In the 130s the Jews give expression to their longing for religious and national independence one last time, in an uprising led by Simon Bar Kochba. After the Romans definitively crush this rebellion, sending the rabbis who supported Bar Kochba to their martyrdom, Jews take this defeat as a lesson that they are meant to wait patiently under foreign domination until such time as God chooses to bring them salvation.

CHAPTER 5

History of the Bible

Suggested reading: Deuteronomy 1–4, 32–34; Joshua 1, 23–24; Judges 2:10–23; 1 Chronicles 28–29

Taking the Bible Apart

The historical questions about the Bible do not end with the history recounted in the Bible. The composition of the Bible's many books involves a long and complex historical process that has been studied intensively for the past two centuries. With textual history, there is even less to go on than with archeology; biblical books rarely announce who wrote them, and when they do, scholars rarely take them at their word. The quest for the settings where the Bible was written has turned generations of scholars into Sherlock Holmeses, forming deductions upon scanty threads of evidence and building theoretical castles in very thin air.

The search for the origins of the Bible leads in numerous directions: to its written origins, starting in smaller blocks of writing to arrive at its current form; to its oral origins, founded in ancient tribal traditions; to its Ancient Near Eastern origins, building upon the writings of the cultures surrounding the Israelites; and to its historical origins, comparing the Bible's account with knowledge gained from other sources of information, such as archeology. Biblical scholarship is as much an art as a science. Scholars build paradigms based upon hypotheses, making intelligent guesses into the age and origin of different traditions in the Bible. They anchor their guesswork upon clues from a slew of different fields. Inner-biblical clues – clues derived from the text of the Bible itself – include language (variations in vocabulary, word forms, and sentence structure over time), place names, quotations and allusions, spelling, and themes (e.g., when would the theme of endogamous (interethnic) marriage, found in several stories in Genesis, have been important historically?). Extra-biblical clues – information relevant to dating the Bible from sources outside the text – come from not only archeology and other writings from the Ancient Near East, but also any field that can persuasively be used to shed light on biblical material, such as anthropology, sociology, psychology, comparative literature, and even geology and climatology. Each reader brings different experiences, intellectual and religious perspectives, and emotional attachments to the study of the Bible in an attempt to discover its meaning. Little wonder that there is so much disagreement over the issue of the Bible's origins.

One of the fault lines in biblical scholarship is the question of how unified or fragmented the Bible is: should it be read as one book or as a pastiche of ancient traditions woven together? The majority of scholars today fall into the latter camp. They treat the Bible like a reverse jigsaw puzzle, dividing the text into smaller pieces and then fitting those into other configurations. This method identifies passages, sometimes as short as half a verse, with different writers and editors who produced the biblical text over hundreds of years. Each writer or editor left a unique historical and religious perspective; therefore, stories about Moses or David display a wide range of viewpoints about the character. The different layers in the Bible do not entirely cohere, so that seams between their divergent positions are evident in the conflicting portraits they present of the ancient Israelite leaders. Marc Zvi Brettler, a prominent member of this new generation of biblical scholarship, explains the current approach by analogy to the work of archeologists:

> [The biblical text] resemble[s] an archeological *tel*, a layered collection of settlements. It presents many of the same problems as archeological *tels*: just as it is not always easy to distinguish definitively between archeological layers, so it is often difficult to isolate groups of verses that belong together. Similar criteria may be used in archeology and texts: artifacts or verses that share certain key elements and differ sig-

nificantly from surrounding material are usually assigned to the same period or author, and the researcher must discover formal indications (e.g., burn layers, formal structural devices) that suggest the boundaries between levels. Archeological *tels* are not always neatly layered, with the oldest layer on the bottom; frequently, older materials are reused by subsequent generations. The same is even more true of texts: we cannot presume that the textual layers are neatly stacked. (Marc Zvi Brettler, *The Creation of History in Ancient Israel*, p. 113)

In this chapter, we will look at some of the layers that scholars believe make up the biblical "tel."

The Quest for Sources: Theories

A careful reading of the Bible stumbles at times against sections suggesting that the Bible is not entirely a unified work. Few of the biblical books are believed to be the work of a single author; each work has its own history of transmission, during which it was edited and often revised or expanded in order to produce the writing that we have today. Within just the first five books of the Bible, there is evidence that the stories were sewn together from multiple sources: some stories contradict each other (e.g., in Genesis 1 man is created last, whereas man is created first in Genesis 2:7, a different version of creation); sometimes the same story is retold with the same and different characters (e.g., the three wife-sister tales); or a single story may contain duplications and internal contradictions (most famously in the story of Noah, which gives different accounts for the number of animals in the ark and days of the flood). For the past 400 years, readers have been openly questioning the traditional attribution of these five books to Moses. In his 1651 magnum opus *Leviathan*, the British Christian philosopher Thomas Hobbes denied Mosaic authorship with this observation:

"[…] *and the* Canaanite *was then in the land* [Genesis 12:6]; which must needs bee the words of one that wrote when the Canaanite was not in the land; and consequently, not of *Moses*, who dyed before he came into it.

Some twenty years later, the renegade Dutch Jewish philosopher Baruch Spinoza claimed in his *Theologico-Political Treatise*, "It is…clearer than the sun at noonday that the Pentateuch was not written by Moses, but by someone who lived long after Moses." Even religious traditionalists in the Middle Ages could not always accept that Moses wrote every word in the Torah, such as the description of his own death at the end of Deuteronomy. The great commentator Rashi gives two explanations for this passage:

> And Moses died there (Deuteronomy 34:5). [Rashi's view:] Is it pos-
> sible that Moses died and wrote "And Moses died there"?! But up to
> this point, Moses wrote; thereafter, Joshua wrote. Rabbi Meir said
> [another opinion]: Can the Torah [that Moses wrote] be lacking in
> anything? For it says (Deuteronomy 31:26): "Take this book of the
> Torah" [implying that Moses had finished writing the entire book
> before his death]. But the Holy One, Blessed be He, says [i.e., gives
> dictation], and Moses writes with a tear.

Rabbi Meir gives a beautiful rendering upholding the traditional belief in Mosaic authorship. Rashi, writing centuries later, regards it more rational to assume that Joshua wrote those last lines.

At this point it may be useful to summarize some of the theories regarding the composition of the Bible. This brief survey will help the reader who would like to enter the world of biblical scholarship, or simply get some idea of scholarly approaches to this exceedingly difficult and crucial issue. The positions outlined here reveal that there is a range of viewpoints in the details, although in the broad outlines there is wide consensus among most scholars who have written over the past century.

Julius Wellhausen (*Prolegomena to the History of Ancient Israel*, 1883). Wellhausen was the chief exponent of what is commonly called the Documentary Hypothesis (also known as "Higher Criticism," in opposition to the linguistic analysis of "Lower Criticism"), namely, the proposition that the Torah was initially composed of distinct sources later woven together into one book. Wellhausen's work stands as the summation of biblical scholarship to his time, rather than an entirely original idea; it became the standard book on the subject, and its widespread readership convinced many people that modern scholars had discovered the Bible's origins. Ever since Wellhausen, the Documentary Hypothesis has served as the main model for the composition of the Pentateuch. Nearly all academic biblical scholars agree with this theory; they argue primarily over questions concerning the setting in which the different sources originated, the dating of the sources, and the prehistory of the material that became the sources.

Wellhausen identified four original blocks that together comprise nearly all the material in the Pentateuch; they are generally referred to as J, E, P, and D. J and E refer to the names that these strands use for God. J is the Jahwist (pronounced Yahwist, *j* in German being pronounced like *y* in English) source, referring to God as Yahweh (also known as the tetragrammaton, the four-letter Hebrew name for God, spelled in Jewish tradition without vowels). E is the Elohist source, which calls God "Elohim," a generic term for God. E consistently avoids the name Yahweh until the revelation at the burning bush. Typically, J is assigned to the royal court during the United Monarchy in the tenth century B.C.E., E to northern priests in the eighth century B.C.E. The relationship between these two sources is complex – for example, there are questions about whether the authors of E knew of J, or if they both derived their material from a common prior source – but scholars generally concur that J and E were combined into a single narrative at an early point, before they joined with the other sources. There is some overlap of material between J and E found in the Bible, but overall there is much more J than E, suggesting that the editors of JE selected more from J and cut out a great deal from E.

P represents the Priestly source, containing all of Leviticus and some of the narrative sections in Genesis, Exodus, and Numbers as well. D includes the book of Deuteronomy, which forms part of a larger history extending through 2 Kings, commonly referred to as the Deuteronomic History. Wellhausen, following accepted scholarly opinion in his time and still today, dates D to the rule of Josiah in the late seventh century. P he regards as a later source, written by priests during the Babylonian exile, in order to recall and record the details of the Temple service, then finished during the Second Temple period. In his estimation, P is the editor who rendered the first six books of the Bible into its final form. Wellhausen's dating of P, and his overall description of Israelite religious history, has come under criticism for displaying a Romantic and Protestant bias. The religion in J and E, which Wellhausen considers earlier and more authentic, is described as spontaneous and voluntary; the later, priestly religion in D and P he views as ritualistic and formulaic, a degeneration leading toward rabbinic Judaism.

Yehezkel Kaufmann (*The Religion of Israel*, 1937–1956). Kaufmann defends the antiquity of P and, implicitly, of Judaism, against Wellhausen and his followers. He points out that P's legal codes, giving detailed instruction for religious rituals, show no awareness of the law codes in D, which surely could not have been the case if P were written after D had been established as the national law. In both narrative and legal sections, P is ignorant of the importance of Jerusalem as a central city containing the only valid Temple – the main features of D. Kaufmann thus establishes that P must have been written before D. Another hand, R (for Redactor), wove the different sources into one, respecting the integrity of the separate traditions to the point of preserving their contradictory aspects.

Richard Elliott Friedman (*Who Wrote the Bible?* 1987). Friedman clearly explains the logic of the Documentary Hypothesis, as well as updating it with his own conjectures about the identity of the source's authors. He sees the sources as each reflecting the consistent perspective of a single author. J wrote within the Judean Court some time between 848 and 722 B.C.E., before the destruction of the north. The extensive sympathy extended to women in J's stories opens the possibility that J was a woman herself, a suggestion pursued further in Harold Bloom's commentary in *The Book of J*. E was "a Levitical priest, probably from Shiloh," writing at some time during the northern kingdom (922–722 B.C.E.). The author of P was a priest in the Temple at Jerusalem, a descendant of Aaron who lived during the time of King Hezekiah and inspired the king's religious reforms. With D, Friedman ventures an even more specific guess: Jeremiah. Jeremiah was a priest who lived during and after the Babylonian conquest, was a follower of Josiah but not of his successors, and was known as a writing prophet because the Bible portrays him dictating his prophecies to his scribe Baruch (Jeremiah 36). Similarly, Freedman identifies R with a biblical character: Ezra. As an Aaronid priest in the Second Temple period, Ezra held authority in religious and legal matters, the areas where the Persians granted local autonomy. Characterized in the Bible also as a scribe, Ezra was capable of producing a Torah book to serve as the official guide for the community. He emphasized P, the largest of the four sources, because it gave the perspective of his group of priests.

Hermann Gunkel (*The Legends of Genesis*, 1901). A younger contemporary of Wellhausen, Gunkel accepts the Documentary Hypothesis but judges it inadequate for understanding the material in the Torah as a whole, and especially in Genesis. Instead, Gunkel regards J and E as collections of pre-literate, oral traditions descending from ancient times. J and E, rather than being original building blocks, are themselves the final result of a long process of development of Israelite traditions. In Gunkel's view, they are collections more than compositions. Inspired by the nineteenth-century fascination with folklore, Gunkel imagines that the stories in Genesis were part of a rich oral culture, recounted by "professional storytellers" or "in the leisure of a winter evening [as] the family sits about the hearth." Only at a late stage, after the oral culture had largely died out, were the individual stories borrowed, combined, revised, expanded, or shrunk to reach their current state in a fixed, written form.

Martin Noth (*A History of Pentateuchal Traditions*, 1948). Noth develops Gunkel's theory of oral composition in a couple of different ways. He believes that at their earliest, the patriarchal stories started as separate traditions each deriving from a particular group located in one particular region. The stories of Abraham, Isaac, and Jacob in Genesis cluster around specific geographical areas that indicate their disparate origin before being joined into one unified composition. Noth then elaborates upon an idea of Gerhard Von Rad, claiming that the current arrangement of the Pentateuch originated in a ritual confession of faith in God's direction of the people, similar to the account of Israelite history recited before a Temple priest in Deuteronomy 26:5–10. The writers of the Pentateuch attached the ancient traditions to a core of historical themes intrinsic to this faith: promise to the patriarchs, exodus from Egypt, revelation at Sinai, wandering in the wilderness, guidance into arable land. Within this template, the ancient oral traditions were molded and expanded until they reached their current form.

Israel Finkelstein (*Unearthing the Bible*, 2001). Finkelstein, an archeologist by training, denies an early date to any of the traditions, JE no less than P and D. Based upon anachronisms within the patriarchal narratives, Finkelstein claims that all of the large literary sources started to be written down no earlier than the eighth century and were mostly completed in the seventh, under Josiah. In his view, that was the first time that Jerusalem possessed a large bureaucracy, a sizable literate populace, and a centralized ideology motivated to produce a national book. The traditions concerning the patriarchs and ancient Israelites must be considered as projections, or retrojections, from a much later age.

Thomas Thompson (*Early History of the Israelite People*, 1992). Thompson is associated with a school of biblical "minimalists" who depart radically from the scholarly consensus. These scholars tend to push biblical dating forward, reaching as late as the Roman empire. In this book, Thompson reckons that the Torah arises in the Persian period. The entire history told in the Bible from the beginnings of time through the Babylonian exile constitutes a projection of the Persian community, according to Thompson, and not historical reality. The Persian empire required each region it controlled to maintain its own religion and Temple. For the Jews living in the Persian territory called Yehud, this demand was particularly difficult, because many different ethnic populations lived on the land side by side, following the transfer of population groups practiced by the Assyrian and Babylonian empires. The history in the Bible thus represents an attempt by the Persian Jewish priests to impose unity upon a population that was badly disunified. The idea of exile and return is a necessary fiction capable of embracing a welter of dislocated groups under one common experience. This new history symbolically encapsulates their shared trauma. Thompson claims that the Persian king Cyrus creates a new ethnic and religious identity under the guise of restoring an old one. The name "Israel," which earlier referred to only one group living in the land of Canaan, now comes to represent the entire nation. Because Thompson thinks the Bible was written by ideologues rather than historians, he maintains that all biblical stories are suspect as depictions of historical reality.

Tradition versus Retrojection

Another way of thinking about the Bible's composition, which may be just as helpful as the theory of the sources, is as a field with two horizons. One horizon is the distant past; a second horizon is the time at which the book was written. Instead of a work stabilized by representing a worldview of one point in time, the biblical text is in constant motion between its present and past, similar to the motion of the angels up and down Jacob's ladder (Genesis 28:12):

The Bible contains numerous traditions passed down from previous generations. Some of them were likely already ancient at the time that they were written down, whereas others may have been changed along the way or perhaps even invented in the more recent past. In the other direction, the writers of the Bible were looking backward toward the distant past that they set out to describe. Their descriptions were colored by the conditions of their day, so that the lives of Abraham, Moses, and Solomon took on characteristics of later eras. In this view, the encounter between ancient traditions brought forward and contemporary concerns cast backward can be discovered in every page of the Bible. It is not always easy to differentiate between early and late; by and large, biblical authors tried to conceal any such distinctions. What follows is an attempt to offer some introductory guidance in sorting out the older from later elements.

Tradition: Bringing Forward

Perhaps the easiest biblical material to identify as genuinely ancient are stories borrowed from the Israelites' Ancient Near Eastern neighbors. Since the discoveries of tablets at archeological sites in the late nineteenth and early twentieth centuries, people have become aware that some stories in the Bible were adapted from tales and writings widespread in that region. The story of a great flood, for example, was extremely popular and found in several different versions, most famously in the epic of Gilgamesh. In another version, a character named Atrahasis builds an ark to save mankind from a flood. These ANE stories undoubtedly exerted a great influence upon the biblical story of Noah's ark. Two good reasons why we know this are that the ANE tablets are hundreds of years older than the Bible, and that the land of Israel does not suffer floods the way the banks of the Euphrates and Tigris do. Another Mesopotamian legend treats the upbringing of mighty king Sargon:

> My changeling mother conceived me, in secret she bore me. She set me in a basket of rushes, with bitumen she sealed my lid. She cast me into the river which rose not over me. The river bore me up and carried me to Akki, the drawer of water. Akki, the drawer of water, lifted me out as he dipped his ewer. Akki the drawer of water, took me as his son and reared me. Akki, the drawer of water, appointed me as his gardener. While I was a gardener, [the goddess] Ishtar granted me her love, and for four...years I exercised kingship.

Obviously, biblical writers exercised great freedom in adapting ANE stories. In this case, it is striking how they transformed this Mesopotamian legend to the Egyptian context of Moses' birth.

Egypt also provided a rich mine for ancient Israelite lore. A couple of Egyptian legends found their way into the biblical story of Joseph. One shows strong similarities with the story of Potiphar's wife (Genesis 39). It tells a tale of two brothers, the older married, the younger not. The younger brother lives with the older, who raises him in exchange for his help on the farm. One day, when the brothers are plowing in the field, the older brother sends the younger back to the house to get more seed. The wife notices how strong the younger brother is and tries to seduce him. Refusing to betray his older brother, he leaves the house. When the two return home later, the wife makes herself sick, accusing the younger brother of attempted rape. Another Egyptian writing relates a tradition that the Nile suffers seven lean years followed by years of plenty, the reverse of Joseph's dream interpretation (Genesis 41:25–32). These and other stories indicate that the ancient Israelites were intimately familiar with the surrounding cultures. They retold popular legends from the Ancient Near East, reworking them over generations until they became cornerstones of a distinct national and religious tradition. The fact that these stories originally were told in other contexts suggests that biblical sagas of the patriarchs did not begin as single, unified biographies. Instead, the composers of these narratives wove together scores of independent legends into a larger whole.

Tablets from Mesopotamia and Egypt give external proof of the antiquity of some stories in the Bible. Such evidence is rare, and so internal criteria are necessary for determining the relative date of biblical passages. One indicator of relative antiquity lies in elements that do not easily fit in with the surrounding story. Some parts of the story may be missing. Here is the Bible's report of Nimrod, the legendary ancestor of Mesopotamian civilization:

> Cush fathered Nimrod; he was the first mighty man on earth. He was a mighty hunter before the Lord. Thus it is said, "Like Nimrod, a mighty hunter before the Lord." (Genesis 10:8–9)

The Bible quotes a saying about Nimrod – perhaps it was widely known at one point – and asserts its truth. Otherwise we learn little about him. Presumably there were ancient legends telling of Nimrod's might and prowess at hunting. The biblical writers felt compelled to mention this important person, in their effort to give some account of universal history, but they had no desire to glorify him by dwelling upon his story. The incomplete quality of this reference is a sign of this story's age. Another example of a truncated tale is the perplexing vignette about the offspring of the "sons of God" and "the daughters of man" (Genesis 6:1–4). Such a story reads like a printer's error, as if a paragraph from Greek mythology has been spliced into the Bible by a drunken editor! Most likely this passage is a remnant of an old polytheistic story that has been imperfectly transformed into the Bible's monotheistic perspective. The story remains in Genesis as an explanation of the great wickedness that God sought to wipe out with Noah's flood.

In this vein, hints of polytheism in the Bible, most notably in Genesis, may indicate that stories have an ancient origin. The word *tehom* in Genesis 1:2, translated as "the deep," recalls the name of the god Tiamat whose body is cut open to create the world in the Babylonian epic known as *Enuma Elish*. The different names of God in Genesis may derive from original deities that were associated with particular locales. For example, the chief god of the Canaanite pantheon was El; this word is used in the Bible to refer to the one God or to other gods, and therefore at times it is ambiguous. In Genesis, *El* often appears in conjunction with other names: *El Elyon* (14:18–20), *El Roi* (16:13), *El Shaddai* (17:1), *El Olam* (21:33), and so on. These compounds may adumbrate a stage in Israel's development between polytheism and monotheism, a time when different divinities were made to appear as faces of one God. Genesis also describes God in more anthropomorphic (human) terms than does the rest of the Bible, reminiscent of the action of gods in polytheistic myth. Adam and Eve "heard the sound of the Lord God walking about in the garden" (3:8); "the Lord smelled the fragrant odor" of Noah's sacrifice after the flood (8:21); God "came down to see the city and the tower" of Babel (11:5). Such language has more in common with Homer than with the rest of the Bible. It is fascinating that the Bible's description of mankind's early history is conveyed in a language reflecting the way of thinking from those earlier times. The story in which God "sought to kill" Moses (Exodus 4:24–26) likewise shows a God "out of character" compared with the rest of the Bible.

Other stories probably passed down from olden times are of the kind called "etiological," namely, stories meant to explain the origins of some place, custom, name, or fact of life. A great many of the stories in Genesis fall under this category, though they can be found as well in later books. Why do people worship at particular locations? Because the patriarchs saw God there. What is the origin of a large salt pillar near the Dead Sea? That was where God punished Lot's wife for looking back at the destruction of Sodom and Gomorrah. Why is it that people speak different languages and are spread out far and wide? Because they defied God with the Tower of Babel. Some stories account for several phenomena at once. The Garden of Eden, for example, offers explanations for a host of worldly affairs: human mortality and interment in the ground, clothing (why do humans alone of all species wear them?), the pain and danger of childbirth (shouldn't God have made childbirth easy if God wanted people to "be fruitful and multiply"? [1:28]), the difficult work of agriculture, man's historical dominance over woman, and not least, the awkward motion of snakes. In other cases, several different stories elucidate the same thing. Genesis provides three accounts of the origin of the name Beer-sheba: it refers to seven ewes that Abraham gave to Abimelech (21:30) in recognition of a well Abraham dug (*be'er* = well, *sheva* = seven); it refers to an oath (*shevuah*, a similar sounding word) between Abraham and Abimelech (21:31 – a different explanation in the very next sentence!); it refers to an oath between Isaac and Abimelech over the same well (26:33). These contradictions may argue for the antiquity of all of the stories. Later editors of the Bible felt compelled to preserve the conflicting traditions instead of judging among them, because they were all considered ancient and valid.

As the legends about Beer-sheba show, etiological stories often climax in a sort of pun, a popular etymology that clarifies the origin of a name. The two different meanings ascribed to *sheba* demonstrate that these etymologies are far from scientific. What matters to the biblical storyteller is the connection drawn by the etymology between the name and the story behind it. The name Moses, for example, is an Egyptian word meaning "son of" and is present in many Egyptian names (such as the dynasty of Thutmose I, II, III, and IV). Indifferent to Egyptian linguistics, the biblical writer invents a Hebrew etymology for Moses – *mashah*, draw out from water (Exodus 2:10) – which provides a lovely link to the adapted legend of the hero rescued from the river and ties into other key moments in Moses' biography (leading the Israelites through the Sea of Reeds, obtaining water for them in the desert). Different motifs of the story may have been old at the time of composition: the drowning of the sons, the hero placed in the river, the role of Pharaoh's daughter, and others. What is marvelous is the storyteller's ability to sew these pieces of tradition into a powerful new literary creation.

Many of the names given in Genesis are eponyms, referring to legendary founders of a group of people or a place. In the United States, for example, Abraham Lincoln is the eponym of Lincoln, Nebraska, and George Washington is the eponym of Washingtonians (people from Washington State). These names refer to heroes deemed worthy of commemoration. Biblical authors go a step further, assuming that all groups of people derived from an individual who gave the group his name. Israel is named after the patriarch Jacob, who was given his new eponym after wrestling with the angel (Genesis 32:29). The twelve tribes took the names of his sons (in the case of Ephraim and Manasseh, grandsons). In Genesis 10, the Bible traces all of humanity back to single ancestors and explains the relations between these groups along one family tree going back to Noah. Most of the names here and in other lists of descendants in Genesis (chapters 5, 11, 25, 36) are probably eponyms as well, even if the groups descended from them are no longer known.

The group's originator stamps his character forever upon his followers. Hagar's son, Ishmael, "shall be a wild ass of a man" (Genesis 16:12), hence Ishmaelites are desert-dwelling, marauding nomads; they wear golden earrings (Judges 8:24) and travel in caravans of camels, trading in goods and people (Genesis 37:28). Why are the Moabites and Ammonites persistent enemies of Israel? Because they were misbegotten offspring of Lot and his daughters (Genesis 19:30–38). The patriarchs' siblings and their families gave their names to some of Israel's nearest neighbors: Abraham's brothers Nahor and Haran become cities in Aram-naharaim (modern-day Syria; see Genesis 11:31–32 and 24:10); his nephew Lot fathers the Moabites and Ammonites; Isaac's brother Ishmael fathers the Ishmaelites; Jacob's brother Esau becomes Edom (explained as a pun on the Hebrew word *adom*, red, after Esau sells his birthright for a stew of red lentils [25:30]), another enduring antagonist of the Israelites. These eponyms thus helped to create a convenient, memorable framework for the comprehension of human history and anthropology.

A further story type passed down from antiquity recounts the triumph of an ancestor through cleverness, and often deception. Since the morality of such trickery appears questionable from the perspective of the rest of the Bible (and to many modern readers as well), these stories can be assumed to derive from an older period that prized different characteristics in its heroes. They remind us of characters like Odysseus and the heroes of folktales, who survive by their wits and are often cruelly indifferent to their enemies. In the wife-sister stories, Abraham and Isaac lie to save their skins. Jacob, the Bible's greatest trickster, outsmarts Esau of his birthright, Isaac of his blessing, and Laban of his daughters and much of his flock. He even wrestles God's angel for a blessing!

Female characters in the Bible are no less capable of triumph through deception. Lot's daughters seduce their father after getting him drunk, since they believe he is the last man alive. Lest we judge them too harshly, the virtuous Jewess Tamar similarly seduces her father-in-law Judah in a desperate ploy to have children (Genesis 38); when Judah discovers her deception, his response is, "She is more in the right than I." In a gesture both morally and religiously suspect, but richly appropriate within the web of deceptions entangling Jacob and Laban, Rachel steals her father Laban's household idols before Jacob and his family flee (31:19). When Laban overtakes Jacob's caravan, Rachel again slyly deceives her father by hiding the idols in a camel cushion she sits on, claiming that she cannot move because "the way of women" is upon her. These triumphs through trickery are never as absolute in the Bible as in mythology: whereas Odysseus gloats unpunished after poking out the Cyclops' eye, Jacob receives in full what he gave, marrying the wrong bride first, serving Laban fourteen years for his two wives, another six for his flock, and later lamenting the presumed death of his favorite son, Joseph. His greatest blow was the early death of his beloved Rachel, which may have been precipitated by Jacob's own mistimed oath to Laban, "With whomever you find your gods, that person shall not live!" Jacob and Rachel's cruel deceptions of Laban, while not undeserved, still are repaid through the crueler irony operating in the mechanics of a moral universe.

One other kind of writing considered among the oldest biblical strata is the poetry, especially the poetry embedded in biblical stories. These poems antedate the narratives surrounding them and may even have given rise to the narratives as a way to include some treasured folk traditions. A colorful example of this pattern can be found in Numbers 21, a chapter discussing Israel's wanderings in the wilderness, containing three such ancient poems. The first one, a quotation from another book entitled "Book of the Wars of the Lord," is enigmatic, missing a crucial verb:

Waheb in Suphah, and the stream-beds, the Arnon,

And the slope of stream-beds extending toward the habitations of Ar,
close by the border of Moab. (Numbers 21:14–15)

This odd description appears after a report that the Israelites "camped
across the Arnon." It is difficult to determine why it was inserted: to add
geographical information? Poetical vividness? Textual proof of the Arnon
River's existence or location? The next campground, Be'er (meaning *well*),
occasions another poem:

> Then Israel sang this song:
> Rise up, O well!
> Sing out to it.
> The well dug by princes,
> Mined by noblemen,
> With a commander's rod, a ruler's staff. (21:17–18)

Here a popular folk song crops up amid Israel's desert wanderings,
which provide an appropriate context within which to preserve a little gem.
The initial stage direction suggests that the song is a national standard;
an analogy would be a Broadway musical in which the characters start
dancing to "Turkey in the Straw." A third, longer poem intrudes several
lines later, after Israel defeats Sihon king of Heshbon in battle:

> Thus say the rulers:
> Come to Heshbon;
> May Sihon's city be built up and secure.
> For fire went forth from Heshbon,
> Flame from Sihon's walled city.
> It consumed Ar of Moab,
> Residents of Arnon's heights. (21:27–28)

This remarkable poem tells nothing about Israel; instead, it sings of Heshbon's triumph over Moab! Here not only does the poem clearly predate
the Bible's composition, but it just as clearly comes from a non-Israelite
source. Nothing better indicates the Bible's interest in preserving a wide
swath of ancient traditions, not only those explicitly considered religious

or sacred. Besides these brief examples, many of the Bible's longer poems, including the Song at the Sea (Exodus 15), Deborah's Song (Judges 5), and Moses' valedictory song (Deuteronomy 32), also contain some of the Bible's most ancient layers.

Finally, mention of the Book of the Wars of the Lord in Numbers 21 reveals the biblical writers' admission that the Bible was not written all at once as the creation of one mind (or Mind). Rather, it represents explicit affirmation that the Bible gathered some of its material from prior sources. Although there are no references to J, E, P, or D in the Bible, biblical writers were not shy about acknowledging sources. In addition to the Wars of the Lord, the Bible cites the Book of the Lineage of Adam (Genesis 5:1), Book of the Upright (2 Samuel 1:18), Annals of the Kings of Israel (1 Kings 14:19 et al.), Annals of the Kings of Judah (1 Kings 14:29 et al.), History of Samuel the Seer, History of Nathan the Prophet, and History of Gad the Seer (all mentioned in 1 Chronicles 29:29). Reference to this wide variety of sources confirms that the Bible made use of all the written materials available in the world of ancient Israel to produce a new kind of national anthology.

Retrojection: Casting Backward

Biblical authors not only collected old stories, they also added to them in significant ways that often changed their meaning. It would be surprising if this were not the case; think about the ways that iconic figures and events from the past – Abraham Lincoln, William Shakespeare, the French Revolution, the civil rights movement – are reinterpreted by each new generation. Our understanding of the past derives in large part from the intellectual and cultural climate of the present, a truth just as valid for the biblical authors writing centuries after the events they describe. In the words of Hermann Gunkel, "The religion of Abraham is in reality the religion of the narrators of the legends, ascribed by them to Abraham." The story of the sons of gods and the daughters of men in Genesis 6 is a good example of how the biblical writers used ancient material for their own purposes. The meaning of the original myth is completely obscure; in its current location, the story is made to signify something new, the widespread corruption of the human race at the time of Noah. Similarly, comparison of biblical stories to tales found in Ancient Near Eastern writings demonstrates that the earlier material was thoroughly reworked to yield a new religious message of ethical monotheism.

One particularly striking example of retrojection, casting a later element backward in time, can be found in the story of the golden calf in Exodus 32. In 1 Kings 12, the first northern king, Jeroboam, creates an Israelite religious system separate from the national Temple in Jerusalem:

> And Jeroboam said in his heart, "Now, the kingdom might return to the House of David. Should this people go up to make sacrifices in the House of the Lord in Jerusalem, the heart of this people will return to their master, to Rehoboam, king of Judah. They will kill me and return to Rehoboam, king of Judah." The king took counsel and made two golden calves. He said to them, "Enough of your going up to Jerusalem! Behold your gods, O Israel, who brought you up from the land of Egypt!" He placed one in Bethel, and the other he put in Dan. (1 Kings 12:26–29)

Jeroboam placed golden calves in the northern temples at Bethel and Dan, where they served the same function as similar objects throughout the Ancient Near East: as a throne or footstool for God. In its original setting the golden calf was no more idolatrous than the cherubim adorning the inner sanctum of the Jerusalem Temple, which provided an exact equivalent as the resting place for God's presence. However, the Book of Kings, like the rest of the Deuteronomic History, was written from the perspective of the southern kingdom against the northern, pitting the Jerusalem Temple against the northern temples. The writer made these ancient northern temples – Bethel, according to Genesis 28:19, was founded by Jacob – appear to be later, polytheistic shrines established when Jeroboam rebelled against the United Monarchy based in Jerusalem. This same shocking quotation of defiance against God – "These are your gods, O Israel, who brought you up from the land of Egypt" – was placed in the mouth of the Israelites during the episode of the golden calf in Exodus 32. The Bible here displays two levels of retrojection: a seventh century southern writer envisions the creation of the northern temples in the tenth century as a pagan revolt; and the argument against the north is inserted into the ancient stories of the Israelites at Sinai. The final effect is to make the northern temples appear doubly sinful, for not only does Jeroboam and his new cadre of priests sin against God, they also repeat an appalling episode of apostasy from Israel's past.

It is hard not to notice that Aaron does not come off very well in the golden calf episode. Traditional Jewish commentators tried to justify Aaron's actions. Rashi, for example, cites earlier interpretations for Exodus 32:5, "And Aaron saw [the statue], and he built an altar before it, and Aaron called out and said, 'Tomorrow is a festival to the Lord'": Aaron feared for his life, lest the people kill him for criticizing them; Aaron altruistically wanted the stench for this bad altar to be upon him rather than on the people; he built it himself to delay its construction, hoping all the while that Moses would return before its completion. The Levites, followers of Moses, emerge clean from this affair. At God's and Moses' instigation, they purge the community of rebels, killing "about three thousand men" (32:28). This scene is one of many in the Torah depicting either Moses, Aaron, Levi, or a different ancestor of priests in a negative light, often to the benefit of another priest. Since scholars believe that much of the Bible was written by priests, they consider the different evaluations of these sacerdotal characters as retrojections of later struggles between groups of priests – in other words, as political allegories. One group of priests, based in Jerusalem, saw themselves as descendants of Aaron; another group, centralized at a northern temple, drew a lineage to Moses. Rarely do the two great leaders come into open conflict. The major exception, besides the golden calf episode, occurs when Miriam and Aaron challenge Moses' preeminence in the nation's relationship with God: "Has the Lord spoken only through Moses alone? Has He not spoken also through us?" (Numbers 12:2).

The competition is usually more subtle. One writer frames God's word, "And the Lord said to Moses," while the other writes, "And the Lord said to Moses and Aaron." The Aaron priests show Aaron brandishing a staff that turns into a snake (Exodus 7:10) and transforms the Nile to blood (7:19); the others portray Moses wielding the staff to the same effects (7:15, 17). In Leviticus, Aaron is the high priest in charge of the

Temple ritual, the people's highest representative to God; the rest of the Torah generally gives the impression that Moses fills that role: "And the Lord would speak to Moses face to face, as a man speaks to his fellow" (Exodus 33:11). Korah, the Levite who leads a rebellion against Moses and Aaron in Numbers 16, was identified with yet another group of Levites, who sang in the Jerusalem Temple (see Psalms 42, 44–49, 84–85, 87–88). The story in Numbers probably reflects a later suppression of Korahites by rival priests.

Another example of retrojection commonly adduced is the Tabernacle. From chapter 25 until the end of Exodus, most of the book concerns the construction of the Tabernacle, conveyed in loving detail. The entire book of Leviticus proceeds to describe the minutia of sacrificial worship at the Tabernacle. The elaborate architectural structure, system of rituals, categories of sacrifices, and hierarchy of worship have appeared, at least since Wellhausen, much more plausibly to represent worship in the Temple of Jerusalem than in any portable desert shrine. In Wellhausen's view, priests during the Second Temple modeled their own religious institution backward in the times of the ancestors (in source P) to establish the antiquity, and hence authenticity, of their rite. With the redating of P, however, this view has come under criticism. Friedman has recalculated the dimensions of the Tabernacle and concluded that it would have fit precisely within the Holy of Holies in the First Temple. He claims that the Tabernacle did indeed exist as described. Because it was considered sacred, it was retained within the precincts of the Temple built to supersede it. According to Friedman, there is no reason not to take the description of Solomon's Temple literally:

> The priests brought the ark of the Lord's covenant to its place, to the innermost chamber of the Temple, to the Holy of Holies, beneath the wings of the cherubim. For the cherubim would spread out their wings toward the place of the ark, and the cherubim would provide covering from above over the ark and its poles. (1 Kings 8:6–7)

The truth may fall somewhere between these two positions. There may well have been an ancient Tabernacle that could not be disposed of when the Israelites built a more durable Temple. Equally plausibly, the detailed lists of sacrificial rituals in Leviticus may have arisen long after the Israelites left the wilderness. More than any other object in the Torah, the Tabernacle embodies the intriguing and mysterious interaction between the forces of tradition and retrojection.

Conflicting impressions of the same figure can offer strong indication that a later hand has retouched the original painting. Such retouching can be found with all three kings of the United Monarchy. King Saul, the least legendary figure of the three, comes in for the harshest treatment. Originally portrayed as a natural-born hero, the tallest, strongest man in Israel, who leads the Israelites to victory, Saul is later depicted as the inferior of Samuel the prophet, who reluctantly anoints Saul as king and rushes to remove the kingship when Saul does not entirely comply with Samuel's decrees (1 Samuel 13, 1 Samuel 15). The depiction of David's heroism extends much longer than Saul's, but he too receives God's criticism from the mouth of a prophet, Nathan (2 Samuel 12). Similarly, the Bible portrays Solomon as the wisest man and Israel's greatest ruler – until, at the end of his life, he sinks into decadence and idolatry. Again it is a prophet, Ahijah of Shiloh, who proclaims the downfall of his kingdom (1 Kings 11:29 ff). All three kings start out as legendary heroes and wind up suffering long, drastic declines punctuated by God's rebuke. Scholars maintain that the books of Samuel and Kings reveal at least two layers: an original courtly narrative representing an official history, and a later, prophetic revision critical of the institution of monarchy from its very inception. The prophetic criticism explains why the monarchy and Temple, institutions blessed by God, were destroyed. The current version of these books is richer for retaining both perspectives.

Similar ambiguity results from conflicting pronouncements concerning God's promise to the House of David. As was discussed in chapter 3, the original covenant to David was a covenant of grant, God's unconditional promise: "Your House and your kingship shall be established eternally before you; your throne shall be secure forever" (2 Samuel 7:16). However, the history narrated in Kings reveals that David's heirs did not rule forever. First, the monarchy split in two, with the House of David ruling over the less populous southern kingdom; second, the Babylonians captured Judah, spelling the end for Davidic kings. Looking backward, the Deuteronomic historians needed to adjust the covenant with the House of David to account for the cataclysmic end of its rule. A sequence of God's statements to Davidic rulers over the span of the Deuteronomic History shows a graduated transition from the promise of eternal rule to the foretelling of utter ruin. This progressive development causes Judah's downfall to appear not as God's abrogation of His covenant, but instead as the inevitable outcome of human corruption and disloyalty.

The slippage begins with David himself. After David arranges to kill his neighbor Uriah so he can marry Uriah's wife, Bathsheba, Nathan the prophet warns him, "Now the sword shall never depart from your House" (2 Samuel 12:10). In Hebrew there are no capital letters, so it is not altogether clear whether "house" refers to David's own family, riven with murderous sibling rivalry, or the sovereign line of the House of David. Nonetheless, the term "forever" here recalls the same term in God's covenant to David five chapters earlier, and suggests that the initial promise is already compromised. When Solomon marries foreign wives and builds temples for them, God diminishes David's covenant still further:

> The Lord said to Solomon, "Because you had this in mind, instead of keeping My covenant and My statutes that I commanded you, I shall surely tear the kingdom away from you and give it to your servant.... But I shall not tear away the entire kingdom. One tribe I shall give to your son, for the sake of David, My servant, and Jerusalem, My chosen." (1 Kings 11:11, 13)

After Solomon, the House of David will rule over only one tribe, Judah. The covenant with David is no longer unconditional; it depends upon the king's fidelity to God's laws.

Once the northern kingdom has splintered off from the south, it no longer rests under the protection of David's covenant: "For Israel tore away from the House of David, appointing Jeroboam son of Nebat as king. Jeroboam led Israel astray from the Lord, causing them to sin a great sin" (2 Kings 17:21). Jeroboam's rebellion is simultaneously political and religious; the north rebels against God's chosen ruler and form of worship.

Jeroboam's descendants wear away God's patience, until God allows the destruction of Israel by the Assyrians. Because the south remains under the control of David's heirs, God is slower to enact the same punishment. Generations of betrayal, though, culminating in Manasseh's pagan worship within the Jerusalem Temple, kindle God's fury:

> [Manasseh] put an idol of Asherah that he had made in the Temple, of which the Lord had said to David and his son Solomon, "In this Temple and in Jerusalem, which I have chosen from all the tribes of Israel, I shall set My Name forever. And I shall no longer cause Israel's foot to wander from the ground I gave to their fathers, *so long as they take care to do all that I commanded them.* (2 Kings 21:7–8; emphasis added)

God's loyalty to David's House now comes to be proportional to the king's loyalty to God's House in Jerusalem. Manasseh's sin inflames God to alter the covenant of grant fully into a covenant of obligation – an obligation that Judah has miserably failed to fulfill. With this new understanding of David's covenant, there no longer exists any limit to God's punishment: "I will wipe Jerusalem clean as one wipes a dish, wiping and turning it upside down" (2 Kings 21:13). The historian has subtly transformed the ancient covenant in harmony with historical realities centuries later.

Editing and Rewriting

This process of retouching older material leads to the final layers of the text, in which stories were edited, and sometimes rewritten, in order to give this diverse material a strong sense of shape and meaning. In Genesis, we've seen how original units, many of them originating as brief legends, came together over time to form larger segments about the lives of the Israelite ancestors. During the composition of the final written document, editors connected different sections of Genesis through the use of lists of "generations" as bridges – for example, the bridge from Adam to Noah in Genesis 5. These lists helped smooth the way for a linear, narrative history from the beginning of the world up to the birth of the people of Israel.

The editors imposed an overall frame upon each biblical book, enabling the individual stories to fit into a larger picture. Exodus recounts the grand narratives of the escape from Egypt and the receiving of the law. Leviticus, a compilation of laws, does not require a narrative structure, but Numbers continues the story through the frame of national wanderings in the desert. Deuteronomy's historical narrative links the laws contained therein to the previous four books. Its frame, Moses' review of his own history with the Israelites as a valedictory address the day before his death, renders the book as a poignant capstone to the early history of Israel, even as the themes in Deuteronomy, such as the emphasis on covenantal fidelity and the legitimacy of one central shrine, anticipate the historical books that follow.

Likewise, the books within the Deuteronomic History divide history into clearly identifiable phases with distinctive characteristics. The frames here, just as in the Pentateuch, enabled the editors to string together many stories with disparate origins. The Book of Joshua describes the conquest and allotment of the land of Israel – conquer and divide, in a reversal of the usual formula. Judges ostensibly tells stories of a motley assortment of tribal chieftains, though not all of them fill that function. Samuel recounts the transition to the United Monarchy; Kings, to the Divided Monarchy. The historians stamped each phase with a strong moral judgment that at times overshadows the actual events and accomplishments of the age. They portrayed periods in black-and-white terms that are quite foreign to the language of historical description today: Kings Jeroboam, Ahab, and Manasseh are unspeakably wicked; King Josiah is the best leader in Israel since Moses. It is perhaps for that very reason, however, that their depictions etch themselves so powerfully in the reader's mind.

The biblical editors worked not only on the macro scale of narrative frames, but also on a micro scale, making small changes in the text when they felt it necessary to create the proper religious tone. Numerous examples of small pious revisions can be found in the Bible, reflecting the editors' discomfort with some of the language from the older traditions. One of the most obvious occurrences is evident in the Hebrew but not in translation, in cases where characters commit blasphemy. After Job has lost all of his children and has been afflicted with a severe skin disease, his wife tells him, "Do you still hold on to your integrity? Curse God and die!" (Job 2:9). The editors refused to leave such a irreverent expression in the Holy Scripture, so they substituted its opposite "Bless God and die!" as a euphemism. (The same euphemism appears in Job 1:5 and 2:5.) A similar euphemism occurs in the prophet Nathan's rebuke of David, after the king has arranged Uriah's death and taken his wife, Bathsheba: "Because you have scorned the enemies of the Lord by this deed, the son that is born to you shall surely die" (2 Samuel 12:14). Scorning "the enemies of" the Lord is no sin; presumably, this term was added to soften the language. In Deuteronomy 32:8 we find a more interesting occurrence of this phenomenon: "When the Most High gave lands to the peoples, / When He separated human beings, / He affixed the nations' boundaries, / According to the number of Israelites." The verse as written is baffling: what relation is there between "the number of Israelites" and global geography? An alternative reading, found in a version of Deuteronomy discovered at Qumran (among the so-called Dead Sea Scrolls), helps resolve the problem: "In relation to the number of divinities." The original verse reflects an ancient theory that each nation has its own deity that serves as a "guardian angel." Biblical editors were uncomfortable with this polytheistic idea, so they reworded the verse as best they could.

Not only did the editors replace troublesome language. On occasion, they inserted sentences to correct an unsavory impression given in a certain passage. One striking example comes in David's deathbed speech to Solomon:

> [2] I am going the way of all the earth; be strong and show yourself a man. [3] Keep the charge of the Lord Your God to walk in His paths and to observe His statutes, His commandments and His laws and His testimonies, as written in the Torah of Moses, so that you prosper in all that you do and everywhere you turn. [4] So that the Lord will uphold His word that He spoke concerning me, "If your sons maintain their path to walk before Me in faithfulness, with all their heart and all their soul, no man shall be cut off from the throne of Israel." [5] Also, you know what Joab son of Zeruiah did to me, what he did to two Israelite captains, Abner son of Ner and Amasa son of Jeter: he

killed them, avenging the blood of war during peacetime; he spilled the blood of warfare on his belt upon his waist, and on his shoes upon his feet. [6] Act according to your wisdom; do not allow his gray hairs to descend to Sheol in peace. (1 Kings 2:2–9)

David was encouraging Solomon to "be strong and show yourself a man" because Solomon would have to kill his enemies after David's death. Uncomfortable with this bit of ruthless political advice as David's final legacy, the pious editors added a typical Deuteronomic message in verses 3 and 4: Solomon should follow God's commandments so that his descendants will retain eternal sovereignty.

Another discordant insertion was made at the end of Ecclesiastes:

In the end, when all is said and done: Fear God and keep His commandments, for this is the sum total of man. For God brings every deed to judgment – upon every hidden thing, whether good or bad. (12:13–14)

Ecclesiastes' editor leaves the reader with a simple, pious message, negating all of the book's skeptical philosophy leading up to it. The idea that God rewards the good and punishes the wicked comes under question, for example, in 3:16: "Another thing I saw beneath the sun: in the place of justice, there is wickedness; in the place of righteousness, there is wickedness." A book filled with such thoughts required more than replacing a word here and there. Nothing less than a final credo, a kind of "deathbed conversion" for the author, would do to render Ecclesiastes a sufficiently pious text for inclusion in the Holy Scripture.

The most obvious examples of editing occur when versions of the same text are found in different locations in the Bible. The differences in context, and the textual changes between the two occurrences, indicate that one book is reusing the same material and interpreting it for a new purpose. For example, Isaiah 36–39 repeats 2 Kings 18:13–20:19 substantially verbatim. In Kings, this section is located within a larger description of King Hezekiah's struggles against the Assyrian army. It shows how God rewarded Hezekiah for his loyalty by destroying the forces of King

Sennacherib of Assyria. The same material in Isaiah cuts off the larger context of the Assyrian war, retaining only the exchanges between Isaiah and Hezekiah. One substantial difference is that a poem of thanks by Hezekiah, written after a recovery from illness, is included in Isaiah but not in Kings. The poem disrupts the narrative; Isaiah 38:21–22, ending in Hezekiah's question, "What is the sign that I shall go up to the House of the Lord?" receives no answer because it is out of context. A comparison with 2 Kings 20:7–8 shows that these sentences in Isaiah belong before 38:7, since Isaiah 38:7 is almost the same as 2 Kings 20:9. Hence, it appears that Kings preserves an older form of this passage, whereas Isaiah borrows it in order to gather all material concerning the prophet in one book.

By far the most extensive reuse of prior material can be found in Chronicles. Written during the Second Temple period, Chronicles repeats large sections from Samuel and Kings; evidently, the authors of Chronicles had these prior works laid out on the table as they composed the new work. The ways that Chronicles departs from them, therefore, manifest the difference in perspective between the Chronicler and the Deuteronomist. One of the distinguishing characteristics of Chronicles is its idealization of the great kings of the past. The Deuteronomist presents a multi-layered picture of David and Solomon as legendary but deeply flawed rulers; Chronicles systematically removes their flaws. It fails to mention, for example, the story of Uriah and Bathsheba, and naturally the prophet Nathan's rebuke is also lacking. The fighting within David's household, among David's sons, and between David and his sons, which occupies most of 2 Samuel 13 through 1 Kings 2, is completely absent from Chronicles.

Chronicles mentions only Solomon among David's sons by name. David describes Solomon's choice to succeed him as follows (1 Chronicles 28:5): "Of all my sons – for the Lord has given me many sons – He has chosen my son Solomon to sit upon the throne of the Lord's kingdom over Israel." No such divine selection takes place in Kings; rather, there it is David who chooses Solomon as king over his brother Adonijah (1 Kings 1:29–30): "The king [David] took an oath, saying, 'As the Lord lives, who rescued me from every strait, just as I swore to you [Bathsheba] by the Lord God of Israel, saying, "For Solomon your son will rule after me, he will sit on my throne in my stead," thus I will do this very day."' Similarly, Chronicles applies an eraser to Solomon's enemies, both Adonijah and his followers. Chronicles rewrites David's deathbed scene discussed above, where David urges Solomon to kill his foes, into an entirely different context well before his death:

> David said to his son Solomon, "Be strong and take courage and act,
> do not fear nor be dismayed. For the Lord God, my God, is with you;
> He will not release nor abandon you until the completion of all the
> work of making the House of the Lord. (1 Chronicles 28:20)

David urges Solomon to muster his resolve – to build the Temple! With no enemies in sight, Chronicles gives little reason why Solomon would need so much courage.

Like his father, Solomon appears in Chronicles to be a perfect king. His wives and the idolatrous temples he built for them, which figure so prominently in Kings, vanish from Chronicles. The fault for the kingdom's division devolves upon Solomon's son Rehoboam. Thus, while Chronicles covers much the same ground as the Deuteronomic History, even copying whole sections when convenient, the final impression it leaves of history contrasts sharply with that of its predecessor. The Deuteronomist regards David and Solomon as great but flawed rulers, whose failings led to the dissolution of their kingdom and snowballed, through ever more corrupt descendants, until both halves of the kingdom were conquered by foreign powers. According to Chronicles, written under the Persian empire, David and Solomon were flawless monarchs, of exemplary piety and character, whose likes one day might return to Israel in a future restoration of Israelite sovereignty.

Putting the Bible Together Again

We've gotten a sense of how biblical scholars carve up the text of the Bible into subunits from different historical hands. At the end of the day, however, unless we are to republish the Bible as J, E, P, D, and a host of other hypothesized sources put forward as self-sustaining documents, we need a way to account for the Bible in its final, current form. After all, this is the form in which people have been reading it and responding to it for some 2,500 years. There is still a book sitting on our desks called the Bible, a book of sufficient power and wonder, despite or because of its torturous prehistory, that it has held countless generations under its spell. How can we put Humpty Dumpty back together? Historical scholarship poses a stark challenge to the way we read this book in our hands. As David Damrosch puts it in *The Narrative Covenant*, "Once one begins to wander in the wilderness of historical study, is there any way back to the wholeness of the unified text?"

Since the 1970s, a literary school of biblical scholarship has attempted to present an alternative to the atomizing tendencies of historically oriented scholars. Some literary scholars of the Bible accuse the historical scholars of drastically reducing the Bible's literary riches to questions of original purpose, or overemphasizing seams and conflicts between sources at the expense of other textual qualities. The effect might be compared to a description of a fine automobile that focused on the welds and ignored the craftsmanship of the parts and the beauty of the overall design. In the words of Robert Alter (in *The Art of Biblical Narrative*):

> What we need to understand better is that the religious vision of the Bible is given depth and subtlety precisely by being conveyed through the most sophisticated resources of prose fiction.... The biblical tale, through the most rigorous economy of means, leads us again and again to ponder complexities of motive and ambiguities of character because these are essential aspects of its vision of man, created by God, enjoying or suffering all the consequences of human freedom.

In Alter's view, the Bible has served as a cornerstone for Western literary art because it is in itself a great work of literature. To read biblical stories only as conveyors of coded messages representing the political views of putative sources is tantamount to ignoring the reasons why people love the Bible, the great appeal of the stories, their insights into the drama of human relations and the challenges of human existence. More important, the Bible's literary qualities are essential to the vision of biblical authors. Biblical writers could convey their messages only through compelling, complicated stories; those literary qualities were not accidental by-products of other historical motives. In other words: you can't understand the Bible *without* understanding it as literature. Most literary scholars do not deny the claims made by source critics; rather, they deny that source criticism provides the most compelling method for reading the Bible.

Meir Sternberg, a pioneer in the field of literary analysis, distinguishes between "source-oriented inquiry," which "address[es] itself to the biblical world as it really was," and "discourse-oriented analysis," which "sets out to understand not the realities behind the text but the text itself as a pattern of meaning and effect." A literary approach to the Bible should look for the kinds of verbal patterns, the play of perspectives of characters and the author, the kinds of ambiguity and irony found in other works of literature, rather than seeking to break up the writing into component parts whose motives and meanings derive from assumptions external to the work. In his view, source critics are too quick to assign unusual features of the text to artificial breaks between sources or to errors of scribes, instead of pondering whether they might be intentional features of literary art. Sternberg claims that biblical historians need to acquaint themselves with the literary qualities of the Bible so that they will be less hasty in splitting the text up into separate, consistent parts and more appreciative of the unity found within biblical stories. He has explored the artful uses of gaps, conflicting perspectives, and repetitions in the Bible in ways that reveal how fully it deserves to be considered a work of literature.

Whereas early literary critics of the Bible threw down the gauntlet at source critics, more recent scholars have attempted to integrate historical with literary approaches into a new synthesis. David Damrosch accomplishes this synthesis through an analysis of the different layers of the text. He starts by describing the original components that came from separate sources, and proceeds to an evaluation of the strategies used to weave them together into the final product. Damrosch regards the Bible in its final form to be as much a work of creative intelligence as the earlier layers, although its artistry may often be governed by different norms than ours, allowing for duplications, contradictions, and disjunctions. He argues that to understand the Bible requires seeing the ways that the different layers come into play with or against each other, forcing the reader to "read a passage three or even four ways at once." The dynamic shifts in perspective between the layers are what make the Bible a book that challenges its readers, again and again, to develop new insights and interpretations.

Damrosch's synthesis meshes nicely with traditional views of the Bible's openness to multiple interpretations. The knowledgeable Bible reader is free to choose among alternative approaches, just as a traditional Jewish reader glides among the great medieval commentaries. Source criticism, literary approaches, archeology, theology – all schools and methods can enrich our own understanding and guide us to explore our own original interpretations. Modern biblical scholarship reveals that the Bible was constructed by numerous authors with different points of view. It shows how arguments about the Bible's meaning originate as arguments within the Bible itself.

CHAPTER 6

Prophecy

Suggested reading: 1 Kings 17–22, 2 Kings 1–10, Amos

Mr. Smith Goes to Jerusalem

If you want to know about the character of the ancient Israelite prophets, Frank Capra's classic 1939 movie, *Mr. Smith Goes to Washington*, would provide a good start. In it, Jimmy Stewart plays a junior senator from the Midwest newly arrived to the halls of the capital. He finds Washington politics to be a cesspool of graft and corruption, a façade of refinement masking greed and exploitation. Smith goes on a mission to clean up the system. He wins few friends, but his own inner sense of morality does not allow him merely to "play the game" like all other politicians. He has no choice but to challenge those in power in the name of the common folk. After a long, bitter struggle waged through a lengthy filibuster, Smith triumphs over politics-as-usual, becoming a national hero, thanks in part to a jaded secretary (played by Jean Arthur) won over to his cause.

Mr. Smith represents a quintessential updated American version of a biblical prophet. Like his ancient role model, Smith comes from a modest background far away from the center of power. The movie emphasizes his roots in a rural society: he has risen to fame by putting out a forest fire, and he is a hero among a young group of nature lovers called the Boy Rangers. Smith's native American lifestyle embodies homespun, honest values that contrast sharply with the oversophisticated, morally bankrupt ways in the capital. Smith did not seek a position of power – at his acceptance speech, he says, "There must be some kind of mistake." Manipulated by Jim Taylor, the all-powerful boss and business tycoon, the state politicians select Smith because they believe that he will fall in line with their goals while retaining the loyalty of the populace. The crooks in power do not realize at first that Smith's genuine belief in the ideals of this country, demonstrated by his adoration for Washington, Jefferson, and Lincoln, render him utterly incorruptible.

When he sees fraud running rampant in Washington, Smith can't stop himself from preaching against it. He wasn't born a prophet; the circumstances of the country impelled him to take up that role. But he was born with the morality, and the gift of expression and inner confidence, that enabled him to become a prophet when the times required one. As a prophet, Mr. Smith stands alone. (The camera usually shows Jimmy Stewart by himself, or the other senators as a group.) He doesn't worry whether other people agree with him or even like him, so certain is he of the justness of his cause. At first no one pays him much attention, and he is made to suffer for his conviction; indeed, the Committee on Privileges and Elections votes to expel Smith from the Senate. Over time, however, people come to recognize the truth of his criticism, and in the end he succeeds in overturning the entrenched system of graft. (The "common people" in the Senate gallery applaud him loudly.) He has healed the country, bringing a renewed sense of joy and hope to the people everywhere.

The parallels between Mr. Smith and the biblical prophets are so numerous and striking that one can assert with confidence that Capra drank deeply from the wellsprings of Jerusalem as he was writing his script. From Smith's origins far from seats of power, his sympathy for the common people, his idealistic identification with the nation and his belief that its true values have been forgotten, to his relentless criticism of holders of power, both economic and political, and his defiance of a system that has rotted – all these characteristics derive from the ancient prophets. Like them, Smith places great stock in the ability of speech to change people's hearts and minds; while condemning the senators to their faces, he simultaneously addresses the rest of the country, through the journalists taking down his story, urging the people to restore the country to its noble ideals of the past.

Perhaps the chief similarity lies in the conviction that the nation's destiny lies entirely in its own hands and is determined by its moral character. A country should look within itself for the causes of its own problems. (The film's message would have been unimaginable a couple years later, when Americans were fighting against the Nazis in the middle of World War 2.) National character is set by those in power; if the political and religious leaders are corrupt, the entire society suffers. As an old Yiddish expression puts it, the fish stinks from the head. For this reason, Mr. Smith *has* to go to Washington, just as the prophets go to temples or royal courts.

Of course, *Mr. Smith Goes to Washington* does tweak the image of a prophet under Hollywood's lens. In the movie, America avoids the doom that the prophets consistently threaten. The movie comes to a happy ending through the "repentance" of Smith's nemesis, Senator Joseph Payne (Claude Rains). The quotation marks around the word "repentance," however, point to the crucial difference between the secularity of the American movie industry and the religious worldview of the Bible. Ancient Israel's corruption represents a sin not only against other people, but also against God; as that sin continues over time, the offense grows heavier until God must punish the entire society. The offense of the U.S. Senate is against the people alone, just as Smith expresses his opinions alone. Mr. Smith gives voice to the people's perspective, succeeding in reforming the system from within. God remains in the heavens, beyond the screen.

Prophets: The True Israelite Leaders

The Bible calls many people prophets, not only those people for whom prophecy was a specialized role. Abraham is the first one in the Bible to be called a prophet; God identifies him as such in a dream to Abimelech, king of Gerar: "Now, restore this man's wife, for he is a prophet, and he will pray for you, that you may live" (Genesis 20:7). The role of intercessor is an essential one for a prophet; prophets often plead with God to protect people when God is about to punish them. As a prophet, Abraham talks to God, receives messages from Him, obtains visions of the future, and conveys human concerns up to God, even possessing the power to reason with God and affect God's actions in the world. Abraham the prophet has a relationship with God: they speak with each other, share secrets, express disagreement. The argument between Abraham and God over the fate of

Sodom in Genesis 18 serves as a paradigm for the way that God and the prophet interact. God considers withholding His plan for Sodom – "Shall I conceal from Abraham what I am going to do?" (18:17) – but cannot keep anything hidden from Abraham because of His love for him. Abraham then proceeds to question God about the justice of destroying Sodom, wringing a number of concessions from God (He will not destroy the city for fifty innocent people, forty-five, …down to ten). At the end of their discussion, God and Abraham come to an understanding, and only then will God carry out the dreaded plan. The prophet's familiarity with God resembles the closeness of best friends. What we don't see Abraham do is transmit God's words to people, the primary task of later prophets. Perhaps Abraham's very existence, as the first monotheist, embodies a prophetic function, acting as a living testimony to a new kind of faith.

The Bible considers Moses to be the greatest prophet of all time:

> No prophet arose again in Israel like Moses, whom the Lord knew face to face, for all the signs and wonders that the Lord sent him to do in the land of Egypt to Pharaoh and all his servants and all his land. (Deuteronomy 34:10–11)

Here the Bible identifies two distinct aspects marking Moses' exceptional status as a prophet: his unique intimacy with God, and his role as a leader whose actions gave witness directly to God's sovereignty in the world. It is noteworthy that Deuteronomy associates in the figure of Moses the role of a ruler and a prophet. Elsewhere in the Bible, king and prophet appear as eternal antagonists. Moses, as prophet, delivers God's message of the Law at Mount Sinai:

> Face to face the Lord spoke with you at the mountain from the midst of the fire. I was standing between the Lord and you at that time, to tell you the word of the Lord, for you were afraid in the presence of the fire and did not go up the mountain. (Deuteronomy 5:4–5)

Remarkably, God attempts to speak to the people "face to face," just as He does to Moses, treating all of the people as prophets! The people cannot

bear such a close relationship with God, so Moses stands between them
to relay God's word. Moses the prophet here appears like a rabbi, leading
his congregation in their dialogue with the Almighty. Throughout his life,
Moses consults with God regarding important decisions, attempting to
implement God's will in human affairs. That translation from the divine
to human realms can be fraught with great peril, as is demonstrated in
particular in the episode of the waters of Meribah (Numbers 20:2–13). In
response to the Israelites' complaint that they lack water, God tells Moses
to speak to a rock and it will produce water. Moses proceeds to strike the
rock, provoking God's anger, resulting in the punishment that Moses
cannot enter the land of Israel. While there are numerous explanations
concerning the exact nature of Moses' transgression, this story illustrates
that the movement from God's word to human action is far from direct.

The Bible describes Moses' two siblings likewise as prophets. God
assigns his brother Aaron to serve as Moses' "prophet" to Pharaoh:

> The Lord said to Moses, "See, I have made you as a god to Pharaoh,
> and Aaron your brother will be your prophet. You shall speak all that
> I command you, and your brother Aaron will speak to Pharaoh, and
> he will send the Israelites from his land." (Exodus 7:1–2)

This is the only occasion in the Bible where a prophet is assigned the task
of relating the words of another person. God assuages Moses' anxiety
about speaking, a kind of anxiety repeated numerous times among later
prophets. Who am I, mere flesh and bone, the prophets ask, to proclaim
God's word? And when I speak, who will believe me when I say that I am
speaking in the name of the Lord? Aaron, as the purveyor of God's word
once removed, apparently has no cause for such anxiety. He is a prophet
only in quotation marks. This passage also emphasizes Moses' closeness
to God – for whom else would God assign his own prophet? – and,
by contrast, Pharaoh's distance from God – Pharaoh should not hear
God's word directly through His prophet, only secondhand, through the
prophet's prophet. Aaron emerges clearly as Moses' second in command,
although elsewhere God speaks directly to Moses *and* Aaron.

Moses' other sibling, Miriam, is also called a prophet:

> Miriam the prophetess, Aaron's sister, took the timbrel in her hand,
> and all the women went out after her dancing with timbrels. And
> Miriam sang out to them,
> Sing to the Lord, for He has risen up in triumph,
> Horse and rider He has cast into the sea. (Exodus 15:20–21)

This passage does not make clear why Miriam is considered a prophet. The explanation may lie in the music and dance, activities associated with a kind of ecstatic early form of prophecy (see below). Another intriguing possibility lies in the poem she sings, the same poem that Moses and the (male, presumably) Israelites have just sung. Did Miriam compose this poem? If so, the Bible may be linking poets and prophets as different forms of conduits for God's word. Poets in ancient times often depicted their work as inspired by a god; compare Homer's invocation to a goddess in the *Iliad* and a muse in the *Odyssey*. In this view, Miriam's "prophecy" would be her ability to tap into God's inspiration by creating poetry. The connection between poetry and prophecy is widespread in the Bible: some major poems, such as Jacob's testament to his sons (Genesis 49) and Moses' valedictory to the Israelites (Deuteronomy 32), contain prophetic visions regarding the future of the nation; and the utterances of prophets, from the gentile prophet Balaam (Numbers 23–24) to Isaiah and the other books collecting the sayings of individual prophets, generally take the form of poetry. The urgent message of the prophets is best conveyed through the force, rhythm and heightened rhetoric of poetry.

It is significant that the Bible counts Miriam as a prophet just like her brothers. Although the overwhelming majority of prophets mentioned in the Bible are men, some of the most important prophets are women. The most surprising female character in the entire Bible is Deborah, who acts as a prophet in Moses' mold:

> Deborah, the wife of Lappidoth, was a woman prophet. She governed
> Israel at that time. She would sit beneath the Palm of Deborah, be-
> tween Ramah and Bethel, in the mountain country of Ephraim; and
> Israelites would go up to her for legal judgment. (Judges 4:4–5)

Like Moses, Deborah is a prophet whose closeness with God elevates her to a position of national leadership. As with Moses, people come to her to decide legal judgments; again like him, she directs the Israelites into battle upon the command of God, even determining military strategy (4:6–7). After the Israelites triumph, she leads the singing of a victory song, just as Moses did. Although clearly the Israelites, like their neighbors, were not accustomed to women rulers, Deborah stands out as Israel's greatest leader during the troubled era of the judges.

Another major female prophet, Huldah, lived at the end of the First Temple period:

> The priest Hilkiah, Ahikam, Achbor, Shaphan and Asaiah went to Huldah the prophetess…and they spoke to her. She said to them, "Thus said the Lord, God of Israel, 'Say to the man who sent you to me [i.e., King Josiah]: "Thus said the Lord: 'Behold, I am inflicting calamity upon this place and its inhabitants, according to all the words of the Book that the king of Judah read, because they abandoned Me, burning incense to foreign gods so as to incite me with all the work of their hands. My anger will be kindled against this place; it shall not be extinguished.'"'" (2 Kings 22:14–17)

Huldah acts more like a prophet of her age than like Deborah or Miriam. She appears to be officially recognized in that role, perhaps even a professional prophet, esteemed for her judgment on matters of utmost national and religious importance. The high priest and the king's retinue have run to consult with her about the new scroll (Deuteronomy – see chapter 4) discovered within the Temple. Her voice sounds like the familiar voices of the classical prophets. When asked her view of the new scroll, she is instantly, fearlessly, and without a shred of doubt able to summon God's very response. (Note her dexterous use, as a conveyor of divine messages, of quotations within quotations.) She recognizes the authenticity of the scroll and considers its sudden appearance as a form of God's indictment of Judah. Thus Huldah is the prophet responsible for establishing the Torah in one of its earliest forms, as well as announcing the destruction of the Jerusalem Temple.

One further prophet who plays a crucial part in Israel's history is Samuel. Samuel is a reluctant prophet, like Moses; God calls him four times before Samuel figures out who spoke to him (1 Samuel 3:4–10). Yet Samuel rises to become the high priest at the temple in Shiloh, and the last of the judge/chieftains who ruled over Israel. Samuel presides over the transition to Israelite monarchy. His status as prophet gives him tragic insight into the fate of Israel under the rule of kings:

> He [Samuel] said, "This will be the governance of the king who will rule over you: he will take your sons and put them in his chariots and on his horses, and they will run before his chariots. He will set over them chiefs of thousands and chiefs of fifty; he will have them plow his furrows and reap his harvest, make his arms and the gear for his chariots. As for your daughters, he will take them for perfumers, cooks and bakers. And your fields, vineyards and olive groves he will take, and give them to his servants." (1 Samuel 8:11–14)

In Samuel's view, it is wrong for Israel to demand a king "like all the nations." As a judge and prophet, Samuel acknowledges that God is the true king, and he is merely God's administrator. A human king, however, recognizes no limits upon his own authority; he feels free to exploit his own people at will. Thus, despite the fact that Israel grows in power under the kingship, Samuel considers this transition as a step in the wrong direction. Kings, guided primarily by their own vanity and lust, will bring ruin upon the country. After Samuel, no Israelite ruler is designated as a prophet. Many of the prophets appear as countercultural rebels, as isolated, even hated outsiders permanently at odds with their society and its leaders. Nevertheless, in their own eyes and in the view of the biblical narrators, prophets are, as Shelley said of poets, "the unacknowledged legislators of the race."

God's Channel

By no means were all Israelite prophets rabble-rousing populist revolutionaries. Such a profile is in fact a relatively late and short-lived development in the history of prophecy. A prophet is, in essence, a conduit of

God's word. The Bible gives indication that some early Israelite prophets channeled God's word in ways more closely resembling those of non-Israelite prophets than of the later Israelite model. Virgil, in The *Aeneid*, describes the process whereby the sibyl would become a mouthpiece for the words of the god Apollo:

> And as she spoke neither her face / Nor hue went untransformed, nor did her hair / Stay neatly bound: her breast heaved, her wild heart / Grew large with passion.... The prophetess / Whom the bestriding god had not yet broken / Stormed about the cavern, trying to shake / His influence from her breast, while all the more / He tired her mad jaws, quelled her savage heart, / And tamed her by his pressure. (Aeneid VI, 76–80, 120–25, Robert Fitzgerald translation)

For the sibyl and many other ancient prophets, prophecy takes place through "spirit possession." The sibyl prepares herself by going into a trance. A god takes over her body, by an act of physical and emotional violence, until her own personality is nullified and the god speaks through her. In this model, prophecy is a kind of inspired madness. Indeed, if madness is considered as brought about by the gods, then the mad person must contain some extraordinary powers, privileged access to the divine realm. It requires only special training to harness those powers for human understanding.

The Bible contains numerous examples of this kind of prophecy. It mentions bands of prophets, some including musicians, who collectively cultivate a trancelike state of spirit possession:

> [Samuel said to Saul:] You shall meet a band of prophets descending from the high place, with harp, drum, flute and lyre before them, and they will be speaking in ecstasy. The spirit of the Lord shall rush upon you, and you shall speak in ecstasy with them – you will become a different man. (1 Samuel 10:5–6)

The expression translated "speaking in ecstasy" is the same word that means "prophesy." In this kind of prophecy, reminiscent of a Dionysian rite, bodily possession alone, certified by a kind of irrational behavior that may have resembled "speaking in tongues," constitutes the act of prophecy. For these ecstatics, prophecy does not require conveying a comprehensible message from God. It is a kind of temporary madness, induced by music and perhaps other means, signifying that the spirit of God has taken control of them. A similar example of ecstatic possession occurs during the time of Moses in the wilderness:

> The Lord descended in a cloud and spoke to him [Moses], and He withdrew from the spirit that was upon him and gave it upon the seventy elders. When the spirit rested upon them, they spoke in ecstasy and did not continue…. And Joshua the son of Nun, Moses' attendant from youth, said, "Moses my lord, shut them up!" But Moses said to him, "Are you jealous for me? Would that all of the Lord's people were prophets, that the Lord would put His spirit upon them!" (Numbers 11:25, 28–29)

This passage portrays this form of prophecy as a mixed blessing. On the one hand, the message is that anyone can be a prophet. God can cause His spirit to descend upon anyone He chooses; prophecy is not limited to a spiritual or social elite. Moreover, whereas Joshua considers this mass prophesying to represent a threat to Moses' leadership, Moses himself finds encouragement in the spread of prophecy; if prophecy is a remarkable intimacy with God, felt within a person's body, then everyone should be so fortunate to know such a state of bliss. On the other hand, the elders appear to be less well equipped to handle God's spirit than Moses is. Their experience of prophecy is confined to a one-time ecstatic outburst. Joshua's anxiety about people who claim the power of prophecy is not unfounded, considering how Israelites do arise to challenge Moses' authority (especially Korah in Numbers 16), and how the Bible devotes great attention to distinguishing false from true prophets (Deuteronomy 13:2–6, 18:15–22, and others). Ecstatic possession is portrayed as a limited dose of prophecy permitted to common people, different in kind from the prophecy of Moses and the great prophets to follow.

This ambivalence turns to outright rejection in the depiction of the prophets of Baal performing a ludicrous parody of ecstatic possession (1 Kings 18:25–29). Verse 29 employs the same verb, prophesy, used earlier to refer to spirit possession. Here, that kind of prophecy stands in stark contrast to the sober prophecy of Elijah. The prophets of Baal act like madmen, performing an odd hopping dance, shouting louder and louder, finally mutilating themselves with knives and spears. They perform these demented rituals *without* experiencing any spirit possession, rather in the hope that Baal will come. But he does not come, because, in the biblical view, he does not exist: "And there was no sound, no reply, no heed." In this passage, ecstatic possession is associated with the barbaric practices for heathen gods. By contrast, Elijah, the true prophet, needs only to offer sacrifice and call out to God in order to receive an answer from heaven. Nevertheless, although the Bible moves away from this early model of prophecy, possession plays a role with several biblical prophets. Like Moses, other prophets are reluctant to serve as God's spokesmen, uncertain of their own speaking abilities. At an early point in their missions, God touches their mouths – a seraph lays a coal on Isaiah's lips, God places a hand on Jeremiah's mouth, Ezekiel eats a scroll God gives him – transforming them into fit vessels for conveying the divine message. Their bodies must be transformed through contact with God as part of the process of becoming a prophet.

Alongside the unpredictable, anarchic experience of ecstatic prophecy, there arises a school of prophecy trained to harness their extraordinary powers for the benefit of society. The term "school" denotes that prophecy was taught, from master to pupil. The notion that prophecy can be transmitted as a body of knowledge is one that many biblical prophets are opposed to, and yet it was undoubtedly the standard conception of prophecy in ancient Israel. These schooled prophets serve as advisers to rulers. The prophet's access to God renders him an expert in crucial affairs of people or nations. At times, Israelite priests fulfill this function as oracular advisers through a prophetic device called the Urim and Thummim, thought to operate something like a Ouija board. Although the exact nature of this device is uncertain, the Urim and Thummim may have been precious stones located on the breastplate of the high priest; when a question was posed to them, one or the other would light up, providing a yes or no answer (Exodus 28:30; mentioned again in 1 Samuel 28:6, Ezra 2:63). Prophets are often expected to give this same kind of yes-or-no answer, as when Kings Ahab of Israel and Jehoshaphat of Judah considered whether to wage war against Aram:

> The king of Israel gathered together the prophets, some four hundred men, and said to them, "Should I go to battle against Ramoth-gilead or refrain?" They said, "Go up! The Lord will give it into the hand of the king." But Jehoshaphat said, "Is there no other prophet of the Lord here, of whom we may inquire?" The king of Israel said to Jehoshaphat, "There is one more man of whom to inquire about the Lord, but I hate him, because he never prophesies good about me, only bad: Michaiah son of Imlah." (1 Kings 22:6–8)

Ahab maintains a large retinue of court-appointed prophets to give him advice in making important decisions, especially in matters of warfare. The Bible portrays his prophets as mass-produced puppets of the king, yes-men cudgeled to produce the correct response in order to stay on the payroll. While this picture is likely a satiric exaggeration, it does suggest that schools of prophecy flourished during the Israelite monarchy, with the purpose of training people in techniques to receive divine guidance in national affairs.

Yet living, authentic prophets could provide a much more nuanced and complete picture of God's will than the Urim and Thummim or Ahab's lackeys. In the person of Nathan, King David's personal prophet, the Bible provides an image of a prophet who is the king's closest confidant, but far from a yes-man. David shares with Nathan his deepest concerns and aspirations. When David contemplates building a structure to house the Ark of the Lord, he asks Nathan his opinion. Nathan at first succumbs to David's will: "All that is in your heart, go and do, for the Lord is with you" (2 Samuel 7:3). That night, God tells Nathan that not David, but one of his sons, will build a Temple. Nathan immediately reports God's judgment to David, and David accepts it. It speaks well of David that he, unlike Ahab, tolerates a prophet who corrects him when necessary. David has faith in Nathan's powers and appreciates the prophet's candor; for his part, Nathan does not hesitate to impart the truth and does not wait on ceremony to confront the king. Most notably, he condemns David after the king has arranged the death of Uriah so he can marry Uriah's wife Bathsheba (2 Samuel 12:1–14). It is typical of their special relationship that David has not called for Nathan when the prophet enters to rebuke him, yet David shows no anger against Nathan but at once admits his guilt.

David's openness to Nathan's harsh words is reminiscent of the double-edged relationship between Shakespeare's King Lear and his wise fool (one of many similarities between these two great literary monarchs). Nathan here serves as David's moral compass, steering him back to God after he has sinned. He seems to understand David better than anyone else. For this reason, Nathan can choreograph Bathsheba's approach to David in her attempt to ensure that her son Solomon, and not Adonijah, who has proclaimed himself king, will succeed David to the throne (1 Kings 1:11ff). Nathan has the best interests of David and his family in mind; he knows that Solomon is destined to rule, and he helps to pull strings backstage to rectify the situation. Through their access to God's design, Nathan and other prophets acquire a heightened awareness of the course of history, seeing where it is flowing properly, and by contrast, where it is hopelessly off track.

At the same time that prophets were serving as court-appointed royal advisers, an altogether different model of the prophet took shape. Prophets in the new mold could also be found giving advice to kings – not because the king relied on them, but because the king could not afford to ignore them. Their prophetic powers made them legends renowned for their spiritual authority. In the passage above with Ahab and his 400 prophets, the king consults the prophet Micaiah, even though he says, "I hate him, because he never prophesies good about me" (1 Kings 22: 8). Egged on by Jehoshaphat, king of Judah, Ahab turns to Micaiah perhaps out of a tacit admission that his court prophets cannot be relied upon to tell the truth. By contrast, Micaiah tells the truth as he sees it, as God informs him, with no regard for the king's response or his own safety. He predicts the king's demise – Israel will be "scattered over the hills like sheep without a shepherd"; and he claims that the king's prophets were tricked into giving the king the wrong advice by a "lying spirit" dispatched by God. Micaiah refuses to bend God's message to the king's will, and he pays the price for his stubborn independence: he earns the king's enmity, receives physical abuse from a rival prophet, and is tossed in prison to feed on "scant bread and scant water." Just as important, he is correct; Ahab plunges into battle and is killed. Within a single story, Micaiah conforms to the main features of this new kind of prophet. He is spiritually gifted, privileged to receive God's word with perfect clarity and accuracy; honest to the point of being brutal, and fearless in speaking truth to power; independent of all social and religious networks, a prophet by nature or God's choice rather than by profession; and made to suffer for speaking truths that offend.

The chief representatives of this version of prophecy are Elijah and Elisha. In the cycles of stories surrounding them, the conflicts present in Micaiah's mission become magnified and intensified. Like a Western gunslinger, Elijah confronts 450 prophets of Baal in a duel of prophetic powers; after he defeats them, he directs the onlookers to slaughter them (1 Kings 18). Ahab, and even more his wicked wife, Jezebel, threaten repeatedly to kill Elijah. Yet Elijah does not hesitate to walk right up to Ahab to prophesy his annihilation:

> Ahab said to Elijah, "Have you found me, my enemy?" And he said, "I've found you. Because of your devotion to doing evil in the eyes of the Lord, I will bring evil upon you and purge you; I will cut off from Ahab every male [literally, he who urinates against a wall], every bondsman and free in Israel.... The Lord also spoke regarding Jezebel, 'The dogs will eat Jezebel within the ramparts of Jezreel. Dogs will devour Ahab's dead in the city; birds of heaven will consume his dead in the field.'" (1 Kings 21:20–21, 23–24)

Elijah does not cite the Lord in the first prophecy here ("I will bring evil upon you"); by this point, his struggle has become personal. Elijah no longer merely conveys God's word; he now fights God's battle himself against the king and queen. These two prophets, Elijah and Elisha, transform the prophetic stance of independence into brazen defiance and rebellion. They create an entirely new image of the prophet. "Image" is indeed an important part of their persona; Elijah is known as a "hairy man with leather belt tied around his waist" (2 Kings 1:8). He wears a mantle that becomes a recognizable apparatus for a prophet; to signify the transference of prophetic authority to Elisha, Elijah throws his mantle over his heir (1 Kings 19:19).

Unlike prior prophets, Elijah and Elisha possess divine powers that overflow into all aspects of their lives. Whereas Moses employed magic only to certify the truth of his prophecy before the people, by turning a staff into a snake and making his hand temporarily leprous (Exodus 4:1–8), Elijah and Elisha work wonders not to authenticate their words but merely because they can, because they are endowed with supernatural abilities. Tales of their magical power are so abundant that they come to outstrip the rest of these prophets' mission from God; more than any other characters in the Hebrew Bible, they appear superhuman. (The Gospels reprise some of these miracles in their depiction of Jesus.) Through magic, they are able to induce rain, revive dead children, kill off brigades of pursuers with fire from God – but also cause bears to mangle boys who taunt them! make barren women fertile, restore bad water by throwing salt in it, make an axe head float, multiply oil and bread, create a dry path in the water by tossing their mantle in it, and as a final display, ascend to heaven in a chariot of fire. Elijah's first words in the Bible bespeak his certainty in his metaphysical prowess: "As the Lord the God of Israel lives, before Whom I stand, there shall be no dew or rain these years except by my word" (1 Kings 17:1). No other biblical figure would make such a claim – except God! Another major difference between Moses' rather modest magic tricks and these prophets' supernatural acts is that Moses' power is short-lived and derived entirely from God. Elijah and Elisha seem to produce magic by themselves, whenever they fancy it. They do not act upon God's prior instructions, nor do they always invoke God as the source of their power, when performing deeds of magic. They often repeat a certain action several times, as if following a formula from a known magic ritual. Their magic powers seem as much dreadful as beneficent, removing them from the all too human plane that makes other biblical characters, including prophets, sympathetic and believable.

Another essential characteristic of these prophets is their charisma, namely, their talent for attracting followers who acknowledge their divine gift. Like some later prophets, Elijah and Elisha seem to veer between complete isolation and social acceptance. Their audacity and antipathy to authority lead them to wander by themselves, never staying at one location for long. Threatened by Jezebel, Elijah flees alone into the wilderness, walking for forty days until he hides in a cave. God encounters him there, asking Elijah why he is hiding. Elijah answers:

> I have been most jealous for the Lord, God of Hosts, for the Israelites
> abandoned Your covenant, ruined your altars and put Your prophets
> to the sword. I alone remain, and they have sought to take my life.
> (1 Kings 19:14)

Elsewhere, however, Elijah does not appear nearly so isolated. Elijah meets Obadiah, Ahab's chief steward, who calls Elijah "my lord":

> Obadiah feared the Lord greatly. When Jezebel was killing the Lord's
> prophets, Obadiah took a hundred prophets and hid them, fifty to a
> cave, and supplied them with bread and water. (1 Kings 18:3–4)

Elijah is not alone; scores of Israelite prophets refuse to serve Ahab and Jezebel, many of them killed in retribution. Obadiah, and presumably the hundred prophets he saves, remain faithful to God, acknowledging Elijah as God's prophet, the leader of a "God faction" against the idolatrous monarchs. Elijah displays his power to rally ordinary Israelites to his side when he commands them to kill the 450 prophets of Baal.

At the end of Elijah's career, cadres of his disciples suddenly appear throughout the land of Israel:

> When the Lord was about to raise Elijah in a whirlwind up to heaven,
> Elijah and Elisha went out from Gilgal.... Disciples [literally, children]
> of the prophets at Bethel went forth to Elisha and said to him, "Do
> you know that today the Lord is taking your master away from you?"
> And he said, "I know as well; hold your peace."...Disciples at Jericho
> approached Elisha and said to him, "Do you know that today the Lord

is taking your master away from you?" And he said, "I know as well;
hold your peace."...Fifty disciples went and stood across from them
far off, while the two of them stood at the Jordan. (2 Kings 2:1–7)

Elijah's final journey with Elisha presents an altogether different portrait
of him than the previous stories about his life. Elijah is depicted as the
leader of a vast network of followers, who are in touch with each other
and aware of their master's every step. When these disciples see that Elijah
ascends to heaven, and that Elisha receives Elijah's magic mantle, they
transfer their loyalty immediately to him. They play minor roles in several
stories concerning Elisha, reminding the reader that tales dramatizing the
prophets' seclusion must be taken with a grain of salt. After all, they must
have had a circle of followers keen on preserving legendary stories – how
else would we know about them? The fact that both prophets gain such
easy access to kings they generally despise – not only Israelite kings, but
in one case a foreign king as well (2 Kings 8:7) – shows that they attained
a high degree of fame and honor. Elisha actually anoints Jehu as king over
Israel. Jehu repays the compliment: he kills Jezebel, Elijah's tormentor, and
quotes Elijah's prophecy about Jezebel's death (2 Kings 9:30–37).

Some of these stories about Elijah and Elisha bring out the prophets'
concern for and familiarity with people in desperate need, a trait seldom
witnessed among previous prophets. Similar stories are told of each
(1 Kings 17, 2 Kings 4). Both encounter impoverished women who have
almost run out of food and money; Elijah makes a little flour and oil
feed a widow and her son a for long time; Elisha prevents a woman from
having to sell her children into slavery by causing a single jug of valuable
oil to fill many vessels. Both revive children who have died, through a
form of mouth-to-mouth resuscitation combined with urgent prayers to
God. With both prophets, the women who have lost their sons defiantly
challenge the prophets; they turn the tables on the prophets, questioning
them the way that the prophets question God. Elisha, for example, had
promised the woman a son, in phrasing very similar to the promise of
God's angel to Abraham and Sarah (Genesis 18:10). When her son dies,
she asks Elisha, "Did I ask for a son from my lord? Didn't I say, 'Do not
mislead me?'" (2 Kings 4:28) The resemblance between Elisha and God's

angel is disconcerting, as if to point out that Elisha is playing the part of God with too much conviction. The mother's actions toward Elisha cut him down a little more to human size. She cracks through his shell of perfection; he shows an unaccustomed warmth toward her. Neither Elijah nor Elisha preaches about the poor and the downtrodden, as do later prophets, but their attention to the needs of these barren and bereft women prefigures the larger social vision of their heirs.

The "Literary" Prophets

The history of Israelite prophecy culminates in the flourishing of the great prophets called "classical" or "literary." The latter term will be adopted here as most descriptive of a group who together created the eternal model for the role, style, and message of a prophet. These prophets are "literary" in several senses: their prophetic activity consists for the most part in preaching, in imparting God's word; they speak often in a style rich in metaphor and in powerful poetic cadences; and their legacy consists of books that bear their name. The order of the books of the literary prophets is significant: three long books – Isaiah, Jeremiah, Ezekiel – followed by twelve shorter works – Hosea, Joel, Amos, Obadiah, Jonah, Micah, Nahum, Habakkuk, Zephaniah, Haggai, Zechariah, Malachi. The three long prophets are chronological, and the twelve short prophets – sometimes called "minor," an adjective reflecting their length more than their stature – are in rough, though not exact, chronological order. Together they form an arrangement that recalls the three patriarchs followed by the twelve tribes. This collection includes an assortment of material, from exalted prophets of great originality to slight and derivative ones (Haggai, Nahum), as well as a satiric tale about an unwilling prophet (Jonah). The schematic grouping of the material raises doubts whether certain books were included merely to complete the count, or vice versa – whether some books were left out because the count was already full. (Scholars generally hold the former, that the material was stretched to fit the scheme.)

The period of the literary prophets begins with Amos and Hosea in the mid-eighth century B.C.E., and ends with Malachi in the fifth century B.C.E. This span exactly overlaps the most traumatic and formative period of biblical history, covering the downfall of the northern and southern

kingdoms, the conquest by the Assyrians, exile in Babylonia, and the restoration under the Persians, as well as the religious reforms and unification
under Josiah, the destruction of the First Temple, and the establishment
of a Torah book as a central authority for national life. The relationship
between these pivotal historical events and the new form of prophecy runs
both ways. Historical pressures gave rise to a new kind of prophet who
could offer strong explanations for Israel's sufferings and the role of God
in human affairs. People considered the prophet's words as essential for
understanding the world they lived in, and therefore they recorded, collected, and preserved them. As the prophets gained in national importance,
their ideas were increasingly read and studied. The role of prophets came
to be regarded as central in national history; during the crucial years of
the writing of the Torah and the Deuteronomic History, references to
prophets were included at every stage. The Bible, as it develops, thus goes
beyond the view of a one-time revelation at Sinai to an expansive prospect
of God's continuing revelation through His prophets.

Literary prophets combine many of the features of previous prophets – independence, access to authority and defiance of authority, intimacy
with God – but the focus changes entirely from their life to their preaching. Overall, there are few stories about these prophets; for some, we
learn so little about them that it is hard to determine when they lived or
where. Instead, we read the speeches that they delivered as God's spokesmen. Although they all speak in the name of God, they do not impart
the same message or share the same vision. Some of the diversity can be
accounted for by the historical situations of the prophets: some prophets inveigh against Israel, some against Judah, predicting their downfall;
others speak against foreign nations, predicting their demise. Some urge
the nation to repent to God and change their ways, and under different
circumstances others console the people with a vision of God's eternal
love. Before the Babylonian conquest, prophets foresee doom and exile;
afterwards, they envision a return to the land and restoration of national
glory. History alone does not account for all the differences among
prophets. Some prophets view history through the lens of monotheistic
worship: the nation will suffer because people are worshipping other gods
or are ignoring their obligations to God. Other prophets create a new

framework for describing God's relationship with Israel, dependent less upon ritual than upon morality. The people can fulfill all of their ritual obligations meticulously and still displease God because they abuse their fellow man. Roughly, the distinctions between ritual versus moral emphasis and condemnation versus consolation form the basic axes for all the literary prophets. These common coordinates make the general features of biblical literary prophets – the "type" – emerge quite strongly from these fifteen examples.

This timeline identifies when the literary prophets lived. Bear in mind that some of them are impossible to place with any certainty (such as Jonah and Joel).

Time Chart of Literary Prophets

8th century	7th century	6th century	5th century
Amos	Nahum	Ezekiel	Haggai
Hosea		Second Isaiah	Zechariah
	Micah	Obadiah	Jonah
	First Isaiah	Zephaniah	Joel
		Habakkuk	Third Isaiah
		Jeremiah	Malachi

All of the books of prophets are thought to have had a history of composition and editing extending beyond the life of the prophet himself. Some of the books reveal more than this kind of retouching. In places there are striking breaks in the course of the book, which scholars take to indicate the presence of works by two, or sometimes three, different authors. For example, Zechariah chapters 1 to 8 contains a series of visions and speeches written in prose and concerning Israel alone; in 9 to 11, there are prophesies against the surrounding nations, written in poetry; and 12 to 14 strikes yet a different tone, largely in prose, offering a vision of the Day of the Lord, when Judah shall survive but other nations and their gods shall be destroyed.

Even more striking is the standard scholarly division of the book of Isaiah into the work of three distinct authors writing in vastly different eras and circumstances. First Isaiah, who produced most of chapters 1 to 39, lived in Jerusalem from around 740 to 700 B.C.E. and prophesied the downfall of the northern kingdom. Second Isaiah, responsible for chapters 40 to 55, most likely composed his prophecies in Babylonia in the mid-sixth century B.C.E. Third Isaiah, author of chapters 56 to 66, represents a dissident sect living in Judah during the Persian period in the fifth century. (Not surprisingly, in recent years even this neat tripartite division has fallen to further subdivisions on the one hand, and interest in the editorial unity of the whole on the other.) The later "Isaiahs" continue to write under the name of the legendary former prophet rather than under their own names, probably because they consider themselves to be Isaiah's disciples and heirs. By adding to the collection of Isaiah's prophecy, these later writers deepen a sense that Israel's greatest prophet was relevant to all times and places.

The prophets deliver their message almost entirely within Israel and to Israel. They rail against the moral breakdown within their own society; they proclaim their concerns to kings, priests, and commoners, all who would listen. On occasion they do prophesy about surrounding countries, often when those came into conflict with Israel. Such prophecies proclaim that the Israelite God is a universal God; though His message was first conveyed to one particular people, His rule extends over all the earth. This is where the universal aspect of their vision comes into play. They declare that at some time in the future – the "end of time" or the "day of the Lord" – God will become known to everyone. The nations will no longer worship other gods; they will acknowledge the sovereignty of God and even worship at God's Temple in Jerusalem. Thus, while the reach of the Law remains exclusively within Israel, the vision of the prophets broadens the Bible's monotheistic moral perspective outward to include other people.

Amos: The Iconoclast Who Set the Mold

Amos serves as an appealing example of a literary prophet because, as the first, he defined the model for those who came after him; and purely as a character, he is among the most colorful personalities in the Bible. The short book in his name establishes many of the stereotypical contours of the classic Israelite prophet. Amos is startlingly original; he sounds like no one who comes before him, presenting himself as a self-made thinker who refuses to accept anyone's authority except his own – and God's. After the procession of betrayals and dour repetitions in the Book of Kings, the piercing, individual voices of Amos and his colleagues breathe a fresh tone into the Bible. While these prophets are far from universally uplifting, spending most of their energy condemning the wrongs in their society, still they manage to avoid being depressing. At their most negative, they know how to rouse the listener with the force of their oratory, fast-moving and rich in rhetoric. The prophets, at their best, raise the audience to view their lives through God's perspective. It might be said that Amos invented at once a new kind of prophet and a new vehicle for God, a new kind of language for God, as well as a new kind of message. With his gutsy defiance of human authority combined with his fierce independence and common-man image, Amos is the Mr. Smith of ancient Israel.

As is typical among the literary prophets, the Bible offers relatively little about the life of Amos. Only Amos 1:1 and 7:10–17 tell us anything about the person behind these sayings. Like most of the books about the prophets, Amos begins with a short biographical frame, commonly called a superscription, announcing his geographical background and the period and location of his prophesying. He comes from Tekoa in Judah and moves north to prophesy in Israel during the reign of King Jeroboam, son of Joash. The editor adds a note that Amos's call to prophesy occurs "two years before the earthquake"; during a period without a standard numerical method to count years, such an observation would surely have imparted great specificity.

The most significant detail in the superscription is the unusual one about his profession: "sheep breeder." Amos's profession factors into his identity as a prophet in several ways. First and foremost, he is not a professional religious figure:

[Amos said,] "I am not a prophet, and I am not a prophet's disciple, but I am a herdsman and tender of sycamore trees. The Lord took me away from the flock, and the Lord said to me, 'Go, prophesy to My people Israel!'" (7:14–5)

Prophecy

Amos's status as an outsider, by both geography and trade, renders him as
a new and more authentic form of prophet, one not compromised by political debts or family connections. He does not recycle messages learned
from somebody else; his words come directly from God:

> A lion has roared – who would not fear?
> The Lord God has spoken – who would not prophesy? (3:8)

This is one of the most astonishing lines in the entire Bible. Amos is saying:
Forget everything you think you know about who is a prophet. A prophet
is anybody who opens up his or her ears to God's word. God speaks to
Amos not because there is anything special about him, but because he
has chosen to listen. Amos is willing to hear God's harsh and naked truth,
and nothing can hold him back from speaking it.

Amos's rural background aligns him with the Israelite "heartland," in
contrast to the denizens of religious or political centers. Amos champions
the poor and skewers the rich. He plays the cowboy, a straight shooter who
acts with confidence and boldness. Amos's roots lie behind his picturesque
language, woven with observations and metaphors from nature:

> Can horses run on a rock?
> Can the sea be plowed with an ox?
> Yet you have turned justice into a poisonous herb,
> And the fruit of righteousness to wormwood. (6:12)

Amos's familiarity with nature, as demonstrated so effortlessly in these and
other expressions, is unparalleled by any other character in the Hebrew
Bible, rivaled only by the authors of Job and some of the Psalms.

The book reveals one more fact about Amos: his brazen preaching gets him into trouble. Amos conducts his attacks at Bethel, one of
the northern temples. His recurrent predictions about the downfall of
the northern kingdom and the end of the current dynasty of monarchs
draw the ire of Amaziah, the main priest of Bethel. Amos seems to be
picking his fight; one might imagine him shouting outside the gates of
the Temple, taunting Amaziah until the priest can tolerate this renegade

no more. (The placement of this story toward the end of the book supports this impression, as if the priest has been listening to Amos from chapter 1.) Amaziah is a close ally of King Jeroboam; the priest considers the prophet seditious and sends a message of concern to the king: "For thus says Amos:'Jeroboam shall die by the sword, and Israel shall surely go into exile from its soil'" (7:11). Amaziah then banishes Amos back to Judah, possibly at the king's behest. Before leaving, Amos thrusts his verbal rapier even deeper:

> Now, listen to the word of the Lord. You say, "Don't prophesy against Israel, and don't preach against the House of Isaac." Therefore, thus says the Lord: "Your wife shall go whoring in the city, your sons and daughters shall fall by the sword, and your land shall be divided with a measuring cord. You yourself shall die on unclean soil, and Israel shall surely go into exile from its land." (7:16–17)

Amos's message to the king is: Don't mess with God's prophets. Especially since none of his threats came true to Jeroboam directly (according to 2 Kings 14:29, this king died peacefully after a long reign and was succeeded by his son), his words ring less as a prediction than as an angry roar of rebelliousness. The king may hold power now, but he should not forget that the real power resides with God, and God can take the power away from the king in an instant.

Like Elijah and Elisha, Amos adopts the stance of an outsider, but unlike them, Amos neither performs miracles nor displays supernatural powers. Instead, the book places the emphasis entirely on the prophet's moral message. His words now lie at the center of his prophetic ministry, whereas his deeds are distinctly secondary. Indeed, some literary prophets are completely bereft of stories; all that remain are their words. Amos is a verbal artist, painting a vivid if damning picture of decadence and moral turpitude. He condemns the rich for oppressing the poor, thereby leading the country into ruin:

Thus said the Lord:
For three transgressions of Israel,

Prophecy

For four, I will not revoke it [the decree]:
For their sale of the righteous for silver
And the needy for the sake of sandals. (2:6–7)

God listens to the poor and the upright; oppression provokes His wrath. Just as God saved the people from slavery in Egypt, God will make them suffer for their own cruelty. Amos paints his canvas in broad strokes: the whole system is rotten; all the rich are villains. The misdeeds of some become projected upon all. He views the rich as slouching in a drunken, callous complacency:

Ah, those who are complacent in Zion,
The confident ones on the hill of Samaria,
Distinguished among the first of the nations,
Much sought after by the House of Israel:...
They who recline on ivory beds,
Who sprawl upon their couches,
Who eat lambs from the flock
And fatted calves from the stalls.
They pluck upon the lute –
Like David, they invent musical instruments.
They imbibe straight from wine bowls
And anoint themselves with choicest oils –
But they don't grow sick over the rupture of Joseph. (6:1, 4–6)

These leading wealthy individuals care only for their own pleasure; they ignore the plight of others and the decline of the nation that they themselves are causing.

Amos seems to address his words to all the people, not just to kings. One of the new aspects of the literary prophets is that the reader almost never knows who the audience is. The prophet rages, more or less, in a vacuum. Where exactly is Amos standing at Bethel? Who is standing near him, if anyone? Who is listening? How do they react? How long did he preach at Bethel – was it for days, months, or years? Are these sermons collected from a brief period, or from Amos's entire career as a prophet?

The reader is even ignorant of his age. Except for the one brief exchange with Amaziah, the book is silent on these matters. The lack of specifics launches the prophet's words into a wide orbit. They are not limited to one time and place; Amos could be speaking to people everywhere. He appears to be preaching to us, the readers, just as much as to an audience of his contemporaries.

The element of prediction, which plays so large a part in the popular conception of prophecy, becomes less important with Amos and the literary prophets. Certainly they do make predictions, but their predictions do not always come true (see Amos's prediction regarding King Jeroboam), a fact that apparently does not matter. In the long term, Amos was right: Israel, the northern kingdom, was vanquished by a foreign nation. For Amos, prediction is less important than moral exhortation, and it frequently serves as a tool of his exhortation. One moment he envisions Israel's destruction as if it has already taken place: "Fallen, not to rise again, is Maiden Israel" (5:2). The next moment he extends hope for averting disaster: "Thus said the Lord to the House of Israel: Seek Me and live!" (5:4). Amos's predictions are vague, not meant as fortune-telling. "But I will raise up against you a nation, O House of Israel" (6:14) – he makes no mention of who will cause Israel's fall or when.

The prophets draw a picture of a possible future rather than foretell an actual future with dead certainty. Their words are meant to inspire fear and loathing, to stir people to action, changing their thoughts and behavior:

> Listen to this, you who trample the poor and destroy the lowly of the earth, saying, "When will the new moon pass, so we can deal in grain; the Sabbath, so we can open up the wheat...tricking with deceptive scales, purchasing the poor for silver and the needy for the sake of sandals, profiting in wheat refuse." The Lord swears by the pride of Jacob, "I shall never forget their deeds." (8:4–7)

With this vicious caricature of the corrupt mentality of Israelite merchants, the prophet intends to provoke the listener's outrage; in this case the audience even receives guidance from God's reaction. The predictions, then, are designed to propel the audience to transform their society before it's too late. These prophets proclaim the power of repentance to restore people's relationship with God and alter the course of history:

> Hate evil and love good, establish justice in the gate;
> Perhaps the Lord, God of Hosts, will show favor to the remnant of
> Joseph. (5:15)

These words sound very different from the classic position of the Deuteronomic History, here spoken by David upon his deathbed to Solomon:

> Keep the charge of the Lord Your God to walk in His paths and to
> observe His statutes, His commandments and His laws and His
> testimonies, as written in the Torah of Moses, so that you prosper in
> all that you do and everywhere you turn. (1 Kings 2:3)

In both passages, the fate of individuals and nations hinges upon their relationship with God. For David, the covenant sets the terms for that relationship, its laws defining the conditions of moral behavior. For Amos, morality appears to have left its moorings in the covenant and become something much more general and all-encompassing.

Part of the attraction of the literary prophets is that they give us a vision of God's mind far more extensive than does any other part of the Bible. Their lengthy speeches delivered in the name of the Lord provide the reader with a powerful picture of divine pathos, God's emotional attachment to His people. Often we find alternating passages expressing God's love and God's wrath. Some speeches convey only one or the other, offering vistas of unadulterated doom or consolation. But the most intriguing passages show a mixture of both anger and affection, of God wrestling, as it were, with conflicting emotions toward Israel. Take a passage cited in part above:

> Hear the word that I take up in mourning over you, O House of
> Israel:
> Fallen, not to rise again, is Maiden Israel;

> Abandoned on her soil with none to raise her up.
> For thus says the Lord God:
> The city that goes forth a thousand shall have a hundred left,
> The one that goes forth a hundred shall have ten left to the House
> of Israel. (5:1–3)

Brutality and tenderness combine here into a plangent lament. God bemoans the fate of Israel, comparing the country to a destitute maiden fallen upon the ground. (The personification of a nation as an abandoned woman is common in biblical laments; compare the Book of Lamentations.) Yet in the next sentence God announces her destiny as a *fait accompli*: thousands of her people will die in battle. Is God crying during this recitation? Just a few sentences later God "flashes destruction upon strongholds" against people "who turn justice into wormwood" (5:9, 7), showing no trace of remorse. God appears to be struggling between righteous indignation and feelings of mercy. Such painful ambivalence deepens as God recalls His history with Israel:

> Hear this word that the Lord has spoken against you, O children of
> Israel,
> Against the whole family I brought up from the land of Egypt:
> "You alone have I known of all the families of the earth;
> Therefore will I visit upon you all of your transgressions." (3:1–2)

Israel's familial closeness to God can backfire against her; God holds her to a higher standard. The feelings of love and protection that Israel feels from God have dulled her sense of obligation. God pays Israel special attention and will not overlook her ethical lapses. But however great God's anger, He can never forget the love at the foundation of His relationship with Israel. In the same sentence that God promises of Israel, "I will wipe it off the face of the earth!" (9:8), He declares, "But I will not wholly wipe out the House of Jacob." God always assures Israel that there will remain a "saving remnant" to rebuild city and farm, court and temple. God of the prophets always leaves some room for hope, because without hope there can be no love and no repentance.

Amos's near exclusive emphasis on social morality, shared by several (though by no means all) of the literary prophets, represents a major difference between this group of books and all other writings in the Bible. As was already mentioned, the prophets by and large ignore the covenant of law so central to national identity since the time of Moses. In the Deuteronomic History, the biblical historians guided by the covenant explain periods of suffering as caused by Israel's infidelity. When Israel breaks the laws, they worship other gods; God grows angry with them, allowing their enemies to defeat them. Amos seems oblivious to this tradition; in his eyes, justice for the vulnerable alone determines national destiny. Amos scarcely mentions idolatry at all, except for a passing reference to astral deities in 5:26 – not one hint of Ashtarte, the Baals, or the other gods that plague Israel throughout biblical history. This absence is all the more remarkable because Bethel, the temple where Amos preaches, is singled out in 1 Kings 12:29 as the seat of a notorious golden calf!

Amos appears uninterested in the entire sphere of ritual, the worship of God too often interfering with true piety. Of course, the laws no less than the prophets demonstrate great concern for the less fortunate members of society, as is evidenced in many requirements on behalf of the "widow and orphan." Such social legislation is joined to a large body of laws regulating religious practices, most of which pertain to sacrifices. Amos, by contrast, considers social morality not equal to, but weightier than, religious ritual in the eyes of God. He believes that the powerful have elevated ritual above morality; his role is to switch the scales. It is shocking how viciously Amos mocks the conduct within the temples to make his point:

> Come to Bethel and sin, to Gilgal and sin abundantly,
> Bring your sacrifices in the morning, your tithes on the third day.
> Burn a thanks offering of leaven, cry your freewill offerings out loud,
> For so you love to do, O children of Israel
>   – declares the Lord God. (4:4–5)

Amos is condemning not the offering of sacrifices per se, but the hypocritical manner in which the rituals are conducted. The outward show of piety lavishly displayed in the temples cannot substitute for righteousness and justice – a criticism of religious ritual that has echoed down through the centuries. Though he does not advocate abolishing the temple ritual, Amos does demote its importance within the hierarchy of religious values. In this respect, the literary prophets represent a significant change in emphasis from the legal and ritual foundation of the Jewish people present in the Bible from Genesis to Kings.

Conclusion

It is remarkable that prophetic books like Amos survived at all. They enshrine a harsh vein of national self-criticism deep within the sacred canon of Israel's literature. Amos has traveled a long way from his humble origins as a sheep breeder to a seat at the head of a large table of revered Israelite prophets. How did Amos and his followers win acceptance by descendants of priests and kings? The prophets seemed to get it right, in the larger picture if not in all details. They predicted the downfall of the northern and southern kingdoms before they happened, and they offered compelling explanations for the causes of those tragedies. The prophets gave new meaning to history, enabling people to interpret events as expressions of the will of God. Further, they extended hope that suffering was a temporary scourge leading to forgiveness and redemption. Some of the pillars of Israel's theological world – the promise of eternity to the House of David and the Jerusalem Temple – did not survive the test of history. The prophets gave the people tools for adapting the monotheistic idea to a period of national trauma. Without them, the religion of Israel might not have survived, and likely would not have possessed the flexibility to form what we know as Judaism.

Why did the great age of prophecy end? The prophets arose during an extended era of historical crisis; the long period of national stability under the Persians may have rendered their grand pronouncements no longer useful or fashionable. They had made their point. The Jews survived exile and moved on. As inhabitants of a quiet Persian satrapy, the Jews remaining in the land of Israel felt less pressure to interpret contemporary historical events, and they grew to mistrust prophets as loose cannons who might lead people astray. The emergent Torah book was now regarded as the anchor for the community's understanding of God's ways. New prophets could only be extraneous and divisive. Eventually, once the wells of inspiration had dried up, prophecy was replaced by apocalypse, a form of divination of the future based upon interpretation of the prophetic writings from the past (see Conclusion, Chapter 9).

Prophets were great religious figures who rose and disappeared within a relatively brief span. In a larger sense, however, the entire Bible has been read for millennia as a prophetic book. The Book replaced people as the nation's prophet. Readers came to believe that the Bible, in its entirety, conveys God's word. People have consulted the Book in moments of personal, collective, and national crisis, seeking to clarify God's will in human destiny. And many people today still consider the Bible as foretelling the future course of history in enigmatic form. No collection of books has had a more profound impact upon the world's understanding of God and religious values than the fifteen books of literary prophets.

CHAPTER 7

Wisdom

Suggested reading: Proverbs 1–9, Job 1–10, Ecclesiastes 1–2

Divine Creativity

Shacharit, the Jewish morning prayer, begins as follows:

> He Who illuminates the earth and those who dwell upon it with
> compassion, and in His goodness renews daily, perpetually, the work
> of creation; how great are Your works, O Lord! You make them all
> with your *wisdom*, the world is full of Your possessions.

This beautiful prayer captures an original sense of wisdom from which all
other meanings derive. Wisdom is God's design in creating the universe.
It encompasses characteristics such as beauty, sublimity, power, creativity, imagination, and artistry. God's wisdom is manifest throughout the
universe: look at the stars, feel the warmth of the sun, observe the waxing
and waning of the moon, notice the order of created beings, ponder the
symmetry of a leaf – all things on earth and in heaven imbue man with a
sense of intelligence pulsing everywhere. God's wisdom is like an architect
who planned out the world from the most awe-inspiring aspects to the
minutest details:

> The Lord acquired me at the beginning of His path,
> Before His works of old.
> I was installed forever,

From the first, from the earth's origins....
When He fixed the heavens, there was I,
When He drew a circle to bound in the deep.
When He firmed up the clouds above,
When the fountains of the deep grew strong,
When He placed a limit for the sea,
So the waters do not transgress His command,
When He designed the earth's foundations –
I was at His side as a master worker [or confidant],
And as a delight every day, cavorting in His presence at all times.
Sporting with the whole of His world,
Finding delight in mankind. (Proverbs 8:22–31)

Here is the classic biblical statement of a primordial wisdom. This passage describes wisdom as a separate entity – Wisdom personified – created by God at the origin of the universe.[1] The Bible may be recalling Egyptian myths of Wisdom as a goddess, named Ma'at, involved in designing the world. Wisdom in Proverbs 8 is a kind of adviser and encourager cheering the process along. The author may consider Wisdom as one of the divine beings alluded to in Genesis, Psalms ("Ascribe to the Lord, O divine beings, / ascribe to the Lord glory and strength" Psalm 29:1), and elsewhere. Since Proverbs 8 is the only place in the Bible where Wisdom takes on this role, it is difficult to know whether to take these verses literally and regard Wisdom as an actual creature, or instead metaphorically seeing Wisdom as an aspect of God's mind. In either case, this hymn to Wisdom portrays God not only as the world's creator, but also as its ever-present gardener, tending nature through His rules. In Wisdom's grand scheme for the universe, humanity might have seemed dwarfed, an insignificant speck in the cosmic whole. But this is not at all the Bible's position. As the exposition of creation in Genesis 1 makes clear, humanity

1.   In this chapter, Wisdom is capitalized when it refers to a personified figure or to the collective tradition of Wisdom writings and the schools where they were taught. It is lower case when referring to a quality, like knowledge, intelligence, etc. Likewise, Proverbs is capitalized only when referring to the book as a whole; when lower case, proverbs refer to sayings composed in a specific form.

is the capstone of the created universe. People act as God's surrogate in controlling the natural world; moreover, their Creator has endowed them with the ability to acquire wisdom for themselves, albeit on a smaller scale, and apply it in their own affairs. "Finding delight with mankind," Wisdom provides a bridge between God's enormous plan for the cosmos and man's modest place within it.

God bestows upon people the same creative spirit of wisdom for the construction of the Tabernacle in the wilderness. The same word for wisdom – *hochmah* – designates the skill of the craftsmen appointed to make the Tabernacle. The emphasis on the artisans' wisdom indicates the importance of this building, but even more, the fact that God is the architect of record: "[The Lord spoke to Moses,] According to all that I show you – the design of the Tabernacle and the design of all its vessels – thus shall you make" (Exodus 25:9). God transfers some of His own wisdom, God's own artistic energy and ability, to Bezalel, the Tabernacle's chief contractor, and his team of workers:

> The Lord said to Moses, "See, I have appointed Bezalel son of Uri son of Hur from the tribe of Judah, and have filled him with the spirit of God, with skill, discernment and knowledge, and all craftsmanship, to make designs, to work in gold, silver and bronze, for engraving stones for settings and for carving wood – to work in all crafts. And behold, I have put Oholiab son of Ahisamach of the tribe of Dan at his side, and in the heart of every skillful man I have given skill, that they shall do all that I have commanded you. (Exodus 31:1–6)

The word here translated as "skill" is in the Hebrew "wisdom"; it bears little resemblance to the usual image we have of a wise person as an old sage filled with advice. It more closely resembles the common notion of "God-given ability." Significantly, the workers already start out as skillful by nature; God bestows upon them an extra measure of wisdom to enable them to work on the Tabernacle. The assembly of the Tabernacle represents the first time that God's wisdom, God's primordial creative power, is given to mankind. The idea of wisdom undergoes a number of further metamorphoses before reaching its predominant form in the Bible.

Solomon The Wise

In the person of Solomon, the Bible presents the epitome of wisdom:

> God gave Solomon wisdom and a great amount of discernment, and
> understanding as vast as the sand on the seashore. Solomon's wisdom
> surpassed the wisdom of all people of the east, and of all Egypt. He
> grew wiser than all other men, wiser than Ethan the Ezrahite, and
> Heman, Chalcol and Darda, sons of Mahol. His name spread to all
> the surrounding nations. He could speak 3,000 proverbs, and his
> songs numbered 1,500. He could speak about trees, from the cedar
> in Lebanon to the hyssop coming out of the wall; and he could speak
> about animals, birds, reptiles and fish. People came from all nations
> to listen to Solomon's wisdom, including kings of the earth who had
> heard of his wisdom. (1 Kings 5:9–14)

This passage succinctly expounds the primary elements of wisdom according to the Bible, and to the Ancient Near East in general. Wisdom
starts with the observation of nature: a wise person knows the difference
between a cedar and a hyssop and can identify the various animals, plants,
fish, and insects. This portrayal implies curiosity, an industrious zeal for
study and mastery through the acquisition of knowledge. The results of
this study, however, appear in quite different form from the conclusions
of modern science: proverbs and songs! Observation of nature does not
yield formulae of protein consumption, or articles on the mating habits of
Canadian elk. Instead, Solomon burnishes his insights into pithy, memorable expressions. His wisdom is derived from nature but descriptive of
people; it offers insight into individual psychology, human society, and
the workings of destiny. The following examples of Sumerian proverbs
illustrate this common kind of Ancient Near Eastern wisdom:

> Into an open mouth, a fly will enter! Like a barren cow, you are looking
> for a calf of yours which does not exist! The dog understands "Take
> it!" He does not understand "Put it down!"

Surely the number of Solomon's proverbs and songs contributes mightily to his reputation as the wisest man. Wisdom is both qualitative and quantitative. Wise people have the mental sharpness, honed with experience, to perceive things that other people would miss. But their wisdom also accumulates; they become more knowledgeable over time. Each day, a wise person becomes wiser. The description of Solomon also suggests that there are two valid methods for obtaining wisdom: one method is to spend time in nature, the ultimate source of all wisdom; but the second, equally valid method is to learn the teachings of the wise. A person who wants to become wise will study Solomon's wisdom, namely, the Proverbs and other traditions passed down in his name. Through the collection and instruction of wise sayings over time, wisdom becomes a collective, social phenomenon.

Another crucial aspect of wisdom brought out in this passage is its international currency. If Solomon's wisdom "surpassed the wisdom of all people of the east, and of all Egypt," then the people of the east and Egyptians must have their own wisdom – quite a lot of wisdom, for Solomon's wisdom to be so impressive. Indeed, the Egyptians in particular were famous for their collection of wisdom, and other societies followed suit in developing their own wisdom traditions. The Bible does recognize the validity of other people's wisdom. The book of Proverbs contains two collections said to derive from non-Jews: Proverbs 30 are "the words of Agur, son of Jakeh, [man of] Massa"; Proverbs 31 include "the words of Lemuel, king of Massa, with which his mother admonished him"! Additionally, Job, one of the wisest men in the Bible, is not Jewish. Certainly, no other biblical genre has such an international nature as Wisdom. What makes wisdom travel so well across borders of language, ethnicity, and religion is its secular character. If we take the passage describing Solomon's wisdom, the Lord acts first – and does not make a subsequent appearance. God creates wisdom and imbues people with the capacity to acquire it; the rest is up to us. Like modern science, wisdom's study of nature comes to be seen as an end in itself, apart from its divine origins. It is significant to note the concepts that don't form part of Solomon's wisdom: laws or Torah, covenant, the land, people, and the history of Israel. Everything particular to Israel, the contents of the rest of the Bible, plays no role in this kind of wisdom. Its non-national, universal makeup accounts for why "people came from all nations to listen to Solomon's wisdom."

Stories about Solomon illustrate essential aspects of the Bible's conception of wisdom. The famous story of two prostitutes who both claim motherhood over the same baby (1 Kings 3:16–28) reveals Solomon's great mental agility. To test who is the real mother, Solomon orders that the baby be cut in two by a sword. The true mother begs to give the baby up rather than see it killed; the other woman urges Solomon to cut the baby in half. Her real baby has died, and she cares more about making the other mother suffer than about the baby's welfare. Solomon demonstrates how his wisdom gives him remarkable insight into human psychology. Most important, wisdom is useful, facilitating the execution of justice.

The majority of stories about Solomon highlight his prowess as an administrator. He establishes a central bureaucracy with order and efficiency that would have made the Prussians envious, assembling a cabinet of officials who supervise different realms of authority, and dividing the country into twelve districts run by appointed prefects (1 Kings 4). He undertakes a massive national construction project, of a scope and ambition grander than those of Baron Haussmann and Robert Moses. The most impressive buildings are the Temple, described in lavish detail (1 Kings 6–7), and the king's palace. Besides these monuments, Solomon erects a series of fortified cities throughout the land, including "garrison towns, chariot towns, and cavalry towns" (1 Kings 9:19), designed to bolster Israel's position as a regional military power. Solomon achieves these results through the imposition of forced labor battalions, organizing men into work gangs responsible for chopping trees, quarrying stone, and performing the heavy work of construction. These levies strengthen the nation's infrastructure, but at the expense of Solomon's popular appeal (see 1 Kings 12:3–4). Finally, Solomon's preeminence in wisdom leads him to become the world's wealthiest man as well:

King Solomon grew to excel all kings of the earth in wealth and wisdom. The entire world sought the presence of Solomon to listen to his wisdom that God had put in his heart. Each one would bring a yearly gift: silver and gold vessels and robes, arms and spices, horses and mules. (1 Kings 10:23–25)

Solomon receives tribute both in recognition of his powers as a guru, and also as taxes waged upon territories under his control, "from the Euphrates to the land of the Philistines and boundary of Egypt" (1 Kings 5:1). The life of Solomon demonstrates that wisdom brings power, riches, and fame – and love. It makes Solomon the most attractive man in the world: he acquires "seven hundred royal wives and three hundred concubines" (1 Kings 11:3), along with the admiration of the Queen of Sheba. In Solomon's ideal hands, wisdom is a practical tool that guides the exercise of power.

As the paragon of wisdom, Solomon is regarded as the source for Israel's tradition of Wisdom literature. Three biblical books are attributed to Solomon – Proverbs, Song of Songs, Ecclesiastes – regardless of the fact that these works were most likely composed over a long period, extending many centuries after Solomon's life. Why was Solomon chosen to embody wisdom? What features of the Bible's biography of Solomon render him as the perfect wise man? After all, Solomon in the Bible does not emerge without some serious blemishes – the forced labor battalions, foreign wives who practiced foreign worship. Two of his achievements stand out in particular. Biblical descriptions of the Tabernacle show that construction was regarded as the activity of the wise. Since Solomon was the king whom God designated to build the Temple, the structure that housed and replaced the Tabernacle, he must have excelled in the kind of creative wisdom mentioned in Exodus. Strikingly, Hiram, the Temple's chief contractor, is described with the same language used for Bezalel: "He was filled with wisdom, discernment, and knowledge to do every task in bronze" (1 Kings 7:14). As Hiram's employer, Solomon fulfills a role similar to that of Moses by carrying out God's plan.

A second accomplishment, equally vital for establishing Solomon's bona fides as the wisest man, is his role in founding Israel's centralized bureaucracy. In forming the instruments of state, Solomon needed to establish the machinery for that bureaucracy to run. One of the most important components of any large government is a class of literate people who communicate messages among the ruler, the members of his court, local prefects and supervisors, as well as foreign governments. In ancient times, scribes filled this function; they were trained in the arts of reading and writing, arts that throughout history, until after the invention of the printing press, were known only to the elite. With the rise of a state capital and a royal court, Israel suddenly had to train a significant number of scribes. Not surprisingly, therefore, among the officials named to Solomon's cabinet are "Elihoreph and Ahijah sons of Shisha – [in charge of] scribes" (1 Kings 4:3). These officials presumably oversaw the rise of scribal schools. While archeology has found no evidence for the existence of such schools in Israel, they are known to have existed in Egypt and Mesopotamia. Scribal schools not only instructed boys how to write, or incise letters on stone; they also trained them for life in the royal court. The Egyptian book of proverbs "Instruction of Amen-em-Opet" concludes:

> As for the scribe who is experienced in his office,
> He will find himself worthy to be a courtier.

Within these schools, students would study proverbs as wise tools to succeed in life conducted among those in power. Students copied proverbs to practice their writing, and they memorized these short sayings to retain as guides for their future behavior. Solomon's reputation as the fount of all wisdom, then, may have derived from his creation of the institutions in charge of teaching and preserving Israelite Wisdom.

Proverbs: The Wise Always Rise

Israelite proverbs are similar in style and function to their Ancient Near Eastern counterparts. Most of them are self-contained units within a single verse, consisting of two parts:

> Honor the wise shall inherit,
> But dullards raise up disgrace. (3:35)

In most proverbs, the two half-verses contrast. Often, the message seems at first deceptively easy; to understand the proverb properly, one must compare the parallel components of the two halves and draw out the implications of the comparison. Here, in one of the simpler proverbs, note the elegance with which honor and disgrace wrap the expression in an envelope pattern. The interesting contrast lies in the choice of verbs: "inherit" versus "raise up." The wise obtain honor almost passively. They don't need to seek honor; it is bestowed upon them like a birthright. Dullards receive disgrace through their own effort; they seek it and take pride in it. The message seems to be: don't seek status, let it come to you as the reward for your actions.

Proverbs traffic in types of people, contrasting the wise with the wicked under a variety of names. The particularity of a proverb's message depends upon the nature of the contrast it draws between the types. As with this proverb, the contrast usually homes in on a psychological insight aimed at helping the student form the correct perspective for the time when he enters society.

In the early chapters of Proverbs, the instruction is directed to a "son." Scholars differ whether to take the word literally, indicating that the proverbs were popular parental advice to children, or instead as a technical term used by a teacher to his students within the wisdom schools. Both scenarios show that proverbs were highly esteemed for their educational value within ancient Israel.

The contrast between the lessons of the proverbs and the teachings of the prophets brings to focus a unique distinction of the Wisdom school. Proverbs are addressed to the individual, not to a group; they are taught in schools, within "the system," not preached at the gates by outsiders; their advice is practical, not moral in nature, advocating virtues such as prudence and diligence more than justice and repentance. Proverbs aim to direct the individual to succeed in the cutthroat world of court intrigue through winning the loyalty of powerful patrons; prophets regard the world of capital politics as narcissistic, corrupt, immoral, and condemned by God. The fact that both kinds of writings proliferate within the same anthology demonstrates yet again the astonishing diversity of perspectives found within the Bible.

Another look at the passage from Proverbs 8:22–31 quoted at the beginning of the chapter reveals the theoretical underpinnings for the varied, seemingly scattershot observations assembled in the Book of Proverbs. Having played a major part in the creation of the world, God's wisdom exists within the very fabric of the universe. The empirical world provides a book of instruction that people can study and learn from. All of nature, animal, vegetable, insect, and human, is of a piece, all created by God and hence governed by the same guiding intelligence. Wise people can grasp God's design wherever they find it and can use insight from experience to advance their position within society. God is the original source of wisdom – "Fear of the Lord is the beginning of knowledge" (Proverbs 1:7) – but only the beginning. Proverbs mentions God relatively rarely, laying the emphasis squarely on human ingenuity. The book conveys optimism that people can gain wisdom through their own initiative, provided they adopt the proper discipline and receive guidance from wise mentors along their path.

The opening verses of Proverbs give reasons why people should study these teachings:

> For knowing wisdom and discipline;
> For understanding words of discernment;
> For acquiring the discipline of intelligence,
> Righteousness, justice, and equity;
> For giving shrewdness to the simple,
> To the young, knowledge and planning.
> The wise man, hearing them, will increase his learning;
> The discerning man will obtain direction;
> For understanding proverb and epigram,
> The words of the wise and their riddles. (Proverbs 1:2–6)

This introduction enumerates the great benefits that proverbs can impart. The path of wisdom is difficult but straight, accessible and advantageous to all. No matter a person's innate ability or stage of life, he or she will improve in mind and character through the rigorous contemplation of proverbs. The simple, those people who are naïve and easily manipulated, learn the shrewdness to discern the intentions of others. The young, who tend to be occupied with concerns of the moment, gain the knowledge to plan ahead. Even people who already are wise and discerning should continue to study proverbs in order to reach higher levels of wisdom. Undoubtedly, wisdom is a lifelong pursuit. One can never become too wise, nor should one be satisfied with the wisdom already attained.

The final verse presents four different forms of wisdom teachings: proverbs, epigrams, words of the wise, and riddles. The differences among them are not spelled out – do they merely point to variations in form, or are they arranged on a continuum of difficulty? – but the categories show something essential about these teachings: they are meant to be pondered, not merely memorized. Their message is not considered obvious; they contain hidden truths accessible to people who have the patience to plumb them. Wisdom teachers may have thought of their material as closer to haikus than to popular adages like "A stitch in time saves nine." To read these teachings rapidly and straight through, which can be mind-numbing, does not do justice to the way that these teachings were intended to be learned.

For sure, the proverbs exhibit a wide range of levels. Some indeed seem designed for the simple, whereas others are pitched to the wise and discerning. The following series conveys a most basic message:

> You should go in the path of the good
> And keep to the paths of the just.
> For the upright shall dwell in the land,
> And blameless will remain in it.
> But the wicked will be cut off from the land
> And the treacherous will be torn away from it. (2:20–22)

Here is a cornerstone of Wisdom teaching: the good will prosper, the wicked will suffer. Act justly in order to succeed in life. This idea may not appear to present a morally elevated perspective – we might prefer the thought that one should do good in order to please God, or because that's the right thing to do – but it conforms with the orientation toward worldly success found throughout Proverbs. To some, this teaching also might seem counterintuitive. What does it take to succeed? Surely most people would not rank goodness high in the qualities needed for social advancement. Ruthlessness, treachery, limitless ambition, and other Machiavellian traits seem much more useful in the spheres of commerce and politics. In light of our modern skepticism on this subject, the Proverbs' position that the upright will "dwell in the land" while the wicked "will be cut off from the land" reveals a radical faith in the goodness of human society.

The Book of Proverbs repeatedly tells of the rewards that come to people who obey its wise instruction. They will be safe and can live with a firm sense of security, knowing that they are exempt from the disaster that befalls the wicked (3:19–26). Wisdom ensures that its male adherents find a suitable mate; it endows them with the strength to avoid the seductions of evil or adulterous women (6:24ff). Wisdom brings people great prestige (4:8–9), even riches (13:4). It teaches courtiers how to win the king's favor (23:1ff). In contrast to the wise, Proverbs displays a rogue's gallery of miscreants doomed to suffer: the dullard, scoffer, lazy, lawless, spoiled, fool, arrogant, scoundrel, lustful, liar, drunk, rebel, hothead, flatterer. Contrasts between the opposites help vividly incise the features of a wise person in the mind of the reader.

Other proverbs are freighted with a kind of darker wisdom more in line with a modern sensibility:

> A heart knows its own bitterness;
> In its joy no stranger can share.
> The house of the wicked shall be destroyed,
> While the tent of the upright flourishes.
> There is an upright path before a man –
> Ending in paths of death.
> Even laughter can grieve the heart,
> And joy can end in sorrow. (14:10–13)

These insights complicate the message that the good thrive and the wicked fail. The wicked person buys the big house; the upright dwell in a mere tent. Yes, the house will fall and the tent will flourish, but the inequity remains. The path to success is not obvious; no matter how wise or righteous a person is, his or her judgment is fallible and may lead to ruin. Even when people achieve success, they don't know how long their luck will run. And the first sentence gives the devastating insight that individuality, so highly cultivated by Wisdom's disciples, is a trap as much as a blessing, cutting us off from giving or receiving emotional succor. It seems a short step to Jean-Paul Sartre's famous line, "Hell is other people." These more skeptical proverbs don't negate the premises of the whole collection, but they do reveal a range and development of thought that render Proverbs rewarding and not to be taken lightly. They help preserve the collection from a tendency toward smugness, certainty, and self-satisfaction.

Proverbs 8:22–36, the passage describing Wisdom as a primordial female being, speaks to the way that wisdom is imagined as a particularly masculine pursuit:

> Now, sons, listen to me…
> Happy is the person who listens to me,
> Keeping watch daily over my doorways,
> Guarding the doorposts of my entrances. (8:32, 34)

A young man should pursue wisdom like a male lover wooing a woman. Proverbs couches the pursuit of wisdom in erotic terms: "Love her [Wisdom] and she will preserve you…. She will honor you if you embrace her" (4:6, 8). This kind of language may have served to stimulate interest among the boys studying in the Wisdom school. It also sought to train their erotic impulses toward faithful, monogamous relationships:

> Rejoice in the wife of your youth –
> A loving doe, a graceful mountain goat.
> May her breasts satisfy you at all times;
> Intoxicate yourself in her love always. (5:18–19)

This is strong stuff. Wisdom is hardly a retiring wallflower! She recognizes that, in the big city, the faithful wife faces stiff competition from the wanton adulteress. In sensuous detail, Wisdom portrays an elaborate seduction scene by a married woman whose husband is away (7:6 ff):

I have sprinkled my bed with myrrh, aloes and cinnamon –
Come, let us drink our fill of love till morning,
Let us delight in lovemaking. (7:17–18)

Becoming wise requires knowledge of all kinds of dangers and temptations in store for inexperienced young men. Without such training, a man "is like a bird rushing into a trap, not knowing his life is at stake" (7:23).

This kind of instruction makes clear that many or perhaps all of the teachings in Proverbs were intended for men only. Nevertheless, although there are relatively few wise women in the Bible, the exceptions are strong enough to suggest that wisdom was not considered the unique preserve of men. In the construction of the Tabernacle, a group of women possessed the same kind of wisdom as Bezalel and his male workers, giving them the skill to make fabrics adorning the structure: "And every skilled [literally, wise-hearted] women spun with her own hands, and brought threadwork of violet, purple, and crimson and fine linen" (Exodus 35:25). Most intriguing are two heroic tales of wise women in 2 Samuel (14:1–24, 20:15–22). The first tells of a wise woman from Tekoa who convinces King David to take pity upon his son Absalom, after Absalom had killed his brother Amnon for raping their sister Tamar. This wise woman acts like the prophet Nathan in 2 Samuel 12: she invents a story designed to win David's sympathy, a story that, once David reflects upon it, convinces him to change his behavior. The second story describes how another wise woman negotiates with David's general Joab to save the town she lives in. Joab's army has laid siege against the town and is prepared to attack; the woman calls down to Joab and discovers his demand, to hand over a rebel who has taken refuge in the city. She then arranges the rebel's beheading; the town hurls his head down to Joab, who removes the siege. At least in the first case, the woman is considered wise not merely because of her role in the story – the woman from Tekoa has a reputation for wisdom before the story begins (14:2). These two women possess a kind of wisdom similar to the kind described in Proverbs, an understanding of human psychology that enables them to devise strategies to placate people in power. However, their wisdom goes well beyond the prudent calculations of Proverbs' young lads. These women display a kind of bravery and brilliance hard to imagine within the narrow path set for the king's courtiers. They demonstrate that wisdom had a wider applicability within ancient Israel than we could gather from Proverbs alone.

Job: Taking Wisdom to Court

The book of Job poses a direct challenge to the optimistic worldview presented in the Wisdom tradition:

> Why do the wicked live on,
> Grow old and become powerful?
> Their children are securely established in their midst,
> Their descendents are before their eyes.
> Their homes are safe from fear;
> God's staff does not come down against them. (21:7–9)

To Job, the picture of human destiny described in Proverbs contradicts the world that he experiences. Line by line, one can discover statements in Proverbs that Job reverses in his complaint. The first two chapters establish the book's premise: what if the most upright man in the world were made to undergo excruciating suffering – the loss of his possessions, the death of his ten children, unrelenting skin disease? The whole edifice of Wisdom teaching would crumble. Wisdom then would not lead a person to life, success, happiness, nor would wickedness surely cause a man's ruin. The hypothetical nature of the frame is important for understanding the message of the book as a whole. Job does not intend to undermine the reader's faith in God or God's wisdom; he means to question it. We can no longer pretend to have such confidence in God's direction of human affairs. What circumstance would have led an author trained in the Wisdom school to write Job? Of course, many people believe that good people do not necessarily prosper, nor that the wicked automatically suffer. However, the image of Job's suffering is so extreme, and the questioning of God's justice so urgent and persistent, that only a great calamity could have caused this book to be written and accepted into the national literature. Job was likely written to express Israel's struggles with God in the aftermath of the destruction of Jerusalem and the Temple.

The book of Job represents the Bible's most extended and powerful discussion of theodicy, the challenge of understanding the presence of God's justice in the world. There are strong Ancient Near Eastern parallels to Job that the book's author adapted in its composition. A text from the Sumerian Wisdom tradition contains the long lament of a suffering man to his god. Another ancient work, known as the Babylonian Theodicy, relates a protracted argument between a sufferer and his friend strikingly reminiscent of the dialogue between Job and his various companions. Apparently, the problem of theodicy is an ancient one; Wisdom traditions throughout the region developed literary forms in response to this potent philosophical dilemma. The fact that theodicy was a problem for polytheists may come as a surprise. It is hard to envision Homer's characters sitting around perplexed why bad things are happening to them. With so many gods who act so unpredictably, inevitably someone will get scorched from a stray thunderbolt. Nonetheless, these ancient writings on theodicy suggest that many polytheists had a strong belief that the world was just, that their god would reward them for good behavior. Their faith in justice, like the Israelites' faith, could be shattered by personal or historical events.

The problem that theodicy posed in ancient Israel may have been similar in kind, but likely much greater in degree, than among its neighbors. Israel possessed no *Iliad* or *Odyssey* to deflect the philosophical quandary of Job; all of its writings portray the universe as created and controlled by one God. Its monotheistic conception, revolving around the relationship between God, the world He created, and people, faced its greatest challenge when the premises of that relationship seemed to topple. God, as it were, had nowhere to hide. Did God control the world? Then He was responsible for inflicting excessive punishment. If God was not in control, then the world was governed by chaos and there was no purpose in praying to a higher power. The author of Job expresses these horrible alternatives, and yet, through the process of argument and the force of his lament, he attempts to restore a sense of God's presence, shorn of some illusions that sprouted from Israelite faith.

Job's friends mistakenly attempt to console Job by explaining his suffering through the teachings of the Wisdom tradition. Eliphaz the Temanite invokes the idea of God's discipline:

Behold, happy is the man whom God rebukes;
Do not reject the Almighty's discipline. (Job 5:17)

Compare:

The Lord's discipline do not reject,
Nor should you loathe His rebuke.
For whom the Lord loves, He rebukes,
As a father the son he favors. (Proverbs 3:11–12)

Eliphaz tells Job to accept his suffering as God's method of correction. Job must have done something wrong; God inflicts suffering only to lead Job back toward the path of righteousness. Job should be happy! His pain is a sign of God's care. It will last only for a moment, and then God will reward him with safety, prosperity, long life, and descendants. Eliphaz's notion of discipline, of course, is wildly disproportionate to the extent of Job's pain; nor does it recognize the possibility that a just person can suffer wrongly, for no reason.

Another friend, Bildad the Shuhite, argues that the authority and antiquity of the Wisdom tradition render it infallible, beyond discussion:

Ask of prior generations,
Pursue the studies of their fathers –
For we are of yesterday, knowing nothing,
Our days on earth are a shadow –
Won't they instruct you and tell you,
Whose words bespeak their understanding? (8:8–10)

In effect, Bildad says to Job, Who are you to question the traditional understanding of God's justice? Our ancestors, who were much wiser than us, believed in it. Their descendants preserved these wise teachings and taught them down through the generations. Do you think you are smarter than all those people? How presumptuous! Bildad takes refuge in an argument that goes against the experiential perspective of Proverbs. According to Proverbs, people should study Wisdom teachings because they will find them useful throughout their lives. Experience proves them to be true; proverbs are the fruit of experience, not divine revelation. By claiming that Job should accept the tradition despite his experience, Bildad inadvertently undermines the logic of the Wisdom tradition that he seeks to uphold.

Another way of phrasing the question of theodicy, one helpful for understanding the book of Job, is as follows: When good people suffer and the wicked thrive, what has happened to God's wise creation? At such times, the wise fabric of the universe shreds into tatters; creation itself comes undone. Without the manifestation of wisdom, God no longer appears to rule the world, and the forces of chaos return to vanquish God's creative powers. Job gives expression to this vision of a world run amok by invoking mythological beasts: Leviathan (3:8), the sea and Dragon (7:12), Rahab (9:13). In Ancient Near Eastern polytheistic myth, gods create the world by cutting open the belly of a god defeated in battle. Hints of this story exist in Genesis 1: "darkness on the surface of the deep" (1:2) – the word for deep, *tehom*, resembles the goddess Tiamat, who was carved up in the Babylonian creation epic; the "great sea monsters" (Genesis 1:21) may remain from a primitive, pre-monotheistic myth of God's battle before the world's creation. The revival of these mythological dragons in Job signifies the reversion to a world stripped of God's control. The world behaves as if God never created it.

Another tack in Job is to reinterpret the meaning of creation:

> Your hands shaped and made me –
> Altogether, round about – then destroyed me.
> Remember: like clay You made me;
> Back to dust will You then send me?
> Did not, like milk, You pour me,
> Like cheese, You curdle me?
> In skin and flesh You clothed me,
> And with bones and sinews You bedecked me.
> Life and love You made by my side;
> Your gracious care watched over my spirit. (10:8–12)

Job describes God's act of creating man, recalling the description in Genesis 2 but going well beyond it in loving detail. Yet in light of Job's affliction, his – and by extension, mankind's – creation appears no longer an act of love, but one of cruelty. In his first words after God inflicts suffering upon him, Job vilifies his own creation, calling for the day he was born to "perish" and return to darkness (3:3–4). The problem now lies with creation itself; it no longer promises God's protective care, but instead the punitive watchfulness of a cosmic Big Brother:

> What is man, that You make much of him,
> That You set Your mind upon him,
> That You summon him every morning,
> Test him at every moment?
> How long will You not avert your gaze from me,
> Will not let me alone, till I swallow my spittle? (7:17–19)

God's attention, so deeply prayed for throughout the Bible, turns from a comfort to a curse in Job's eyes. The alternation of third and first person highlights the universal significance of Job's condition.

To the hard questions raised by theodicy, Job does not give a straight-forward answer. The purpose of the Book of Job may lie more in framing the problem than in finding a solution. Job's author felt the need to voice his despair in the face of great loss; under extreme circumstances, the questioning of God's justice is permitted, even required. Job takes God to court, literally, "suing" God to obtain an answer to his questions:

> O, that I knew how to find Him!
> I would come right to His place.
> I would set forth my case before Him,
> Filling my mouth with arguments.
> I would know with what words He would answer me,
> And understand what He could say to me. (23:3–5)

At the climax of the book comes God's answer in the form of a "voice from the whirlwind," a long, majestic poem asserting God's dominion over nature (Job 38–41). God's response to Job has evoked numerous interpretations, with many people finding it unsatisfactory. But the speech may be intended less as an answer to a question than as an affirmation to a challenge. There is a God; God did create the world; the world is indeed full of God's wisdom; human understanding, however, is not always able to fathom it. God takes people down a notch from the high level promised to them in Proverbs. Proverbs gives man an unrealistic, inflated view of himself. Job ends his dialogue with God by acknowledging God's mastery over the world and, by comparison, man's insignificance:

> I know that You can do everything;
> No purpose is beyond Your reach....
> Therefore, I despise myself, repenting
> Upon dust and ashes. (42:2, 6)

But does Job accept man's condition? It's hard not to hear a residue of deep bitterness in Job's self-loathing conclusion.

Ecclesiastes: Taking Wisdom Apart

If it is surprising to find a book as defiant of accepted tradition as Job in the Bible, the book of Ecclesiastes gives an even greater shock. Ecclesiastes is a doubter let loose in the china shop of Israelite faith, a preacher dismissive of all creeds and pieties as worthless delusions. Schooled in the Wisdom tradition, Ecclesiastes acts like a grownup courtier raised by the Wise who rebels against everything his teachers taught him. He marshals the experiential mode of Wisdom against the optimistic, self-help style formulas of Proverbs. In short, Ecclesiastes is Israel's great debunker. As a kind of ancient H.L. Mencken or Jon Stewart, he might have felt more at home as a modern media commentator than anthologized in the Bible. And yet his appearance in the Bible is precisely what makes him so unexpected and rewarding.

Ecclesiastes is thought to have lived in the third century B.C.E., during a period when many Jews were heavily influenced by the culture of the Hellenistic Greeks, whose empire controlled the entire region. Ecclesiastes exhibits some similarities with the Greek philosophical school known as

Skepticism, which started to flourish at this time. He presents his findings as observations generated by a quest for wisdom. He sets his mind "to search and explore with wisdom everything made beneath the heavens" (1:13); he samples different experiences to see what they can teach him. "I explored the matter in my mind, stimulating my flesh with wine" (2:3). No other biblical character would try such an experiment, let alone write it down! He is constantly examining, noting, finding. The book reads like a philosopher's diary. Ecclesiastes' experience prompts him toward pessimistic conclusions. He makes no effort to find the silver lining in the cloud:

> Again I noticed all who are made oppressed beneath the sun. Here are
> the tears of the oppressed, with none to comfort them; and power in
> the hands their oppressors, with none to comfort them. So I praise
> the dead who died long ago more than the living who are still alive;
> and better off than both is he who does not yet exist, who has not
> seen the evil deeds being done beneath the sun. (4:1–3)

For such dour reflections, any congregation would fire Ecclesiastes after his first sermon from the pulpit – surely not allow him to occupy a permanent room within the mansion of Holy Writ.

Ecclesiastes does not subscribe to the cosmic view of Nature envisioned in the Wisdom tradition. According to Proverbs, Wisdom planted within Nature a treasure house of knowledge, setting up the world with rules so that the wise can prosper and the wicked perish. Ecclesiastes describes Nature in starkly different terms:

> The sun rises, and the sun sets –
> And races back to the place where it rises again.
> Going southward,
> Spinning northward,
> Spinning, spinning circles the wind,
> And on its rounds the wind returns....
> What has been – that shall be,
> What has been done – that shall be done;

There is nothing new
Beneath the sun! (1:5–6, 9)

For Ecclesiastes, Nature is a pinwheel spinning around and around over and over in the same way day after day. Life is distilled into a tautological equation: $x = x$. It has nothing to teach us. Wisdom is a mirage: there is no sense in pursuing it, we cannot acquire it, much less store it. The famous passage beginning "To everything there is a season" (3:1–8) teaches the same lesson: life consists of endless, meaningless repetition. Ecclesiastes is the anti-Wisdom teacher, warning us against following the traditional precepts.

In Hebrew, the author of the book is called Koheleth, a word related to *kahal*, meaning "assembly." The exact meaning of the name is uncertain, appearing nowhere else in the Bible; it may refer to the author as a speaker before a congregation, a preacher, or alternately, as an assembler of sayings, a thinker. Although Solomon is not mentioned explicitly, the reference to the "son of David, king in Jerusalem" in the caption implies that he is the author. Jewish tradition assigns the book to Solomon's waning years, when he grew tired of all his wives and fortune and saw his legacy threatened by Jeroboam's insurrection. Modern scholars regard Solomon as a mask worn by the writer; Solomon, the embodiment of the Wisdom tradition, is the only person with the authority to call its bluff. Imagine the effect if, in his later writings, Karl Marx had renounced communism, Adam Smith opposed capitalism, or Thomas Jefferson condemned representative democracy as folly. Such is the impact of Ecclesiastes: as the author of Israelite Wisdom, Solomon now authorizes its demise:

> I, Koheleth, was king over Israel in Jerusalem. I set my mind to search and explore with wisdom everything made beneath the heavens. 'Tis a sorry business, which God gave men to keep busy. I have seen all the work that is done beneath the sun, and observe, all is emptiness and pursuit of wind:
> What is bent cannot be made straight,
> what is lacking cannot be counted. (1:12–15)

"Beneath the heavens," that is, in God's created world, is precisely where Wisdom is supposed to be found. Its pursuit, according to centuries of tradition, *is* the path of knowledge and happiness! By having Solomon, the wisest man, look back so sourly upon his efforts to acquire wisdom, the author brilliantly punctures the whole tradition in a few lines.

Trained in Wisdom's pattern of thought, Ecclesiastes often formulates his observations as proverbs. His proverbs bring to mind classical Wisdom teachings only to overturn them entirely. Ecclesiastes evokes the tradition in the spirit not of debate but of travesty. A contrast with Job's allusions to Proverbs is instructive. Job argues with the tradition because he wants it to be true and is devastated to find that it is not. Ecclesiastes long abandoned his faith in Wisdom. He cites proverbs only to mock them. They serve as compost recycled into new, cynical observations:

> In the place of justice there is wickedness,
> In the place of righteousness there is wickedness. (3:16)

The book of Proverbs draws a sharp contrast between the just and righteous on the one hand and the wicked on the other. Ecclesiastes tears down this and all such distinctions. The just may prosper, but so may the wicked; in the end, both meet the same fate. All of human wisdom cannot guarantee a person's happiness or secure a lasting legacy. From Ecclesiastes' death-haunted perspective, "man's superiority over beasts is nil, since all is emptiness. All go to the same place; all came from the dust and all return to the dust" (3:19–20). At times, Ecclesiastes presents a thought that could have been taken from Proverbs:

> There's an advantage to wisdom over folly
> Like the advantage of light over darkness;
> The wise man has his eyes in his head,
> But the fool walks in darkness. (2:13–14a)

He offers this aphorism, in the contrastive style of Proverbs – wisdom–folly, light–darkness, vision–obscurity – like a jeweler examining a diamond, considering its value rather than asserting it. Under his microscope, he sees only flaws: "But I also realized that the same fate will happen to all" (2:14b). The great leveler, death, flattens all human distinctions, causes all achievements to crumble into dust. In its extreme fatalism and passivity, Ecclesiastes is far removed from all other biblical perspectives.

When Ecclesiastes does offer advice, after the fashion of Wisdom, his advice is opposite in nature from that in Proverbs. Starting from his pessimistic appraisal of life, he tries to steer his audience to make the best of a bad lot. The worst thing a person can do is to work hard in order to obtain wealth or knowledge:

> For what does a man have from all the labor and thought he toils over beneath the sun? All his days are painful, his business gives him grief; even at night his mind is not at rest. That too is emptiness! (2:22–23)

Since we are here, we might as well derive a little pleasure: "There is nothing better for a man than to eat and drink and give himself joy for his trouble" (2:24). The rich should enjoy what they have, while they have it; a poor person should also find pleasure where possible. Even though the rich have more to take pleasure in, they may not be any happier: "Sweet is the worker's sleep, whether he eats little or much; but the rich man's plenty does not let him sleep" (5:11). Ecclesiastes advises people to form couples, for utterly practical, unromantic reasons:

> Two are better off than one, for they have a good recompense for their labor. For if they fall, one can lift up his fellow; but if one alone should fall, there is no second to lift him. Further, if two lie down, they are warm; but one alone, how can he get warm? And if one is attacked, the two can stand against him. (4:9–12)

Safety, health, earnings: Ecclesiastes sells human partnership like an insurance broker. His vocabulary lacks those words that portray the appeal of human partnership: love, companionship, intimacy, children, family. In Genesis 2, man and woman come together in order to complete each other.

Ecclesiastes considers human partnership – the sex of the partners is not specified – purely as a matter of convenience. A life lived alone would be more "brutish, nasty and short," to quote Hobbes. These examples show that when Ecclesiastes gives advice, he doesn't place much stock in it. He knows his advice isn't great; there just isn't anything better for him to recommend. Unlike standard advice givers, Ecclesiastes is utterly non-prescriptive. He doles out wisdom more as a spur for people to question other sages than to attract followers himself.

Finally, the form of the three Wisdom books is crucial for conveying their meaning. Proverbs is compiled as an advice list. Life's meaning is clear; the task: memorize these sayings to achieve success. Job is structured in dialogues (really alternating monologues), highlighting a clash between wisdom and experience, the ideal of God's justice and the reality of the world's injustice. Ecclesiastes seems to ramble; his arguments circle around and around. The structure of words, like the structure of reality, leads nowhere for him. Similarly, the grammatical form of each book provides an index upon their different perspectives. Proverbs are typically in the third person (Happy is he …), or in the second person imperative, supporting the book's didactic aim. Job uses the second person increasingly over the course of the book, to attack his interlocutors and challenge God. Ecclesiastes couches his thoughts in the first person because he has no objective wisdom to impart. For him, wisdom starts and ends with experience: what the I sees, the I knows, nothing more. His experiments and observations leave him feeling trapped within the helpless confines of his own fragile self.

Conclusion

In these three books, biblical Wisdom unfurls the life cycle of a philosophy: its statement, questioning, and negation. The presence of all three in the same collection may provoke frustration in readers turning to the Bible for a straightforward message. But the breadth of biblical writings and the longevity of their composition inevitably yield works that disagree with each other. Enclosed side by side under the same covers, Proverbs, Job, and Ecclesiastes find themselves clenched in an eternal argument. The underlying wisdom of the Bible's Wisdom tradition lies in the way it reveals the mobility of ideas, their energy and capacity for change. As long as they remain vital, each generation receives, evaluates, and transmits them in an altered form. Some generations are content to accept them piously from their forebears; at other times those ideas give rise to doubts, criticisms, and repudiations. Later generations may look back at such debates wearily, declaring all words on the subject as vanity. Yet just by continuing the conversation, these jaundiced teachers preserve the ideas they reject, giving people who come after them a chance to discover and interpret them afresh.

Although the kinds of writing and issues found in the Wisdom tradition seem so remote from the grand national and theological narratives in the Pentateuch and the Prophets, in one sense Wisdom played a crucial role in forming the Jewish conception of Torah. In postbiblical Jewish interpretation, the primordial Wisdom that accompanied God in the creation is identified with Torah. God created Torah at the beginning of His course; the Torah was God's guide in creating the world. The Torah as a whole, not just the book of Proverbs, is regarded as the instrument of God's wisdom. Study of the Torah becomes the path for obtaining that wisdom, for understanding God's design for the world. As God's creation of the world and intervention in human affairs recede further back in time, the books that tell of God's acts and words grow increasingly important for the spiritual life of the Jewish community. The Torah, in all its meanings and manifestations, serves as a path leading us back to God's wisdom.

The popularity of biblical Wisdom lies in the way it opens up the perspective of the individual within Israelite religion. In other biblical genres of writing, individuals are expected to act their part in the whole. For the legal writings, the historians, and the prophets, every person has the same obligation to obey God through certain forms of worship and behavior. These writings view people first and foremost as members of the nation; their fate hinges upon the history of the entire society. In the Wisdom tradition, by contrast, people start out as individuals, with their own abilities, backgrounds, challenges, and goals. The individual has a destiny of his or her own, apart from the collective fate of the nation. Thus Wisdom embodies a certain democratic spirit lacking in the rest of the Bible. Each person has the ability to rise, to succeed; Wisdom is addressed to everyone with access to its teachings, not just to kings; it tells people that their individual experiences and choices are meaningful; and it conveys the belief that the power to find direction, achieve status, win friends, and gain wealth lies in their own hands. This focus on the individual is what makes Wisdom such an important voice within the choir of biblical writings.

CHAPTER 8

Poetry

Suggested reading: Psalms 1, 9, 10, 23, 24, 47, 48, 78, 101, 105, 137, 150;
Song of Songs

Biblical poetry speaks with an emotional directness not often found in
contemporary poetry. Unlike biblical proverbs, which couch their message
in riddles requiring time to consider their meaning, most poems in the
Bible convey their message simply and powerfully:

> How long will my enemy rise above me?
> Pay attention, answer me, O Lord, my God! (Psalm 13:3–4)

> Give thanks to the Lord, for He is good,
> For His kindness endures forever. (Psalm 118:1)

This is not to say that the poems lack beauty and subtlety. Within a limited
scope of poetic forms, the Psalms[1] and other biblical poetry give voice to
the gamut of human emotions, from love, contentment, and exaltation
to despair, mourning, and vengefulness. Their intensity and expressive-
ness give them an appeal especially in private, solitary moments. Jewish
tradition encourages the individual to read Psalms regularly as a means
to purify the mind and concentrate one's faith. Biblical poetry also serves
as the great source for Jewish prayer, providing the material for much of

---

1. The word "psalms" is capitalized when referring to the Book of Psalms or when it is
followed by a number – Psalm 103; it is lower case in all other uses.

203

the synagogue service. In the manifold ways that the Psalms and other poems address God with all kinds of human concerns, these poems provide a model for the ongoing dialogue between people and God that is so central to Judaism and Christianity.

Poetry is interwoven throughout the Bible; it can be found in stories, the historical writings, the prophets, and the Wisdom writings. In the Hebrew, sometimes poems are clearly demarcated by being written down in a special pattern. Moses' valedictory song (Deuteronomy 32) is written in two columns, whereas Moses' Song at the Sea (Exodus 15) and the Song of Deborah (Judges 5) are written in a braided pattern alternating three and two as follows:

⎯⎯⎯⎯⎯   ⎯⎯⎯⎯⎯⎯⎯⎯   ⎯⎯⎯⎯

⎯⎯⎯⎯⎯⎯⎯⎯   ⎯⎯⎯⎯⎯⎯⎯

⎯⎯⎯⎯⎯   ⎯⎯⎯⎯⎯⎯⎯⎯   ⎯⎯⎯⎯

⎯⎯⎯⎯⎯⎯⎯⎯   ⎯⎯⎯⎯⎯⎯⎯

The scribes who wrote down the Bible usually made no distinction between poetry and prose. The translator is required to determine what constitutes a poem, and the choice is not always obvious. Sometimes as little as half a line can intrude a mini-poem into a prose passage:

> In the six hundredth year of Noah's life, in the second month, on the
> seventeenth day of the month, on that day,
>> All the wellsprings of the great deep burst
>> And the casements of the heavens were opened.
>>>> (Genesis 7:11, in Robert Alter's translation)

The elevated language suggests that these two lines might best be read as poetry. Why break up a prose passage with so brief a verse? Here the poem marks a climactic moment, capturing the awesome grandeur of the scene described. According to scholars, this line of verse may have been taken from an original poetic version of the Noah story that existed prior to the biblical account.

Translators often disagree over which passages are poems. Genesis 7:11, for example, is not typeset as poetry in the Revised Standard Version (rsv). The Jewish Publication Society (jps) Bible prints Genesis 15:1 as follows:

> Some time later, the word of the Lord come to Abram in a vision.
> He said,
>
> "Fear not, Abram,
> I am a shield to you;
> Your reward shall be very great."

Most other translations render this sentence entirely as prose. In translating Genesis 9:6–7, jps is more cautious, setting only the first sentence as poetry:

> Whoever sheds the blood of man,
> By man shall his blood be shed;
> For in His image
> Did God make man.
> Be fertile, then, and increase; abound on the earth and increase
> on it.

By contrast, Robert Alter considers both sentences to be part of the poem:

> He who sheds human blood
> by humans his blood shall be shed,
> For in the image of God
> He made humankind.
> As for you, be fruitful and multiply,
> swarm through the earth, and hold sway over it.

Part of the difficulty lies in the fact that biblical poetry lacks meter, which so clearly stamps Western verse as distinct from prose. The chief characteristics of poetry in the Bible, parallelism and terseness (described below), can also be found within passages that are clearly not poetry. The consensus today is that poetry and prose in the Bible are not absolute entities but exist on a spectrum, with poetry exhibiting greater parallelism and terseness than prose. Translators – and readers – must differentiate between prose and poetry by relying on their own sensitivity to the linguistic properties of biblical Hebrew. Such distinctions are difficult if not impossible to make in translation.

Psalms: Parallel Lines Meet

²ᴬ I will thank the Lord with all my heart;
  ²ᴮ I will tell of all Your wondrous deeds.
³ᴬ I will rejoice and exult in You,
  ³ᴮ I will sing to Your name, O Most High. (Psalm 9)

Biblical poems are by and large built up of self-contained verses. It is extremely rare for a sentence or a thought to spill over from one verse to the next. Each verse, in turn, contains two half-verses, on occasion three to provide some variety (for example, 9:6). These half-verses nearly always bear a strong resemblance to each other. The second half-verse repeats the thought in the first one, rephrasing it in different words. Often, the similarity between the two halves goes beyond the idea to a correspondence in grammar, words (synonyms), sometimes even sounds. The system of relationships between half-verses is known as biblical parallelism. Parallelism is a phenomenon found in poetry of many cultures throughout the world. Some scholars even consider parallelism to be the chief characteristic of all poetry. Nevertheless, it was through the study of biblical poetry that the term "parallelism" was first coined.

These two verses from Psalm 9 give a clear picture of biblical parallelism. The action described in the A line is repeated in the B line. Each of these four half-verses begins with a verb in the first person future tense (called the imperfect in biblical Hebrew grammar). To "thank" finds an equivalent in to "tell"; "rejoice and exult" is matched by "sing." The object too, is always God. Despite the high similarity between these four lines, their divergences are crucial to the poem. Part of the poet's artistry resides in his ability to harness the resources of language to create variety and interest within the structure of parallelism. Each line highlights something different: the human heart, God's wonders, exalted feelings, God's majesty. The first two half-verses emphasize the speaker, the second two, God. These two sentences as a whole are parallel to each other, with verse 3 substantially repeating verse 2. Yet within the repetition, the variation creates a certain dynamic that prevents the parallelism from becoming dull. The move from third person to second ("the Lord ... Your wondrous deeds") imbues the speaker with a sense of getting closer to God. While verse 2 announces the basic theme, verse 3 elevates it to a higher register. 3A employs two verbs, 3B two references to God, thus increasing the energy of the act of praising. These four half-verses rapidly build in intensity upward to a focus on God's elevated power as *Elyon,* the Most High.

James Kugel has described the relationship between half-verses in biblical parallelism as "A, and what's more, B." B doesn't merely repeat A; it usually adds some new information that provides emphasis, concreteness, or elaboration. In our example, 2A and 3A relate a general action or feeling of the psalmist, whereas 2B and 3B convey a more specific action. The B half-verses answer the question of how the verbs in A will be fulfilled. Other verses in Psalm 9 demonstrate different aspects of this relationship between halves:

> ^{16A} The nations have sunk in the pit they made;
>> ^{16B} In the very net they hid, their foot has been caught.
> ^{18A} Let the wicked return to Sheol,
>> ^{18B} All the nations forgetful of God!

16B brings to life the personification of the nation in 16A. A person might read 16A without calling the metaphor completely to mind. Compare this sentence: "The United States is mired in financial troubles." Most people reading that would not envision the underlying metaphor, of a person stuck in the mud. 16B does not leave the reader a choice; the details force the reader to imagine the action through their specificity. 18B adds clarity not to the verb but to the subject of the sentence. Who exactly are the wicked? The nations who forget God. The identity of the wicked is still vague – do they include all polytheists, or only those who attack Israel? –

but 18b does limit them to members of foreign nations. An examination of other biblical poems would reveal numerous additional ways that B complements and furthers the message stated in A.

In Chapter 2 on storytelling, we saw that terseness is an important characteristic of all biblical writing. Biblical style is typically spare, relating only as much information as is necessary to understand the story; it eschews ornamentation, adjectives and adverbs being rare, precious commodities; and it leaves out a great deal, such as Moses' childhood or how Pharaoh discovered that Moses killed the Egyptian. Poetic terseness in the Bible is of a different kind. The language is typically clipped, eliminating participles and conjunctions that smooth the process of reading:

> You rebuke [the] nations
> > You destroy [the] wicked
> > > Their name You blot out
> > > > Forever and ever. (9:6)

In Hebrew this sentence is even more condensed than in English, because the subject "You" is contained in the verb, and the pronoun "their" in the noun "name." Each action is told in two words – even the article is dispensable. The actions appear as simultaneous, occurring quickly all in one stroke. Bang bang bang: the terseness gives a much greater impression of God's might than is possible in prose.

Biblical prose is highly linear and sequential, moving from one event in time to the next through the ever-present *and* that begins sentences (made famous by the King James Bible). Biblical poems don't move so smoothly. They don't typically tell a story, so they lack the connective tissue holding prose together. The short half-verses bond together in parallelism, in turn making the transition between one line and the next relatively weak. Each line in a poem acts more like a brick in a wall than a length of rope in a cable. This kind of composition, combined with the density of the language, makes biblical poetry more difficult to read than prose, as we might expect. In the JPS translation, for example, most pages of the Psalms contain the footnote "meaning of Hebrew uncertain." Translations almost never reflect the terseness of the original. Through

their interpretation, the translators typically smooth out the features of
the Hebrew poem that make it challenging.

Another example from Psalm 9 reveals how poetic terseness can
yield sentences that are hard to understand at the basic levels of grammar
and meaning. This technical discussion, it is hoped, will shed light on
the unseen complexity of biblical poetry. We start with a word-for-word
translation of the Hebrew:

> The enemy [singular] finished [plural] ruins forever and cities You
> uprooted gone [is] their memory they. (9:7)[2]

There are at least four challenges to an interpretation of this sentence. (1)
There is one verb and two subjects – does "finished" go with "enemy" or
"ruins"? (2) How to tie together the pile of nouns strewn about in the first
part – enemy, ruins, cities? (3) Does "forever" describe "ruins" or "finished"
(i.e., is it to be taken as an adjective or an adverb)? (4) How to incorporate
the redundant "they" into the second part? Here are two translations:

> The enemy is no more –
> ruins everlasting;
> You have torn down their cities;
> their very names are lost. (JPS)

> The enemy have vanished in everlasting ruins;
> their cities thou hast rooted out;
> the very memory of them has perished. (RSV)

Both translations reflect some of the thickets in the original, while ignoring more of them in favor of sound and sentence structure in English.
Both ascribe the verb to "the enemy." The problem with doing so is that

---

2.   An additional cause of difficulty is the lack of punctuation or cases in biblical Hebrew.
     Sentence divisions, as well as a system of notation indicating grammar, were added
     to the Hebrew text in the Middle Ages; they do not necessarily reflect the text's
     original meaning.

the verb "finished" in the Hebrew is plural while the subject "enemy" is singular. On occasion a singular noun in the Bible does take a plural verb, so this solution is not impossible. RSV makes the issue clear by assigning a plural verb, "have vanished," thus transforming "enemy" into a collective noun. By contrast, JPS turns the verb into the singular. Nevertheless, there is a plural noun lying adjacent to the verb that is a strong candidate to be the subject: ruins. Evidently, the translators thought that it makes more sense to say "the enemy vanished" than "the ruins vanished," since ruins are already destroyed objects. Besides, if the verb goes with "ruins," "the enemy" will be left hanging with nothing to go with it. But the plural form of "ruins" and "finished" requires consideration that those two words belong together.

Another feature contributes to this theory: the "and" before "cities." Both translations delete this conjunction, breaking the line into three half-verses like 9:6 analyzed above. This breakdown destroys the neat envelope structure of verb-noun-noun-verb (vanished-ruins-cities-uprooted), called a chiasmus, very common to biblical style, as well as the parallelism between "vanished" and "gone," both verbs placed at the beginning of a clause. Additionally, both versions transform the adverb "forever" into the adjective "everlasting," a departure from the original. A rendering more faithful to the Hebrew might look like this:

> The enemy – vanished are the ruins forever and the cities You uprooted;
> gone is the memory of them themselves.

Even their ruins have vanished; hence there is nothing left to remember them by. This version clearly reveals the emphasis on disappearance: the enemy is out of sight and out of mind. The verse now begins and ends with a grammatically extraneous noun and pronoun, creating another envelope structure. A chart of the relations within this one line of verse would look like this:

A1, B1	A2, B2	A3, B3	A3, B3	A2, B2

The enemy – vanished are the ruins forever and the cities You uprooted;

A2	A3	AI, BI

gone is the memory of them themselves.

A = parallelism   B = envelope

This verse gives some indication of the intricacy and internal patterning woven into biblical poems.

To compensate for the self-enclosed nature of verses, which hinders a sense of connection and movement, many of the Psalms fall into a standard three-part structure. They begin with an appeal to or praise of God, move toward a description of the poet's enemies and troubles, and conclude with a call for God to help. These sections often correspond to a progression in time, representing the author's past, present, and wished-for future. This three-part movement might best be thought of in musical terms, like the parts of a sonata. The structure might create the impression of sameness to an untrained ear, although a devotee will find considerable variety of mood, message, length, and tone among the Psalms. Psalm 9, which serves as an excellent example because it is an ordinary psalm in many respects, clearly divides into three: verses 2–3, 4–19, 20–21. The author conveys a strong sense of contentment throughout. The opening section is all praise: God's in the heavens, all's right with the world. Whatever enemies lurk, God strikes down in judgment; from their very first mention in verse 4, they "stumble to their doom." The concluding call for God to "strike fear" into enemy nations thus lacks urgency, asking God not to change course but to continue the good work.

Psalm 10 strikes the opposite note. It begins not in praise but provocation: "Why, O Lord, do You stand far off, hiding in times of trouble?" This poet is so perturbed by his enemy that he cannot bring himself to praise God; he rushes into a description of his woes. Verses 2–11 portray the enemy's arrogance, wiliness, power. God has not intervened to strike him down; indeed, "His ways prosper at all times; Your judgments are far above him; he snorts at all his foes" (10:5). Just as the poet rushed right into the second movement, he does the same for the third; he cannot wait until the end to call upon God's aid: "Rise up, O Lord! O God, lift Your hand!" (10:12). (Remarkably, Psalms 9 and 10 are two parts of one psalm; see below.) Psalm 23 plays upon this structure to an entirely different effect. It projects complete serenity and confidence in God. God is a "shepherd," accompanying the poet on earth – not "Most High" or "far off." Scant reference is made to the psalmist's troubles: God provides a rod and staff to comfort him "through the valley of the shadow of death," and prepares a table before him "in the presence of [his] enemies." The author has no need to implore God for help, so sure is he that he "shall dwell in the house of the Lord" all of his life. Overall, the psalms share a common perspective on life, alternating between the difficulty of human conflict and the expectation of God's salvation. Within this framework, however, can be found a full range of emotional expression.

Several other kinds of structure are evident in the Psalms. One method obvious in the Hebrew but not in translation is the alphabetic poem, in which the first letters of the verses run through the Hebrew alphabet (9–10, 25, 34, 37, 111, 112, 119, 145). Except for Psalms 9–10, whose alphabetic scheme links two psalms with strikingly different moods, alphabetic poems do not exhibit the progression between distinct sections seen in other psalms. They focus entirely on one theme, praise of God, the alphabet device suggesting a sort of completeness, like books that promise to cover a city "from *a* to *z*." The poet's cleverness in handling the challenge of the device engages the audience's attention sufficiently to overcome the repetition of theme and lack of movement. Psalm 119, by far the longest psalm, provides the other exception – each letter begins eight verses (aaaaaaaa, bbbbbbbb, etc.), forming separate stanzas that stand apart almost as separate poems. Psalm 136 contains another obvious structural device, the repetition of the same half-verse in each line: "His steadfast love is eternal." Presumably this psalm was sung in a call-and-response pattern, a form so richly developed in music of the African-American church.

Still other psalms rely on key words to provide structure. In several, the word *selah* marks the break between stanzas of roughly equal length (for example, see Psalm 140). *Selah* derives from a word meaning "lift up," and it serves as a kind of chant-sound, a musical punctuation. The word "hallelujah" betokens its own form of poem. Meaning "praise the Lord," hallelujah occurs as the first or last word of a poem, and usually as both. Hallelujah poems urge people to join in praising God; they call on all people, animals, and created things to sing praise and they elaborate on

God's wondrous acts. Another linguistic structural element is the repetition of phrases or whole sentences, as in Psalm 8: "O Lord, our Lord, how majestic is Your name throughout all the earth!" The poem begins and ends with this statement. When uttered first, it appears as a premise; as a concluding observation, it summarizes what has just been demonstrated in the body of the poem.

The superscriptions, the introductions that come before a majority of the psalms, relate specific information about the kind of composition that follows. Their exact meaning is unknown today, as if, like the Italian used for musical scores, they were written in a language other than biblical Hebrew. These captions refer to a plethora of psalm types: *mizmor, michtam, maskil, shiggaion*, song of ascents, prayer, song, praise. Some of these terms likely give musical information about the song – the kind of tune, the manner in which it was sung, its liturgical or instrumental setting. They would serve a function similar to the names of the numerous kinds of dances designated in eighteenth-century classical music. Others may speak to the song's purpose – a song of ascents, for example, being designated for priests and pilgrims during major festivals. Many psalms refer to a leader, perhaps a choirmaster, suggesting a purely vocal setting. Some comments offer special instructions that may allude to specific rituals: *al tashheth, almoth labben, ayalet hashachar, shoshannim, lehazkir*. Above all, the superscriptions indicate that psalms are musical compositions intended to be sung. They mention instruments, all unrecognizable today, that would accompany the song: the *gittith, nehiloth, sheminith, alamoth,* and *mahalath*. As opposed to the superscriptions, the songs themselves invoke a variety of familiar instruments:

> Praise Him with the blast of horn;
>> Praise Him with lute and lyre.
> Praise Him with tambourine and dance;
>> Praise Him with harp and pipe.
> Praise Him with resounding cymbals;
>> Praise Him with loud-clashing cymbals. (150:3–5)

The reference to dance further broadens our vision of how these psalms were performed. Psalm 150 gives a picture of a raucous, festive atmosphere. By contrast, psalms such as 119 are hard to imagine being sung at all. The collection, including works spanning hundreds of years, displays an extraordinary musical and emotional range.

Psalms: Settings

According to tradition, the Psalms were written by King David, just as King Solomon is said to be the author of the Proverbs and other Wisdom books. David's reputation as a musician comes right at the beginning of his story: "Whenever the evil spirit from God came upon Saul, David took the lyre and played with his hand. Saul found relief and felt good, and the evil spirit departed from him" (1 Samuel 16:23). Music in the Bible not only is considered pleasant, it also carries great spiritual power. A few of David's songs are embedded in the historical books: his lament over Saul and Jonathan (2 Samuel 1), a song of praise for delivery from enemies (2 Samuel 22, repeated with some changes as Psalm 18), and a final poem at the end of his life (2 Samuel 23). Several Davidic psalms indicate the specific occasion in David's life when the poem was written (3, 7, 18, 34, 51, 52, 54, 56, 57, 59, 60, 63, 142). Psalm 51, a plea for repentance and purification, David wrote "when Nathan the prophet came to him after he had come to Bathsheba" and killed her husband, Uriah. These psalms open up a personal and more pious side of David than we find in biblical history. We overhear him speaking to God, acknowledging his sins, begging for mercy and forgiveness, as well as seeking God's help when he finds himself in narrow straits.

Whether David actually wrote the poems attributed to him, and if so which ones, is impossible to determine. History has produced rulers who were also fine writers; for example, one of the greatest medieval Hebrew poets, Shmuel Ha-Nagid, served as vizier charged with leading the royal army of Granada. But whatever David's musical talent, it is also likely that David was a magnet for psalms because of his reputation as *the* songwriter. Consider how much attention is paid to any new couplet thought to have been penned by Shakespeare; David held that kind of status in ancient Israel.

Within the book of Psalms itself, less than half are called "psalms of

David." The second section of the Psalms concludes, "End of the prayers of David son of Jesse" (72:20); although there are some individual psalms of David that come after, this line demonstrates ancient acknowledgement that David did not write the entire book. In the next section of the Psalms, nearly all are said to be "of Asaph" or "of the Korahites." Regarding Asaph, we learn elsewhere that he founded a musical group of Levites:

> When the builders had laid the foundation of the Temple of the Lord, they stationed priests clad in their vestments with trumpets, and Levites sons of Asaph with cymbals to give praise to the Lord, in the manner of King David of Israel. They sang songs praising and giving thanks to the Lord, "For He is good,
> for His kindness for Israel endures forever." (Ezra 3:10–11)

The Psalms are believed to have originated as songs sung by choral guilds of Levites – such as the "sons of Asaph" – in the First Temple. (1 Chronicles 25 mentions the sons of Heman and Jeduthun as well.) Ezra ascribes the establishment of these guilds to King David, and as he tells it, the Levites returned to duty as singers in the Second Temple. The Asaphites sing a line taken directly from the Psalms (106:1, also 136:1), with one addition, "for Israel" (Ezra 3:11), which may have been inserted to reflect the nationalist mood at the Temple's rededication.

Most psalms give no indication of their original setting, of who wrote it or for what occasion. As with the Proverbs, the Psalms' lack of context makes them appear universal, applicable to all. Their generality renders them particularly appropriate as prayers that speak to congregations of pilgrims or individual supplicants within the Temple precincts. A prayer of distress such as Psalm 10 would express the pain of someone bringing an offering in the hope of changing his fortune, or perhaps of the nation at times of distress. The distinction between personal and communal psalms is difficult to make, since even psalms voiced in the first-person "I" may well have been sung by a congregation or by a singer or choir standing as the representatives of a larger community. In addition to the lamentations, many psalms contain hymns of thanksgiving, giving thanks and praise to God. Sigmund Mowinckel, a leading scholar of the psalms, considered a number of these hymns as forming part of a liturgy for a great annual New Year's festival proclaiming the enthronement of God. In his view, Psalm 47 was sung at a procession which reenacted God's ascension to kingship over the earth:

> God ascends with a shout;
>> The Lord, to the sound of the horn.
> Sing to God, sing out!
>> Sing to our king, sing out!
> For king over all the earth is God;
>> Sing a hymn.
> God rules over the nations;
>> God sits on His holy throne. (47:6–9)

Some psalms give more specific information about the way they were used; their ritual or historical context was an essential aspect of their meaning and so it remains discernible today. One evident and colorful example is Psalm 101:

> My eyes are on the trustworthy men of the land,
>> To remain with me.
> He who walks in the path of integrity –
>> He shall minister to me. (101:6)

Here we find an inaugural hymn, a kind of Israelite oath of office, in which the king promises to pursue truth and justice while opposing arrogance and corruption.

Psalms 24 and 48 both evoke their setting within the ceremonies conducted at the Temple. In Psalm 24, the poet seems to be staring up at the walls of Jerusalem as he speaks:

> Who may ascend the mountain of the Lord?
> Who may stand in His holy place? –
> Clean of hands and pure of heart is he,
> Who has not sworn falsely by Me or taken a deceitful oath. (24:3–4)

This psalm may have been recited as a call and response (a style as known as antiphonal) by a priest and worshipper approaching the Temple. As they get closer, the song reaches a climax in an address to the entrance of Jerusalem: "O gates, lift up your heads!" The speaker in Psalm 48 takes a different path toward the city:

> Walk around Zion, circle it.
> Number its towers,
> > Observe its ramparts,
> > > Go between its citadels,
> So that you retell it to the next generation. (48:13–14)

This invitation to encircle the city may have been given following a victory in battle ("See, the kings joined forces…" 48:5), or as part of the celebrations for a pilgrimage holiday. Either way, the psalm describes Jerusalem as a special place to encounter God, a sanctuary receiving God's protection.

Those psalms suggest their setting in office (king) or geography (Jerusalem). Some others give strong indication of their position in time. Of these the best known is Psalm 137:

> By the rivers of Babylon,
> There we sat down and wept,
> When we remembered Zion. (137:1)

This song could have been written only during the Babylonian exile in the sixth century B.C.E., when Israelites were forcibly exiled from their land. Although Jews remained in Babylonia for thousands of years afterwards, they were allowed to return to the land of Israel after the Persians defeated the Babylonians; hence the psalm dates from between 586 and 539.

Psalms 78 and 105 are historical psalms, retelling crucial portions of Israel's past in regard to its relationship with God. Despite the similarity of subject, the two poems take opposite approaches: for the author of Psalm 78, Israel could do nothing right, constantly rebelling against God, whereas in the idyllic picture of Psalm 105, Israel has no role in its history except as the beneficiary of God's protective care. Both poems read like miniature Torahs, reviewing some of the key events from the first five books through one very strong filter. The conclusion of Psalm 78 reveals when it was composed through its description of the fates of the northern and southern kingdoms:

> [God] spurned the tent of Joseph,
>> And did not choose the tribe of Ephraim.
> He did choose the tribe of Judah,
>> Mount Zion, which He loved. (78:67–68)

The psalm contrasts the destruction of the northern temple at Shiloh with God's eternal love and protection for "His Sanctuary" in the south – Jerusalem. Therefore it must date between the destruction of Israel in 722 B.C.E. and the destruction of Jerusalem in 586. Psalm 105 is not as transparent; it finishes in a more general fashion:

> He gave them the lands of nations,
> The savings of peoples they inherited,
> That they might keep His statutes
> And uphold His teachings. (105:44–45)

We find not a hint of a split between north and south. The poet writes from a perspective in which such internal struggles do not exist. Perhaps the poem dates from the United Monarchy, before the division between the kingdoms, though it may just as likely come from much later, projecting a nostalgia for a time when God's role in human affairs was abundantly obvious. Whatever the occasion, the psalm's message is plain and didactic: observe God's law.

During the Second Temple period the Book of Psalms came together into the form we have today – a psalter. The Psalms are the world's first prayer book. In the course of their transformation into the new collection, these poems take on a kind of significance they had not known during the First Temple. Psalm 1, appended to the written collection, declares how the editors wanted people to regard these poems:

Happy is the man who does not walk in the counsel of the wicked,
Does not stand in the path of sinners,
Nor sits in the company of scoffers.
Rather, the teaching of the Lord is his pleasure,
And he studies His teaching day and night. (1:1–2)

The distinction between the wise student of God's teaching and an assortment of bad characters – the wicked, sinners, scoffers – derives from the vocabulary of the Wisdom tradition and is not typical of the Psalms. Psalm 1 is thus known as a Wisdom psalm. The Psalms now become regarded as the "teaching of the Lord" – in Hebrew, the word used is *torah* – which people should study "day and night." These are no longer occasional musical numbers, a songbook to be riffled for material appropriate to the circumstances at hand. The editors of the collection consider them to possess a depth and importance akin to other sacred writings. Their success in promoting the study of the Psalms is seen in the New Testament, which quotes Psalms more than any other book of the Old. Evidence of the influence of Israel's Wisdom school is sprinkled throughout the Psalms, from psalms attributed to Solomon (72, 127) and the wise men Heman and Ethan the Ezrahites (88, 89; compare 1 Kings 5:11), to Wisdom terminology predominant in several other psalms (including 19, 32, 34, 37, 49, 73, 78, 112, 119, and 128). Besides Psalm 1, the most important indicator of the book's new status is its division into five parts, analogous with the Torah. The book's editors may have regarded the Psalms as a religious complement to Proverbs, with Proverbs providing Wisdom's map to earthly success and the Psalms charting a path to achieve success with the Lord. With this editorial revision, the Psalms shift from material for public recitation to a text for private contemplation. The Psalter changes from holy songs to Holy Writ.

Song of Songs: A Delightful Puzzle

Lovers of poetry and people in love may choose the Song of Songs as their favorite book of the Bible. The poem's inclusion in the Bible is just as remarkable, in a different way, as the inclusion of Job and Ecclesiastes. How could such earthy hymns to romantic love find their way into the world's greatest collection of religious writings? The problem did not go unnoticed in the ancient world. For sure, the early rabbis debated whether this poem belonged among the Jews' canon of sacred texts. The book's attribution to Solomon likely guaranteed its sacred status, but there remained the problem of how to understand it. The literal meaning of the Song was unreadable to people who studied the Bible for its religious significance. Ultimately, the poem gained acceptance as an allegory, a work that speaks in code. Jews read the Song as expressing the love between God and Israel; Christians saw in the same book the love between Jesus and the Church. For both religions, allegory saved the poem by transforming a celebration of physical love into the expression of heightened spiritual experiences and mysteries. Rabbi Akiva in the early second century C.E. crystalized this new understanding of the book:

> No man in Israel ever disputed the status of the Song of Songs…for the whole world is not worth the day on which the Song of Songs was given to Israel; for all of the writings [of the Bible] are holy, but the Song of Songs is the holy of holies (Mishnah, Yadayim 3:5)

The allegorical impulse found in Rabbi Akiva was more heated the stronger the resistance of the material. The Song of Songs stands in stark contrast to the theocentric nature of most other biblical poetry, with God not mentioned at all in the book's eight chapters.

Although Rabbi Akiva's approach governed Jewish commentary through the centuries, the Song provided the model for both religious and secular poetry in the Jewish tradition. Among the former, the medieval poem "An'im Zemirot," a song that catalogues allegorical interpretations of the Bible and is sung weekly in many synagogues, recounts the Song's description of the male lover in its portrait of God:

> His head appears as pure fine gold…
> His locks are jet-black ringlets. (see Song 5:11)

The first Hebrew wine poem, penned by Dunash ben Labrat in tenth-century Cordoba, borrows imagery from the Song for quite different purposes:

> He said, "Do not sleep! Drink old wine,
> Amidst myrrh and lilies, henna and aloes,
> In an orchard of pomegranates, palms and vines...." (compare Song
> 4:13–14)

Awareness of the Song's sensual qualities revived with the growth of Hebrew poetry in Spain when ben Labrat and many others wrote under the influence of Arabic secular poetry. Within the Bible, the Song's celebration of romantic and erotic love enriches the entire anthology by embracing one of the most important aspects of human life.

In light of the other writings in the Bible, it is difficult to identify in which social circles this great poem originated. Scholars have proposed a motley assortment of theories, attempting to locate the Song within ancient Israel's inhospitable soil. Tradition, of course, attributes the song to Solomon: "The Song of Songs, by Solomon" (1:1). As with Ecclesiastes, scholars believe the Song was written centuries after Solomon. In both books, the writers play at being Solomon – Ecclesiastes, for the king's reputation as wise; the author of the Song, for his legendary appeal to women and his taste for luxury. Solomon's name may also indicate that the poem began within the royal court, perhaps as a love manual among Wisdom circles.

Another theory holds that the Song consists of folk songs popular among rural Israelites. This hypothesis takes its cue from the rustic elements within the Song itself, the talk of shepherds and vineyards, as well as the poem's remarkable familiarity with nature to a degree rarely seen in other biblical books. It is bolstered by comparisons to similar folk songs attested in the modern Middle East. Early rabbinic literature attests to the Song's widespread popularity and use on diverse occasions: carousers would recite it at "banqueting houses," and young women would sing verses while dancing in the vineyards to court eligible bachelors.

A third approach looks at the resemblance between the Song and

Ancient Near Eastern fertility rites. ANE poems tell of the quest of a goddess who searches for her dead lover, often a king, and revives him through her love. Some of the language in the Song seems taken directly from these much older fertility songs. The most recent scholarship, based upon linguistic analysis of the Song, points to a late date, during the Hellenistic period in the third century B.C.E. In this view, the poem's secular celebration of the body, its frank acceptance of eroticism, reflects the Greek influence of the poet's milieu. The depiction of rustic innocence within sophisticated poetic form recalls the idylls of Theocritus, a third-century B.C.E. Greek poet who lived in Alexandria, Egypt.

Another puzzle hovering over the Song: is the poem a unified whole or a miscellany of poems stitched together? The converse of this question is, does the Song have one author, or did an editor collect its pieces and hew them into their current shape? The book presents a variety of voices and kinds of songs. Most of it consists of a duet, with the lovers not speaking directly to each other so much as alternating monologues. Only rarely do they seem to respond to each other:

> "I am the rose of Sharon,
> The lily of the valleys."
> "Like a lily among thistles,
> So is my darling among the young women."
> "Like an apricot tree in the forest stands,
> So is my beloved among the young men." (2:1–3)

They speak in similes and metaphors about their feelings, painting verbal images of each other. The poem has some of the elements of drama, yet there is no real action from beginning to end. The woman – called the Shulammite, probably meaning of Jerusalem – searches for her beloved in and around Jerusalem; her brothers (1:6) and watchmen (5:7) try unsuccessfully to prevent her; she enlists the help of "daughters of Jerusalem" (5:8), who serve as a chorus; at the end of the poem, the lovers have found each other. And yet even these shreds of action appear more as literary motifs than as anchors for an actual story. The dramatic element of the poem is thoroughly overwhelmed by the lyrical, the play of poetic invention. The Song possesses the kinds of shaping devices one would expect to find in lyric poetry: development of imagery and theme; verbal repetition, such as "Daughters of Jerusalem, swear to me" (2:7, 3:5, 5:8, 8:4); and a sense of closure via the similarity between the end and the beginning, in this case through the mention of Solomon. If viewed as drama, the Song seems to fall apart; considered as lyric, the whole hangs together beautifully as one artistic composition.

The Song's emphasis on pure poetic creativity renders it a timeless source of pleasure and inspiration. Contrast it with other presentations of human artistry in the Bible – with Bezalel, builder of the Tabernacle, for example. Bezalel works within the strict constraints of the design that God gave him. The lover-poets in the Song have no limits other than their own human ingenuity. Their verbal play describes their love and simultaneously enhances it; their excitement over their love and over their poetic wit merge into one and the same thing. The metaphorical language of the Song conveys the erotic nature of the relationship. It is powerfully sensual, richly suggestive without crossing the line into explicitness or crudeness. The poem's imagery is drawn mostly from nature, an Edenic nature meant to awaken the listener's senses: fragrant spices, succulent fruits, ripe produce, vibrant young animals; orchards, groves, vineyards, hills, pastures all abounding with life. Woven into this tapestry are metaphors from human art, especially jewelry and architecture. There is no distinction between the human and natural worlds; both become projections of the lovers' desire. The subtle and clever ways that the figurative language cloaks and reveals the erotic intentions make the Song seem both innocent and sophisticated at the same time.

The atmosphere of cleverness and invention engages the lovers to carry out a fantasy by means of role-playing. Their love transforms the world outside and the world inside themselves. Through their imagination, the lovers are free to become whomever they like in relation to society and each other. One moment they pretend to be herders of sheep and goats (1:7–8); the next, they are the king and his lover (1:12). Magically recreated through the eyes of her lover, the woman becomes a "daughter of nobles" (7:2) whose every body part has been shaped by an artist. In her loving, jealous gaze, the man is a veritable King Solomon, his name alone sufficient to drive young women into a frenzy (1:3). In addition to adopting these personae, the lovers play a verbal game in which they dress each other by finding comparisons for parts of the body (4:1–7, 5:10–16, 6:4–9, 7:2–7). Despite the similarity of these four poems, there are crucial differences that reward reading them as an ensemble: notice that the second poem belongs to her – how remarkable to find in the Bible a woman artist depicting a man; the first three start with the head and move down, while the last poem reverses direction. Once the man finishes his last verbal portrait, he rejects the detachment of the artist and paints his love all over again as food waiting to be consumed:

> Let your breasts be like grape-clusters from the vine,
> The scent of your breath like apricots,
> And your mouth like good wine. (7:9–10)

Only at the end of the Song do the lovers strip off their masks as a gesture that the game is over, the lovemaking is about to commence:

> Solomon had a vineyard in Baal-hamon.
> He gave the vineyard over to watchmen;
> For its fruit, each would take in
> A thousand pieces of silver.
> My vineyard, my very own, is right here.
> Let Solomon keep his thousand,
> And the guards of his fruit their two hundred! (8:11–12)

By renouncing his disguise, the male lover states that the reality of his love exceeds the fantasy of Solomon's thousand women and thousands of shekels. Poetic flights of fancy have raised the lovers' sense of enthusiasm and anticipation. The elaborate charade must in the end yield to reality for its effect to endure. The actors behind the costumes remain completely unknown – any couple may try these on.

The nature of the relationship between the lovers has perturbed numerous commentators. Is the couple married? Do they consummate their love? Is the poem describing, even advocating, sex outside of marriage?

The Song is a poem, not a political or ethical tract, and as such it does not argue any cause nor offer easy answers. The man calls his beloved "my sister, my bride" (4:9 and elsewhere), by which he surely does not mean to suggest an incestuous relationship. "Sister" indicates intimacy, and "bride" in all likelihood means a form of partnership other than marriage – perhaps betrothal, whether formal or informal. The beginning and end of the poem leave little doubt that the couple have not yet wed. In chapter 1, the brothers try to prevent her from seeing him; she surreptitiously arranges to meet him while they are both out pasturing flocks. Chapter 8 begins with a cry to satisfy a love that is still thwarted:

> If you were only as a brother to me,
> Nursed at my mother's breast:
> I could find you in public and kiss you,
> And no one would despise me. (8:1)

Surely this is not the frustration of a married woman. Yet the Song does include a wedding poem, 3:7–11 (opinions differ whether verse 6 is part of this poem), in which Solomon, surrounded by warriors as groomsmen, seated in a structure of royal opulence, receives a crown from his mother on his wedding day. Is this scene a part of the fantasy acted out by the young lovers?

The question whether the lovers have consummated their love is harder to ascertain, since the poem describes the stages of their relationship entirely through metaphor and simile. Nonetheless, certain verses strongly suggest that their love has been fulfilled:

> I have come to my garden,
> My sister, my bride;
> I have plucked my spice – even myrrh,
> Eaten my honey – even honeycomb,
> Drunk my milk – even wine. (5:1; see also 6:12)

If love is a feast waiting to be consumed (recall 7:9–10), this lover has "tasted his fill." The poem ends on an open, circular note, with the woman urging her lover to flee at dawn before he is caught (8:14, largely a repetition of 2:17). The ending promises that the cycle of desire, consisting of re-unions and partings, quests and evasions, frustration, anticipation, and satisfaction, will continue indefinitely.

One final, intriguing piece of the puzzle lies in the dominant role that women play in the Song. The woman speaks the first and last words of the poem, and the majority of those in between as well. The chorus consists of women; besides the lover, the only men in the poem are brothers, watchmen, and herders, shadowy figures who do not speak and are largely ineffective. The poem mentions no fathers, only mothers. Solomon's mother crowns him at the wedding canopy (3:11). The Shulam-mite asks to bring her lover back to her "mother's house, that she may teach me" (8:2, also 3:4). In the realm of love and courtship, according to the Song, women rule. This impression is far removed from the treatment of the subject elsewhere in the Bible. The Pentateuch describes men as the active determinants of marriage. Laban gives Jacob Rachel and Leah as payment for his services (Genesis 29); Deuteronomy considers situ-ations arising after "a man takes a wife" (22:13, 24:1, 24:5); and Numbers 30 shows women graduating from the control of their fathers to that of their husbands. These passages reveal a world where men are in charge, women have little say in their destiny, and there is no room for romantic attraction. Does the Song represent a truer picture of the reality in an-cient Israel? Does it complicate the understanding of marriage that we receive from historical and legal texts in the Bible? Or is the Song merely a poetic fantasy with no relation to reality? Does the book's sensitivity to the perspective of women suggest that a woman wrote it? Whatever the answers, the Song of Songs is a radiant poem that enhances the Bible's value for our own culture and lives today.

Conclusion

Biblical poetry, characterized by compressed language delivered in pairs of similar lines, is found in nearly every book of the Bible, not only those identified as explicitly poetic. Translations of the Bible typically print most of the literary prophets as poetry, since the same poetic charac-teristics – parallelism, terseness, heightened rhetoric and figurative lan-guage – flourish there in abundance. Undoubtedly, these basic features originated in ancient Hebrew oral poetry and continued for centuries into the period of written composition. Biblical poetry possesses simple, flexible means of achieving rhythm and force. It is adaptable to all occasions, ranging from prophetic exhortations, pleas for divine aid, and solemn Temple ceremonies to battle victories, musical celebrations, and secular love poetry. A testament to the enduring appeal of biblical poetry is the fact that it remained a cornerstone of the Western literary heritage long after poetry had adopted the Greek and Roman standard of meter and feet. In the nineteenth and twentieth centuries the biblical model helped inspire the move back to "free verse" among the resolutely anti-clerical Walt Whitman and his heirs:

> The parallelism which constituted the peculiar structural device of Hebrew poetry gave the English of the King James version a heightened rhythm without destroying the flexibility and freedom natural to prose. In this strong rolling music, this intense feeling, these concrete words expressing primal emotions and daring terms of bodily sensation, Whitman found the charter for the book he wished to write. (Bliss Perry, quoted in Paul Zweig, *Walt Whitman: The Making of the Poet*)

Whitman, along with countless poets throughout the centuries, has shown that the poetry of the Bible can be immediate, vital, and beautiful to people in all eras.

CHAPTER 9

Conclusion

This book covers the major kinds of writing in the Bible, representing most of the material found therein. A few genres have not been discussed so far because they are present in smaller units. Nevertheless, it is important to describe them briefly at this time to fill out the picture.

Tale

The books of Ruth, Esther, and Jonah are closer to the form known today as the short story than to the kind of storytelling described in Chapter 2. These tales are self-contained, with a clear beginning and end. Their protagonists undertake a dangerous mission that leads them away from their home and society to an encounter with a powerful person. As with tales generally, the climactic encounter leads to a happy conclusion, with the danger being averted for the individual as well as for an entire community. The writing style is very different from the kind exhibited in the story of Moses' growth to manhood in Exodus 2. The sentences tend to be longer, the depictions more elaborate, and the descriptive details more copious.

Dirge

The Book of Lamentations consists of a collection of five dirges bemoaning the destruction of Jerusalem by the Babylonians. Laments are found elsewhere in the Bible – in the Psalms, in David's moving elegy for Jonathan and Saul in 2 Samuel 1, or his pitiful wail for Absalom in 2 Samuel 19, "O my son, my son Absalom!" – but Lamentations presents the most sustained example of the form. Four of the dirges are in the alphabetic structure found also in Psalms, suggesting a kind of list incorporating the entirety of Israel's pain. The narration, alternating between objective description, some of the most gruesome in the Bible, and the expression of individual anguish and complaint, gives voice to collective experience. The poet speaks on behalf of the nation, or channels historical events through the personification of Jerusalem as a downcast woman. Different hands likely composed the five poems; they may have been sung originally at the ruins of the Jerusalem Temple during a national day of mourning.

Apocalypse

With the exception of a few passages from the prophets considered apocalyptic by some scholars, the Book of Daniel is the only certain example of the form in the Hebrew Bible. The word "apocalypse" derives from a Greek word meaning "to uncover," and apocalyptic writings claim to reveal secret knowledge that God had previously hidden from people. Daniel receives elaborate visions followed by schematic keys to their interpretation. His visions foretell the course of world history through the rise and fall of kingdoms. Unlike the prophets, whose visions were far simpler, expressed general warnings about social injustice in poetic imagery, and were delivered orally, Daniel traffics only in writing and lacks the prophets' fiery emotional cadences. Like the purveyors of the Bible codes today, Daniel plumbs the writings of his predecessors for concealed messages relevant to his own time. Historical references in Daniel's predictions place the book in the second century B.C.E., making it the latest writing in the Hebrew Bible. Subsequently, apocalyptic writing became more popular, and it is represented in the New Testament in the Book of Revelations.

The Bible is a book of questions. As the book of Proverbs explains, the Bible envisions life as a perpetual quest for knowledge and wisdom. The Bible does not yield answers easily; the answers that the reader learns become platforms for launching further questions. Biblical stories demand the reader's full power of inquisitiveness. One must constantly probe the text to uncover the swarm of questions milling just below the surface, then attempt to thread different passages together to discover creative ways of forming answers. The more knowledge that the reader brings to the Bible, and the more familiar he or she is with its contents, the better the questions the reader can pose, and the better the answers that can be wrung.

The true significance of the Bible lies not in what scholars or theologians have written about it. Rather, it lives in the insights that you, the informed reader, bring to it in your own encounter with its stories, poems, and sayings. Only when the Bible is read and reread with fresh eyes does it remain a vital force in our spiritual lives; only when people come together to discuss it does it offer meaningful truths for our society. Don't rely on what other people have told you about the Bible. Pick it up and discover its wonders for yourself.

Bibliography

This list consists of works referred to in this book or consulted in the course of writing it. Books are listed in the first category in which they are useful, though many books shed light on several genres and proved helpful in the writing of more than one chapter.

A = written primarily for an academic audience
G = accessible to a general readership
* = recommended as a next step

General

Ackroyd, P.R., and C.F. Evans, eds. *The Cambridge History of the Bible*, Vol 1. Cambridge: Cambridge University Press, 1970.   G

Buber, Martin, and Franz Rosenzweig. *Scripture and Translation*. Trans. Lawrence Rosenwald with Everett Fox. Bloomington: Indiana University Press, 1994.   G

Driver, Samuel R. *An Introduction to the Literature of the Old Testament*. Gloucester, Mass.: Peter Smith, 1972.   G

Gottwald, Norman. *The Hebrew Bible: A Socio-Literary Introduction*. Philadelphia: Fortress Press, 1985.   G

Greenspahn, Frederick E., ed. *Essential Papers on Israel and the Ancient Near East*. New York: New York University Press, 1991.   G

Levenson, Jon D. *The Hebrew Bible, the Old Testament, and Historical Criticism.*Louisville: Westminster John Knox Press, 1993.   G

*———. *Sinai and Zion: An Entry into the Jewish Bible*. San Francisco: Harper & Row, 1987.   G

Sanders, James A. *Torah and Canon*. Philadelphia: Fortress Press, 1972. G

Trible, Phyllis. *God and the Rhetoric of Sexuality*. Philadelphia: Fortress Press, 1978. A

Translations Mentioned

Alter, Robert. *The Five Books of Moses*. New York: W.W. Norton, 2004.

The Holy Bible, Containing the Old and New Testaments (King James Version) (1611). New York: American Bible Society, 1978.

The Holy Bible: Revised Standard Version (1946). New York, Meridian, 1974.

Tanakh, A New Translation of the Holy Scriptures According to the Traditional Hebrew Text. Philadelphia: Jewish Publication Society, 1985.

Storytelling

* Alter, Robert. *The Art of Biblical Narrative*. New York: Basic Books, 1981. G

——— and Frank Kermode, eds. *The Literary Guide to the Bible*. Cambridge, Mass.: Harvard University Press, 1987. G

Auerbach, Erich. *Mimesis*. Princeton, N.J.: Princeton University Press, 1953. G

Bloom, Harold, and David Rosenberg. *The Book of J*. New York: Grove Weidenfeld, 1990. G

Damrosch, David. *The Narrative Covenant*. San Francisco: Harper & Row, 1987. G

Fishbane, Michael. *Text and Texture: Close Readings of Selected Biblical Texts*. New York: Schocken Books, 1979. G

Freud, Sigmund. *Moses and Monotheism*. Trans. Katherine Jones. New York: Knopf, 1939. G

Frye, Northrop. *The Great Code: The Bible and Literature*. New York: Harcourt Brace Jovanovich, 1982. G

Pardes, Ilana. *The Biography of Ancient Israel: National Narratives in the Bible*. Berkeley: University of California Press, 2000. G

———. *Countertraditions in the Bible: A Feminist Approach*. Cambridge, Mass. Harvard University Press, 1992. G

Sarna, Nachum M. *Exploring Exodus*. New York: Schocken Books, 1986.   G

———. *Understanding Genesis*. New York: Schocken Books, 1966.   G

Sonnet, Jean-Pierre. *The Book Within the Book: Writing in Deuteronomy*. Leiden, Holland: Brill, 1997.   A

Steinmetz, Devora. *From Father to Son: Kinship, Conflict and Continuity in Genesis*. Louisville: Westminster John Knox Press, 1991.   A

Sternberg, Meir. *The Poetics of Biblical Narrative*. Bloomington: Indiana University Press, 1985.   A

Trible, Phyllis. *Texts of Terror: Literary-Feminist Readings of Biblical Narratives*. Philadelphia: Fortress Press, 1984.   G

Zornberg, Aviva Gottlieb. *The Beginning of Desire: Reflections on Genesis*. New York: Image Books, 1995.   G

Law and the Ancient Near Eastern Background

Cross, Frank Moore. *Canaanite Myth and Biblical Epic*. Cambridge, Mass. Harvard University Press, 1973.   A

Dalley, Stephanie, trans. *Myths from Mesopotamia*. Oxford: Oxford University Press, 1989.   G

Douglas, Mary. *Purity and Danger: An Analysis of Concepts of Pollution and Taboo*. New York: Praeger, 1966.   A

Fishbane, Michael. *Biblical Interpretation in Ancient Israel*. Oxford: Clarendon Press, 1985.   A

Gordon, Cyrus H., and Gary A. Rendsburg. *The Bible and the Ancient Near East*. 4th ed. New York: W.W. Norton, 1997.   G

Levinson, Bernard. *Deuteronomy and the Hermeneutics of Legal Innovation*. New York: Oxford University Press, 1997.   A

*Pritchard, James B. *Ancient Near Eastern Texts Relating to the Old Testament*. 3rd ed. Princeton, N.J.: Princeton University Press, 1969.   G

Weinfeld, Moshe. *Deuteronomy and the Deuteronomic School*. Oxford: Clarendon Press, 1971.   A

History

Albright, W.F. *The Biblical Period from Abraham to Ezra*. New York: Harper & Row, 1949.   G

Brettler, Marc Zvi. *The Creation of History in Ancient Israel*. London: Routledge, 1995.   A

*Finkelstein, Israel, and Neil Ascher Silverman. *Unearthing the Bible*. New York: Touchstone, 2001.   G

*Friedman, Richard Elliott. *Who Wrote the Bible?* Englewood Cliffs, N.J.: Prentice Hall, 1987.   G

Gunkel, Hermann. *The Legends of Genesis: The Biblical Saga and History* (1901). Trans. W.H. Carruth. New York: Schocken Books, 1964.   G

Halpern, Baruch. *The First Historians: The Hebrew Bible and History*. San Francisco: Harper & Row, 1988.   A

Kaufmann, Yehezkel. *The Religion of Israel* (1937). Trans. Moshe Greenberg. New York: Schocken Books, 1972.   G

Noth, Martin. *A History of Pentateuchal Traditions*. Trans. Bernhard W. Anderson. Englewood Cliffs, N.J.: Prentice Hall, 1972.   A

*Shanks, Hershel, ed. *Ancient Israel*. Washington, D.C.: Biblical Archaeology Society, 1988.   G

Thompson, T.L. *Early History of the Israelite People: From the Written and Archaeological Sources*. Leiden, Holland: Brill, 1992.   A

Van Seters, John. *Prologue to History: The Yahwist as Historian in Genesis*. Louisville: Westminster John Knox Press, 1992.   A

Wellhausen, Julius. *Prolegomena to the History of Ancient Israel* (1878). Trans. J. Sutherland Black and Allan Menzies. New York: Meridian Books, 1957.   A

Prophecy

Blenkinsopp, Joseph. *A History of Prophecy in Israel*. Louisville: Westminster John Knox Press, 1983.   G

———. *Prophecy and Canon: A Contribution to the Study of Jewish Origins*. Notre Dame, Ind.: University of Notre Dame Press, 1977.   G

Buber, Martin. *The Prophetic Faith*. Trans. Carlyle Witton-Davies. New York: Macmillan, 1949.   G

Heschel, Abraham Joshua. *The Prophets*. New York: Harper & Row, 1962.   G

Muffs, Yochanan. *Love & Joy: Law, Language and Religion in Ancient Israel.* New York: Jewish Theological Seminary of America, 1992.   A

Wisdom
Crenshaw, James L. *Old Testament Wisdom: An Introduction.* Louisville: Westminster John Knox Press, 1998.   G
Day, John, Robert P. Gordon and H.G.M. Williamson, eds. *Wisdom in Ancient Israel.* Cambridge: Cambridge University Press, 1995.   A
Glatzer, Nahum N., ed. *The Dimensions of Job.* New York: Schocken Books, 1969.   G
Gordis, Robert. *Koheleth – The Man and His World.* New York: Jewish Theological Seminary of America, 1955.   G
Levenson, Jon D. *Creation and the Persistence of Evil.* Princeton, N.J.: Princeton University Press, 1988.   G

Poetry
Alter, Robert. *The Art of Biblical Poetry.* New York: Basic Books, 1985.   G
Berlin, Adele. *The Dynamics of Biblical Parallelism.* Bloomington: Indiana University Press, 1985.   A
Bloch, Ariel, and Chana Bloch, trans. *The Song of Songs.* Berkeley: University of California Press, 1995.   G
Fisch, Harold. *Poetry With a Purpose.* Bloomington: Indiana University Press, 1988.   A
Kugel, James. *The Idea of Biblical Poetry.* New Haven, Conn.: Yale University Press, 1981.   A
Mowinckel, Sigmund. *The Psalms in Israel's Worship.* Trans. D.R. Ap-Thomas. Grand Rapids, Mich.: William B. Eerdmans, 2004.   G
*Sarna, Nachum M. *On the Book of Psalms: Exploring the Prayers of Ancient Israel.* New York: Schocken Books, 1993.   G

Hebrew poetry influenced by the Song of Songs can be found in the following:
Carmi, T., ed. and trans. *The Penguin Book of Hebrew Verse.* New York: Penguin, 1981.

Scheindlin, Raymond P. *The Gazelle: Medieval Hebrew Poems on God, Israel, and the Soul*. Philadelphia: Jewish Publication Society, 1991.

———. *Wine, Women and Death: Medieval Hebrew Poems on the Good Life*. Philadelphia: Jewish Publication Society, 1986.

Biblical Citations

Exodus

Index

A

Aaron 36, 73, 82–83, 116, 129–30, 147

Abimelech 51, 79, 123, 145

Abraham 30–37, 41–42, 51–53, 55–58, 78–80, 92, 123, 145–46

Adam and Eve 78, 122

Ahab and Jezebel 98–99, 102, 134, 154–56, 158–59

Albright, William F. 80

Alt, Albrecht 89

Altars 33, 66–67, 98, 129

Alter, Robert 34n, 139, 204, 205

Amphictyony 92

Ancient Near East 50, 55–56, 61, 62, 64, 65, 67, 75, 76, 79, 80, 91, 101–2, 104, 111–2, 119–20, 128, 178, 182, 190, 192, 222,

Apocrypha 10, 107

Archeology 75–76, 79–81, 85–86, 88–89, 91, 95–96, 101–4, 106–7, 112, 119, 182

Assyria 55, 61–62, 81, 99–103, 105, 118, 133, 136–37

B

Babylonia 64, 70–71, 79, 100–1, 104, 106–7, 115, 116, 118, 121, 131, 161, 163, 190, 192, 217, 229

Bar Kochba, Simon 109

Bathsheba 94–95, 132, 135, 137, 155, 214

Bezalel 177, 181, 188, 223

Bible, meaning of word 8

Bloom, Harold 20, 116

Brettler, Marc Zvi 112–13

Burning bush 25, 28, 36, 38, 56, 60, 82, 115

C

Cain and Abel 23, 40, 78

Canaanites 41, 86–91, 95, 113, 118, 122

Capra, Frank 143–45

Christian interpretation 11–15

Codex 14

Covenant (brit) 15, 50–69, 72, 78, 82, 92, 100, 131–33, 169, 171, 179

Covenant Code 68

About the Author

Elliott Rabin is the director of education at Makor, a program of the 92nd Street Y in New York City. He earned a Ph.D. in comparative literature with a specialty in Hebrew literature from Indiana University, and he has taught classes in literature, religion, Jewish culture, and Hebrew language at universities and community centers in Indiana, Louisville, and New York City. He resides in New York with his wife and daughter.